THEORY AND INTERPRETATION OF NARRATIVE
James Phelan, Peter J. Rabinowitz, and Robyn Warhol, Series Editors

Narrative Theory
Core Concepts and Critical Debates

DAVID HERMAN

JAMES PHELAN

PETER J. RABINOWITZ

BRIAN RICHARDSON

ROBYN WARHOL

 THE OHIO STATE UNIVERSITY PRESS | COLUMBUS

Library of Congress Cataloging-in-Publication Data
Narrative theory : core concepts and critical debates / David Herman ... [et al.].
    p. cm. — (Theory and interpretation of narrative)
Includes bibliographical references and index.
 ISBN 978-0-8142-5184-3 (pbk. : alk. paper) — ISBN 0-8142-5184-6 (pbk. : alk. paper) — ISBN
978-0-8142-1186-1 (cloth : alk. paper) — ISBN 0-8142-1186-0 (cloth : alk. paper) — ISBN 978-
0-8142-9285-3 (cd-rom)
 1. Narration (Rhetoric) I. Herman, David, 1962– II. Series: Theory and interpretation of narrative series.
 PN212.N379 2012
 808.036—dc23
                         2011049224

Cover design by James Baumann
Text design by Juliet Williams
Type set in Adobe Minion Pro
Printed by Thomson-Shore, Inc.

9 8 7 6 5 4 3 2 1

CONTENTS

PREFACE

If we were to compile a list of Frequently Asked Questions about narrative theory, we would put the following two at or near the top: "what is narrative theory?" and "how do different approaches to narrative relate to each other?" *Narrative Theory: Core Concepts and Critical Debates* addresses both questions and, more significantly, also demonstrates the extent to which the questions themselves are intertwined: how one defines narrative theory shapes one's understanding of how the different approaches are related, and vice versa. At the same time, the structure of the book reflects our assumption that promoting dialogue among practitioners in the field is the best way to address both of these interlinked questions.

Thus, in Part One, we address the first question by taking turns exploring core concepts of narrative theory—authors, narrators, and narration; plot, time, and progression; space, setting, and perspective; character; reception and the reader; and issues of value—from four distinct theoretical perspectives. Jim Phelan and Peter Rabinowitz demonstrate a rhetorical approach to narrative theory; Robyn Warhol, a feminist approach; David Herman, an approach emphasizing the interconnections between narrative and mind; and Brian Richardson, an antimimetic approach focused on a tradition of storytelling that violates conventions of realism and conversational storytelling and that thus calls for the development of an "unnatural" narratology. In addition, Part One demonstrates the interpretive consequences of our four perspectives by focusing on the analysis of four particular narratives: Phelan and Rabinowitz work with Mark Twain's *Huckleberry Finn,* Warhol explores Jane Austen's *Persuasion,* Herman examines Ian McEwan's *On Chesil Beach,* and Richardson investigates Salman Rushdie's *Midnight's Children*. Then, in Part Two, we address the second question—"how do different approaches to narrative relate to each other?"—by taking turns discussing one another's contributions to Part One. In effect, we revise this second question by making it much more pointed: "how does my/our preferred approach relate to the other three approaches?" In staging this dialogue, Part Two not only highlights some key debates in contemporary narrative theory but also provides a navigational aid for readers seeking to orient themselves within the general landscape of narrative studies.

Of course, there are many other *Approaches to This and That* books on the market, and, in fact, some of us have had a hand in producing such books. *Narrative Theory* is fundamentally different for two reasons. First, our contributions are the latest chapter in conversations that the five of us have been having for years. Although the sections in Part One were written independently of one another, we each worked with a strong sense of (and respect for) what the others would be saying, and with a commitment to framing our arguments in terms of this continuing discussion. What we have, then, is four separate voices working not in absolute independence but rather in counterpoint. Second, for all our disagreements (some of them contentious), we all consider ourselves to be contributing to a shared project: developing ways of understanding what stories are and how people engage with them. Consequently, as will become especially clear in Part Two, it is not surprising that issues on which we disagree are flanked by other issues where our positions converge, overlap, or intertwine in complicated ways. To put this second point another way, the "navigational aid" that we offer here aims not to steer our readers in particular directions but rather to give them the means to pick their own routes through major debates within the field—routes that may well differ from any of ours.

We have written *Narrative Theory* for teachers, graduate students, and advanced undergraduates as well as for specialists in narrative theory. Given its combination of theory and interpretation, its range of approaches and illustrative narratives, and its unusual feature of having the co-authors responding directly to one another's contributions, we hope that the book could be the basis for courses (or a substantial part of courses) in narrative fiction, narrative theory, or literary theory. At the same time, we believe that specialists can benefit from the book's compact presentation—and demonstration—of four approaches to narrative, as well as our conversation in Part Two about the possibilities and limitations of those approaches. Indeed, as we explain below, we view the book as (literally) an invitation for readers at all levels to engage in a broader discussion about core concepts and critical debates in narrative theory.

Our organization in Part One allows readers to choose different paths through that section depending on their own backgrounds and interests. Because we take turns addressing key concepts, readers concerned with comparing approaches can readily consider similarities and differences between, say, rhetorical and feminist conceptions of plot, just as they can juxtapose the treatment of character or space in an approach that foregrounds issues of narrative and mind against their treatment in an approach that concentrates on experimental, antimimetic narratives. And because we arrange the approaches in the same sequence (rhetorical, feminist, mind-oriented, antimimetic) within each chapter, readers who want to trace a single perspective through several different concepts will easily be able to do so.

We should also note that although we have each developed analyses that are meant to reflect current practices within different traditions in the domain of narrative theory, we have written our contributions with a view to articulating our own take on the issues. Thus rather than acting as spokespersons for an entire group or school, where appropriate we have made it a point to note ways in which our own positions differ from the positions of others developing the same general approach—with those very differences indicating productive areas of debate within as well as across approaches. Finally, we recognize that the four approaches discussed here do not cover the entire field and that there are many theorists doing valuable work that does not fit comfortably under any one of the four rubrics we use to describe our work. But we happily acknowledge this limitation because it underscores the diversity and vitality of contemporary narrative theory. In that spirit, we view Part Two as only the starting point for a broader dialogue about the core concepts, methods, and goals of narrative theory, and we invite all our readers to contribute to the blog that The Ohio State University Press has generously created for purposes of further discussion. The web address is https://ohiostatepress.org/Narrative_Theory_Debates. Your participation, we are confident, will add greatly to the further development of our individual and collective thinking even as it expands the frontiers of our field.

ACKNOWLEDGMENTS

The co-authors wish to acknowledge the professionalism of and proactive support provided by the staff at OSU Press, including Laurie Avery, Sandy Crooms, Maggie Diehl, Kathy Edwards, Malcolm Litchfield, and Juliet Williams. They also thank the two external reviewers, Susan Lanser and Gerald Prince, for their productive comments on an earlier draft of this study. In addition, they are grateful to the OSU faculty and graduate students who offered feedback during a panel discussion that was sponsored by OSU's Project Narrative in November 2009; the discussion afforded the co-authors an opportunity to present preliminary versions of their contributions to chapter 4. We are also deeply indebted to each other. As Robyn put it first, each one of us is grateful for "the brilliance, forbearance, and generosity of spirit" exhibited by the others, and it has thus been a privilege for all of us to work together on this project.

Jim Phelan and Peter J. Rabinowitz thank the OSU Department of English and its chair, Richard Dutton, and Hamilton College and its Dean of Faculty, Patrick Reynolds, and its Associate Dean, Margaret Gentry, for support that helped make this collaboration possible. They also thank Corinne Bancroft, Katie Berlent, and Michael Harwick for helpful advice; and Ivy Akumu, Lindsay Martin, and Brian McAllister for proofreading and other assistance.

Robyn Warhol would like to thank the participants in the 2011 Curiosities: The 19th Annual British Women Writers Conference held in Columbus for their responses to her section on Character. She is grateful to the graduate students and core faculty of Project Narrative for making her feel so much at home at OSU and for teaching her so much more than she already knew about narratology.

David Herman thanks the American Council of Learned Societies, as well as OSU's College of Arts and Sciences and Department of English, for supporting his work on this project. He is also grateful to the following people, either for their direct assistance with his work on this study or, more generally, for the example they have set as scholars and mentors in the larger field: Porter Abbott, Jens Brockmeier, Richard Gerrig, Matti Hyvärinen, Barbara Johnstone, Elinor Ochs, John Pier, and Amy Shuman. He also thanks the students whose challenging questions and stimulating insights have shaped the arguments he outlines in his contributions to this book, and whose energy and enthusiasm are a constant source of inspiration. Most of all, however, he is grateful to Susan Moss for the many ways in which she supported his work on this book.

Brian Richardson wishes to thank fellow Unnatural Narrative Theorists Jan Alber, Henrik Skov Nielsen, and Stefan Iversen for their collegiality, inspiration, and advice, and Nancy Stewart for timely editorial assistance. He thanks the University of Maryland's College of Arts and Humanities for a grant that allowed him to work on this project.

PART ONE

Perspectives

Rhetorical, Feminist, Mind-Oriented, Antimimetic

1

Introduction
The Approaches

Narrative as Rhetoric
James Phelan and Peter J. Rabinowitz

As rhetorical narrative theorists, we look at narrative primarily as a rhetorical act rather than as an object. That is, we see it as a purposive communication of a certain kind from one person (or group of persons) to one or more others. More specifically, our default starting point is the following skeletal definition: *Narrative is somebody telling somebody else, on some occasion, and for some purposes, that something happened to someone or something.* Every part of this definition after "is" deserves further commentary—and we will provide such commentary in the following chapters. Before we do so, however, we'd like to start out by identifying six main principles that underlie our approach.

1. Narrative is often treated as a representation of a linked sequence of events, but we subsume that traditional viewpoint under a broader conception of narrative as itself an event—more specifically, *a multidimensional purposive communication from a teller to an audience.* The focus on narrative as *purposive* means that we are interested in the ways in which the elements of any narrative (e.g., character, setting, plot structure) are shaped in the service of larger ends. The focus on narrative as *multileveled communication* means that we are interested not simply in the meaning of narrative but also in the experience of it. Thus, we are as concerned with narrative's affective, ethical, and aesthetic effects—and with their interactions—as we are with its thematic meanings.

Of course, the underlying rhetorical situation varies in different kinds of narrative. For instance, in fictional narratives such as *Adventures of Huckleberry Finn,* the occasion/teller/audience situation is at least doubled: shortly after the events (before he lights out for the Indian Territory), Huck tells his story to his audience for his own purposes, while at a much later historical moment, Twain communicates both Huck's story and Huck's telling of it to *his* audience for *his* own purposes. (As actual readers, we read it on yet another occasion—and attending to the differences that these different occasions make is one way in which we bring history into rhetorical analysis.) To put these points another way, a fictional narrative is a single text combining multiple tracks of rhetorical communication. As this way of describing the communication implies, the rhetorical approach is ultimately most concerned with the author's telling to his or her audience. We will come back to these tracks of communication and the roles of various audiences in them in chapter 6.

In nonfictional narrative, the extent to which the rhetorical situation is doubled will depend on the extent to which the author signals her difference from or similarity to the "I" who tells the story and the extent to which the author posits an internal audience different from his or her readers. Sometimes authors of nonfiction speak directly in their own voices (as, for example, Joan Didion does in *The Year of Magical Thinking*), but at other times authors of nonfiction distance themselves from their narrators (as, for example, Frank McCourt does in *Angela's Ashes*). Sometimes an author of a nonfictional narrative will address a specific audience who is clearly distinct from the author's larger audience (think, for example, of an elegiac narrative addressed to a deceased subject, such as Marilyn Hacker's poetic tribute "Elegy for a Soldier, June Jordan, 1936–2002").

We characterize our definition as "default" rather than "definitive" for two reasons.

(a) We believe it captures essential characteristics of most of those works that are widely considered to be narratives in our culture, even as we recognize that individual narratives may not conform exactly to every element of the definition. Thus, for example, we say "something happened," because the telling of events typically occurs after their occurrence. But we also recognize that the telling can sometimes be simultaneous with the events (as in J. M. Coetzee's *Waiting for the Barbarians*) or before the events (as in narratives written in the future tense, such as Lee K. Abbott's "As Fate Would Have It"—which also shifts from the default of the indicative mood to the subjunctive).

Characterizing the definition as "default" helps us recognize both that there will be deviations *and* that such deviations tend to be significant.

(b) We do not believe that there is a single, best definition of narrative. Rather, any definition, because it implies a particular orientation, brings with it a particular set of emphases and serves a particular set of interests. That is, any definition highlights certain characteristics of individual narratives while obscuring or even effacing others. Our default definition reflects our special interest both in the multidimensional purposes of narrative acts and in the relationships among authors, narrator(s), and audiences.

2. In interpreting narrative, rhetorical narratologists adopt an a posteriori instead of an a priori stance. Rather than declaring what narratives invariably do or how they invariably do it, we seek to understand and assess the variety of things narratives have done and the variety of ways they have done it. In practical terms, this principle means that rhetorical narrative theory does not preselect for analysis particular issues such as gender or cognition or particular kinds of narratives such as those deploying antimimetic elements of story or of discourse—though of course we recognize that some narratives give special prominence to those issues or elements. More generally, rhetorical narrative theory maintains its interest in how narratives seek to achieve their multidimensional purposes even as it strives to be sufficiently flexible to respond to the diversity of narrative acts.

3. In explaining the effects of narrative, rhetorical narrative theory identifies a feedback loop among authorial agency, textual phenomena (including intertextual relations), and reader response. In other words, our approach assumes that texts are designed by authors (consciously or not) to affect readers in particular ways; that those authorial designs are conveyed through the occasions, words, techniques, structures, forms, and dialogic relations of texts as well as the genres and conventions readers use to understand them; and that since reader responses are ideally a consequence of those designs, they can also serve as an initial guide to (although, since misreadings are possible, not as a guarantee of) the workings of the text. At the same time, reader responses, including affective and ethical ones, can be a test of the efficacy of those designs. Thus, for example, we would expect any adequate analysis of the Phelps farm episodes of *Huckleberry Finn*—the episodes in which Tom Sawyer orchestrates an unnecessarily elaborate plan by which he and Huck free Jim—to account for the tedium most readers experience as they slog through the seemingly interminable section and the disappointment they feel in Huck's ethical decline in his relationship with Jim. For that

reason, we find many thematic defenses of Twain's design to be unpersuasive: they neglect the evidence of readerly response or regard it as less significant than the thematic meanings they find in the design. We will return to this issue in more detail in chapter 7.

4. We regard the progression of a narrative—its synthesis of textual and readerly dynamics—as the key means by which an author achieves his or her purposes, and we therefore look to a study of progression for key insights into understanding how a narrative works. Since we are interested in why the narrative text is the way it is and not some other way, we are interested in understanding the principles of its construction. Coming to understand the principles that underlie its progression from a particular starting point to a particular ending point provides an excellent way to understand a narrative's design and its purposes.

 Textual dynamics are the internal processes by which narratives move from beginning through middle to ending, and readerly dynamics are the corresponding cognitive, affective, ethical, and aesthetic responses of the audience to those textual dynamics. The bridge between textual dynam- ics and readerly dynamics is formed by narrative judgments of three kinds: interpretive, ethical, and aesthetic. These judgments constitute a bridge because they are encoded in the narrative yet made by readers, and, once made, their various interactions lead to readers' multilayered responses. (For more on these responses see point number 6.)

5. With regard to fictional narrative, the approach identifies three key audiences involved in the rhetorical exchanges, though it is just as accurate to say that it focuses on the actual audience (the flesh-and-blood readers, both as individuals and as a group) and two primary positions that the actual audience typically adopts. First, readers typically join (or try to join) the authorial audience, the hypothetical group for whom the author writes—the group that shares the knowledge, values, prejudices, fears, and experiences that the author expected in his or her readers and that ground his or her rhetorical choices. Second, the actual audience *pretends* to join the narrative audience, the audience that receives the narrator's text—an audience that exists in the narrator's world, that regards the characters and events as real rather than invented, and that accepts the basic facts of the storyworld regardless of whether they conform to those of the actual world. The narrative audience does not necessarily accept the narrator's portrayal as accurate, any more than the reader of a nonfictional text necessarily accepts everything represented as true; but the narrative audience does, as its default position, accept the world presented in the text as a "real" one. With some narratives (e.g., epistolary novels), it may also be useful to distinguish between the narrative audience and the narratee, the intratextual audience specifically addressed by the narrator. The terms are sometimes used almost as synonyms, but the differences are often significant. The narrative audience is a role that the actual reader takes on while reading; the narratee, in contrast, is a character position in the text, one that the narrative audience in a sense observes. Thus, when we begin Mary Shelley's *Frankenstein,* we do not pretend to be Mrs. Saville, to whom Captain Walton is addressing his letters; rather, we pretend to be a narrative audience that views her as a real person and that, in a sense, reads over her shoulder.

One final (for now) note on audiences that also applies to our other analytic concepts. Our approach is profoundly pragmatic, in the everyday rather than philosophical sense, and when studying particular texts, we're apt to glide over distinctions that don't bear significant interpretive weight. Thus, for instance, although *Huckleberry Finn* begins with a direct address to "you," the narratee is not characterized, and the distinction between narrative audience and narratee does not have a sufficient payoff for us to use it in our analysis of Twain's rhetorical communications.

6. Audiences develop interests and responses of three broad kinds, each related to a particular component of the narrative: mimetic, thematic, and synthetic. Responses to the mimetic component involve readers' interests in the characters as possible people and in the narrative world as like our own, that is, hypothetically or conceptually possible and still compatible with the laws and limitations that govern the extratextual world. These responses to the mimetic component include our evolving judgments and emotions, our desires, hopes, expectations, satisfactions, and disappointments. Responses to the thematic component involve readers' interests in the ideational function of the characters and in the cultural, ideological, philosophical, or ethical issues being addressed by the narrative. Responses to the synthetic component involve an audience's interest in and attention to the characters and to the larger narrative as artificial constructs, interests that link up with our aesthetic judgments. The relationship among an audience's relative interests in these different components will vary from narrative to narrative depending on the nature of its genre and progression. Some narratives (including most so-called realistic fiction) are dominated by mimetic interests; some (including allegories and political polemics such as *Animal Farm*) stress the thematic; others (including the *nouveau roman* and much postmodern metafiction) put priority on the synthetic. But the interests of many narratives are more evenly distributed among two or three of the components (Dostoevsky's novels, for instance, promote both the mimetic and the thematic). Furthermore, developments in the course of a narrative can generate new relations among those interests. Indeed, many narratives derive their special power from shifting our attention from one kind of component to another: Nabokov's *Bend Sinister,* for instance, has the effect that it does in part because, in the closing pages, the mimetic is drowned out by the synthetic. In *Huckleberry Finn,* our main interest is in the mimetic and thematic components, with the synthetic remaining in the background.

In the chapters that follow we will elaborate on these six principles and demonstrate their consequences for interpreting—and evaluating—the novel that Ernest Hemingway claimed was the fountainhead of all American literature.

A Feminist Approach to Narrative
Robyn Warhol

Like feminist theory itself, feminist narrative theory has consistently increased in its scope of interest. What began as a "feminist narratology" that focused on the impact of culturally constructed gender upon the form and reception of narrative texts has broadened to feminist narratolog*ies* that include race, sexuality, nationality, class, and ethnicity as well as gender in their analysis of texts. As I use the term now, in the wake of the third-wave critique of white-liberal feminism and in opposition to the postfeminist assumptions that prevail in the U.S. mainstream, "feminism" denotes the conviction that dominant culture and society are organized to the disadvantage of *everyone* who does not fit a white, masculine, middle- or upper-class, Euro-American, not-yet-disabled, heterosexual norm. Feminist analysis today must take what Kimberlé Crenshaw named an "intersectional" approach because white privilege, class privilege, heteronormativity, and other positions of relative power complicate hierarchies of gender. As a feminist, I recognize that the "patriarchy" we understand to underwrite male dominance relies on the collusion of women and other marginalized groups even though it serves only a small minority of the people in the world: if everyone who is disadvantaged by it were to end the collusion and positively revolt, patriarchy would not stand a chance. As it is, however, patriarchal arrangements still govern Western culture and institutions, including (and for our purposes especially) the institution of literary theory and criticism.

As the original feminist narratologists pointed out, classical narratology developed in a pointedly masculinist academic culture, based on theories developed by men who grounded their models in the study of male-written texts. The idea behind feminist narratology was that examination of non-mainstream texts could yield generalizable observations about narrative that might be invisible in the mainstream canon. That idea was based on the feminist assumption that texts are always linked to the material circumstances of the history that produces and receives them, an assumption that contradicted the formalist stance of classical narratology and that through the intervention of such influential figures as Gerald Prince has come to be accepted within the broader practice of narrative theory, especially as it is applied to ethnically marked or postcolonial texts.[1] Because the term "narratology" still connotes for many a theoretical approach cut off from questions of history and context, some critics—myself among them—have begun using "feminist narrative theory" or "queer and feminist narrative theories" to name the field.

My assigned task in this book is not to provide a detailed history or overview of the many ways in which feminist narrative theory has come to be in
use today, but rather to demonstrate my own reading practice by bringing
feminist theory together with narrative theory as I look closely at a favorite text of mine, Jane Austen's posthumously published *Persuasion* (1818).
One of the great advantages of narrative theoretical criticism for feminism
is its self-consciousness about methodology, its insistence on being clear
about what questions we bring to bear upon texts and about how we will go
about answering them. Ironically, apolitical narratology's self-consciousness
combines well with feminist criticism's explicitly political agenda. Foundational narrative theorists (e.g., Gérard Genette) did not pretend to be making objective or even empirical pronouncements in their descriptions of how
texts are put together, and Genette's work especially reflects his awareness
that another critic might find different patterns in Proust.[2] It is a small step
from admitting that one's observations are affected by one's subjective position to identifying that position's affiliation with a specific set of convictions,
like feminism. In this sense feminist criticism and narrative theory form a
suitable match.

Of the varieties of theoretical orientation represented in this volume,
feminist narrative theory has most in common with the rhetorical and antimimetic approaches and least in common with cognitive narratology. Rhetorical narrative theory, like feminist narrative theory, considers the narrative
text not just to represent but actually to constitute a transaction between an
author and a reader. For rhetorical narrative theorists like James Phelan and
Peter J. Rabinowitz, however, considerations of gender, sexuality, race, or class
are only incidental to the fact that a genuine communication occurs when a
person picks up a narrative text and reads it. Feminist narrative theory takes
that communication as a given but tries always to frame its analysis with as
much socio-historical context as can be known for the author and readers in
question. Antimimetic narrative theory can also overlap in productive ways
with the feminist approach, in that many modern and postmodern experimental narratives, from Virginia Woolf's *The Waves* (1931) to Jeanette Winterson's *Written on the Body* (1994) to Alison Bechdel's *Fun Home* (2006),
are thematically linked to gender and sexuality, and the very act of writing
outside generic realist boundaries has been seen by many feminist novelists
and theorists as itself a subversive gesture.[3] An antimimetic critic like Brian
Richardson will often attend to the sexed and gendered implications of the
forms he analyzes, though the question of feminist politics is not central to
his method. Of the contemporary approaches current in narrative theory,
cognitive narratology of the kind that David Herman practices is the least

closely linked to feminist narrative theory, because the study of processes in the human brain necessarily privileges similarities among people over differences. The fact of difference—and more importantly, the fact that social inequities are still grounded in culturally produced differences—means that feminist narrative theorists are not yet willing to make the jump from the culturally constructed to the universal, which seems to resonate with the essentialism most poststructuralist feminists strive to undermine. Still, work such as Frederick Luis Aldama's in neuroscience and narrative joins up with feminist narrative theory through its interest in the affective and emotional impact of narrative texts, as well as its attention to the impact of cultural difference on the activity of reading.[4] Nothing in any of the other contemporary versions of narrative theory prohibits attention to gender, sexuality, class, or other politically significant and historically grounded differences. What chiefly sets feminist narrative theory apart is its insistence[5] on placing those issues at the center of the inquiry.

Looking over what I have written for this volume, I can draw some generalizations about what I do when I am practicing feminist narrative criticism. In the analysis of *Persuasion,* I tend to look primarily for ways in which Austen's novel deconstructs binary oppositions underlying mainstream assumptions about gender, sexuality, and class. That is, if the dominant culture of Austen's period promoted the ideology of separate spheres—assigning public life, professions, and power to men and relegating women to domesticity, marriage, and submission—I am interested in reading Austen's novels as responses to and critiques of that ideology. This goes far beyond the time-honored feminist practice of examining "images of women" in order to expose stereotyping and to praise authors' ability to move outside expected sex roles in creating their characters. Even the most stereotypical of Austen's characters embody contradictory traits that complicate her novels' representations of gender and sexuality. In the spirit of poststructuralism, the feminist narrative critic seeks to identify those contradictions and to resist reconciling or resolving them, always keeping in mind the complexity of narrative technologies for endowing a literary character with an interiority and a persona.

At the thematic level of analysis, I confess I am always alert to anything I can see as signs of feminism in Jane Austen's texts. This is attributable partly to my conviction—reinforced by biographical evidence—that Austen either read Mary Wollstonecraft or was exposed secondhand to her ideas about the rights of women, and partly to my sincere wish (shared, I believe, by many contemporary Austen fans) for my favorite author not to have been an instrument of patriarchal oppression, in her day or in ours. I do not look so much for characters' expressions of feminist sentiment (though in *Persuasion* I find significant ones) as I do for narrative practices that pull against received notions of what is suitable to a female character's life or a female novelist's text. When in the early 1980s D. A. Miller revealed the resistance to conventionally neat marriage-plot closure in Austen's novels, he set a pattern for feminist narrative critics of her work. At the same time that it constitutes a critique of gender norms in society and in narrative, Austen's feminism can become manifest as a defense of the values her world and ours have tended to decry as excessively feminine. Granting ample narrative space, for example, to the minute and seemingly trivial details of women's conversations in domestic settings adds up to a literary form quite distinct from what Austen's male contemporaries like Sir Walter Scott were writing. For the feminist narratologist as for Miller, theme is always manifest in form. Deviations from formal norms make deviations from dominant ideology visible.

In the same spirit, I am also looking for positions the text takes on class, race, and the history of colonialism, as well as gender and sexuality. Many feminist critics, having learned from bell hooks to read "from margin to center," scrutinize details that nonfeminist criticism might find trivial or peripheral. In studying Austen, this means paying attention to what is *not* represented in the text as well as to what is. The anonymity of servants, the scarcity of working-class or impoverished characters, the implicit beliefs about income, privilege, and status in Austen's storyworld all *signify*, in the sense of the word that Austen herself employed. Edward Said famously showed how *Mansfield Park* (1814) both acknowledges and ignores the fact that Sir Thomas Bertram's Antiguan slaves enable the existence of the upper-class British lifestyle the novel posits as normal and desirable. Feminist theory suggests, however, that considerations of colonialism and race must also take gender, sexuality, and class into consideration, as Susan Fraiman has shown in her brilliant response to Said's argument—not a rebuttal, really, but a trenchant revision of his reading. Class, race, nation, gender, sexuality, ethnicity, dis/ability: feminist narrative theory tries to keep as many of those balls in the air as possible, accepting responsibility for critiquing narrative manifestations of all categories of oppression based on socially constructed identities.

Interdisciplinary feminist theory underlies the attitudes and practices I have been describing, just as it provides a gender-centered platform from which to view elements of narrative such as plot, perspective, voice, and space. Feminist epistemology, feminist geography, feminist historiography, and feminist ethnography are politically engaged modes for framing research in fields such as philosophy, history, and the social sciences which strive to account for truth. Feminist literary and cultural criticism benefits from the insights of these theoretical approaches, though always keeping in the foreground the fact that texts are not reproductions of "reality" but rather are representations. What can be deduced from literary texts are attitudes toward gender oppression, not facts about how it occurs in the material world. But feminist narrative theorists also keep in mind the fact that literature has its own impact on the material world and that popular texts like the novels Jane Austen wrote can work to constitute real people's gendered assumptions and behaviors as much as to reflect them. "Real" gender does not exist—gender is always and only a virtual construction (or, as Judith Butler calls it, a performance) built along a continuum between material practices and reading practices. The more we can understand about narrative's role in the constitution of gender, the better positioned we are to change the oppressive ways that gender norms work in the world. As she can in so many other matters having to do with how to conduct ourselves, Jane Austen can help.

Exploring the Nexus of Narrative and Mind
David Herman

My contributions to this volume outline an approach that focuses on the nexus between narrative and mind, using Ian McEwan's 2007 novel *On Chesil Beach* as a case study. Research on the mind-narrative nexus, like feminist narratology, work on narrative across media, and other approaches to narrative inquiry can be described as a subdomain within "postclassical" narratology (Herman, "Introduction" to *Narratologies*). At issue are frameworks for narrative research that build on the ideas of classical, structuralist narratologists but supplement those ideas with work that was unavailable to story analysts such as Roland Barthes, Gérard Genette, Algirdas J. Greimas, and Tzvetan Todorov during the heyday of the structuralist revolution. In the case of scholarship bearing on narrative and mind, theorists have worked to enrich the original base of structuralist concepts with research on human intelligence either ignored by or inaccessible to the classical narratologists, in an effort to throw light on mental capacities and dispositions that provide grounds for—or, conversely, are grounded in—narrative experiences.

To explore these interfaces between stories and the mind, I use the idea of *narrative worldmaking* as a central heuristic framework, drawing on the pioneering insights of Nelson Goodman, Richard Gerrig, and other theorists. In my usage of the term, worldmaking encompasses the referential dimension of narrative, its capacity to evoke worlds in which interpreters can, with more or less ease or difficulty, take up imaginative residence.[6] I argue that worldmaking is in fact the hallmark of narrative experiences, the root function of stories and storytelling that should therefore constitute the starting-point for narrative inquiry and the analytic tools developed in its service. Yet the structuralist narratologists, for their part, failed to investigate issues of narrative referentiality and world-modeling, not least because of the Saussurean language theory they used as their "pilot-science." Of key importance here is Saussure's bipartite analysis of the linguistic sign into the signifier and signified[7] to the exclusion of the referent, as well as his related emphasis on code instead of message—that is, his foregrounding of the structural constituents and combinatory principles of the semiotic system of language over situated uses of that system. By contrast, in the years since structuralism, convergent research developments across multiple fields, including discourse analysis, philosophy, psychology, and narrative theory itself, have revealed the importance of studying how people deploy various sorts of symbol systems to refer to, and constitute, aspects of their experience. Building on this work, the approach I outline in this book assumes that a crucial outstanding challenge for scholars of story is to come to terms with how narrative affords methods—indeed, serves as a primary resource—for world-modeling and world-creation.

A focus on narrative worldmaking studies how storytellers, using many different kinds of symbol systems (written or spoken language, static or moving images, word-image combinations, etc.), prompt interpreters to engage in the process of co-creating narrative worlds, or "storyworlds"—whether they are the imagined, autonomous worlds of fiction or the worlds about which nonfictional accounts make claims that are subject to falsification. As this last formulation suggests, although narrative provides the means for creating, transforming, and aggregating storyworlds across various settings and media,[8] different kinds of narrative practices entail different protocols for worldmaking, with different consequences and effects. I argue that illuminating these protocols will require bringing scholarship on narrative into closer dialogue with developments in the sciences of mind. More than this, however, I suggest that moving issues of worldmaking to the forefront of narrative inquiry opens up new directions for basic research in the field, in part by underscoring the need to reframe the kinds of questions theorists ask about narrative itself.

In this respect, my emphasis on narrative worldmaking takes inspiration from Ludwig Wittgenstein's later philosophy, or rather what has come to be called the *metaphilosophy* embedded in texts such as the *Philosophical Investigations*. According to this metaphilosophy, the role of philosophy is to dispel, through analysis of the way particular expressions are used in particular contexts, conceptual problems caused by overgeneralization of any specific usage—as when expressions involving numbers are conflated with expressions involving physical objects, such that numbers start to be treated as things (Horwich 165–67).[9] Put another way, the later Wittgenstein's central metaphilosophical insight is that the grammar with which a question is formulated, or the language in which a problem is cast, can close off other ways of surveying a given area of inquiry or mapping out a problem space being investigated. Similarly, in reorienting narrative theory around questions of worldmaking, and in turn situating storyworlds at the nexus of narrative and mind, I seek to recontextualize existing heuristic schemes for narrative study, or rather shift to an alternative vantage point from which those schemes' underlying "grammar" can be surveyed anew.[10] Hence my contributions have been designed to serve not just narratological purposes, by suggesting how a focus on worldmaking affords productive strategies for studying stories, but also metanarratological purposes, by using this same focus to reassess the terms in which questions about narrative have been formulated up to now.[11]

For example, in the chapters that follow and also in my response to my coauthors' contributions in Part Two, I revisit the grammar of questions about narrative premised on the concept of mimesis. On the one hand, if mimesis is defined narrowly as imitation or reproduction, the very concept becomes untenable—since there can be no direct representation of the world, no bare encounter with reality, without mediating world-models.[12] On the other hand, if mimesis is defined as part of a family of strategies for deploying world-models, then the concept cannot do the work my coauthors try to get it to do—for example, when they set mimesis up as a standard or touchstone against which "antimimetic" stories, or the "synthetic" and "thematic" dimensions of narrative, can be measured. But changing the grammar of the question—asking not about mimesis or its absence but about how story designs can be arranged along a scale corresponding to more or less critical and reflexive methods of worldmaking—opens up new avenues for narrative inquiry. Along similar lines, my focus on issues of worldmaking leads me to reconsider (ways of asking) questions associated with the narrative communication diagram, a widely used heuristic scheme that has given rise to the constructs of the implied author and the implied reader, among others. Shaped by the anti-intentionalist arguments of the Anglo-American New Critics, these constructs are embedded in a grammar that can be surveyed from a different position when processes of worldmaking, which are grounded in defeasible or possibly wrong ascriptions of intentions to story creators, become the key focus. This new vantage point suggests how the communication diagram not only proliferates heuristic constructs but also reifies them—obscuring how the constructs at issue are ways of describing phases or aspects of the inferential activities that support worldmaking, not preconditions for understanding stories. Again, then, by keeping the focus on narrative's root function as a resource for world-modeling and world-creation, new ways of formulating questions about stories suggest themselves. I argue that these questions cannot be fully articulated, let alone addressed, in the terms afforded by previous nomenclatures and the grammar of inquiry with which they are bound up.[13]

By the same token, my emphasis on worldmaking as a framework for exploring the mind-narrative nexus has required that I tweak the template designed to provide readers with a basis for comparing and contrasting the four approaches covered in this volume. Unlike the other three approaches, my approach treats the creation of and (more or less sustained) imaginative relocation to narrative worlds not as a way of analyzing issues of space, setting, and perspective in particular, but rather as a core aspect of all narrative experiences—as an enabling condition for storytelling practices as such (see also Herman, *Basic Elements* 105–36). In turn, narrative worldmaking is imbricated with—both supports and is supported by—basic mental abilities and dispositions that constitute focal concerns of research on the interconnection between narrative and mind. Hence in my approach, time, space, and character can be redescribed as key parameters for narrative worldbuilding. Through acts of narration, creators of stories produce blueprints for world construction. These blueprints, the complexity of whose design varies, prompt interpreters to construct worlds marked by a particular spatiotemporal profile, a patterned sequence of situations and events, and an inventory of inhabitants.[14]

Accordingly, extending scholarship that adapts ideas from psycholinguistics, discourse analysis, and related areas of inquiry to characterize processes of narrative understanding,[15] I suggest that engaging with stories entails mapping discourse cues onto WHEN, WHAT, WHERE, WHO, HOW, and WHY dimensions of mentally configured worlds; the interplay among these dimensions accounts for the structure as well as the representational functions and overall impact of the worlds in question. I emphasize throughout how the making of storyworlds depends on the reader or interpreter, and I expand upon that claim in chapter 6 while using chapter 7 to explore the broader contexts and consequences of such worldmaking practices. Narratives do not merely evoke worlds but also intervene in a field of discourses, a range of representational strategies, a constellation of ways of seeing—and sometimes a set of competing narratives, as in a courtroom trial, a political campaign, or a family dispute (see Abbott, *Introduction* 175–92). Under its profile as a reception process, then, narrative worldmaking entails at least two different types of inferences: those bearing on what sort of world is being evoked by the act of telling, and those bearing on why (and with what consequences) that act is being performed at all.

I should also emphasize at the outset that although I explore issues of broad relevance for the study of narrative and mind, a mind-oriented approach to narrative inquiry can be pursued along lines different from the ones sketched here. For one thing, my example narrative is a (monomodal) print text, and different tools are needed to explore the mind-narrative nexus in storytelling practices that recruit from more than one semiotic channel (see Herman, "Directions"). Further, whereas my approach is synchronic rather than diachronic, focusing on acts of narrative worldmaking that it is currently within humans' capacity to perform, evolutionary-psychological perspectives explore ways in which features and uses of narrative can be traced back to mental abilities that have evolved over time (Austin; Boyd; Easterlin; Tooby and Cosmides).[16] What is more, in contrast with researchers (e.g., Hogan) who have appealed to the neurobiology of the brain to posit mapping relationships between aspects of narrative production or processing, on the one hand, and specific structures and processes in the brain, on the other hand, my approach remains situated at the person level—the level of the medium-sized, human-scale world of everyday experience (Baker, *Persons* and *Metaphysics;* see chapter 5 of this volume and also my response in Part Two). Since narratives and narrative scholarship both have much to say about this world of everyday experience, by focusing on the person level I seek to substantiate one of the basic assumptions of my approach: namely, that the study of narrative worldmaking can inform, and not just be informed by, understandings of the mind.

THE CASE STUDY
McEWAN'S *ON CHESIL BEACH*

I use *On Chesil Beach* to examine key aspects of stories and storytelling from a perspective that foregrounds issues of worldmaking; focusing on these issues will allow me to outline, in turn, strategies for investigating the mind-narrative nexus. I have chosen McEwan's novel[17] for a number of reasons, including its powerful exploration of how interpersonal conflicts are rooted in larger familial and social contexts, and its reflexive investigation of the way stories provide scaffolding for making sense of one's own and others' actions (see Herman, "Storied"). I discuss these and other aspects of McEwan's text in the chapters that follow; however, according to the needs of the discussion, I alternately zoom in on and back out from the novel, which I sometimes use as the basis for theory building and sometimes as a means for testing the possibilities and limits of an approach oriented around issues of worldmaking—and for gaining a new vantage point on the grammar of narrative inquiry itself. In any case, a brief synopsis of the novel here will help lay groundwork for the ensuing analysis.

On Chesil Beach opens in medias res with two inexperienced and underinformed newlyweds trying to navigate the complexities of their wedding night on the eve of the sexual revolution in England in 1962. The first sentence sets the scene: "They were young, educated, and both virgins on this, their wedding night, and they lived in a time when a conversation about sexual difficulties was plainly impossible" (3). The first part of the novel explores the characters' states of mind as they sit down to dinner in their honeymoon suite in a Georgian inn on the Dorset coast. For Edward Mayhew, the groom, and the son of a father who is headmaster of a primary school and a mother who suffered brain damage because of a freak accident on a railway platform, the idea of having sex with his new wife is at once tantalizing and a source of worry. But for Florence Mayhew (née Ponting), a professional musician-in-the-making whose mother is a professor of philosophy and whose father owns an electronics company, the prospect of consummating her marriage with Edward causes a deep, paralyzing anxiety.[18] Thus, whereas Edward "merely suffered conventional first-night nerves, [Florence] experienced a visceral dread, a helpless disgust as palpable as seasickness" (8).

From this point until the final ten pages of McEwan's 203-page novel, the narrative alternates between, on the one hand, periodic shifts back in time that provide information about the main characters' family backgrounds, life stories, and courtship and, on the other hand, a detailed, blow-by-blow recounting of the events of the present moment. The present-day events lead up to what proves to be a disastrous attempt at sexual intercourse by Edward and Florence and an angry, marriage-ending exchange on the beach—Chesil Beach—afterward. Then, in the final portion of the novel, the pace of narration speeds up drastically, covering some forty years of story time in about 5 percent of the page space used previously to narrate events lasting just a few hours. Most of this final section is refracted through the vantage point of Edward, who eventually comes to the realization that though all "[Florence] needed was the certainty of his love, and his reassurance that there was no hurry when a lifetime lay ahead of them" (202), on that night on Chesil Beach he had nonetheless "stood in cold and righteous silence in the summer's dusk, watching her hurry along the shore, the sound of her difficult progress lost to the breaking of small waves, until she was a blurred, receding point against the immense straight road of shingle gleaming in the pallid light" (203).

Antimimetic, Unnatural, and Postmodern Narrative Theory

Brian Richardson

Fictional representation may take several forms. There is a realistic tradition, which I will call "mimetic," that attempts to provide narrators, characters, events, and settings that more or less resemble those of our quotidian experience. Tolstoy's *Anna Karenina* is a paradigmatic example of this form; it attempts to reproduce in the fiction the salient features of typical people and the historical world of mid-nineteenth-century Russia. By contrast, antimimetic or antirealist modes of narrative representation play with, exaggerate, or parody the conventions of mimetic representation; often, they foreground narrative elements and events that are wildly implausible or palpably impossible in the real world. Nabokov's *Ada, or Ardor* (1969), for example, opens by quoting a mistranslation of the first sentence of *Anna Karenina* and goes on to construct a parallel universe, Antiterra, that regularly parodies various literary representations of the actual world. It should be noted from the outset that most postmodern works of fiction are antimimetic narratives; insofar as they problematize their own ontological status, they are by that very fact antimimetic.[19]

Virtually every narrative has two aspects, one mimetic, the other artifactual; one concerning what is represented, the other how it is represented. Furthermore, nearly every narrative represents some portion of the world we inhabit in one way or another, and it does so in a particular manner. That manner of representation may be conventional or unconventional, stylized or straightforward, unmarked or outrageous, clumsy or artistic; it is always constructed. Mimetic narratives typically try to conceal their constructedness and appear to resemble nonfictional narratives, while antimimetic narratives flaunt their artificiality and break the ontological boundaries that mimetic works so carefully preserve. Henry James once objected to Anthony Trollope's narrators' unnatural practice of suggesting to the reader that the events in the novel did not really happen and that they could therefore give the story any turn they chose; James felt such admissions were "a betrayal of a sacred office," even a "serious crime," by the novelist (30). Insofar as a work strives to adhere to a mimetic framework, such a practice is a significant violation, even a betrayal. But of course the author of a work of fiction *can* give the events any turn he or she prefers; at these moments, Trollope is following instead the more playful, antimimetic role of the anti-illusionistic writer who acknowledges the fictionality of the fiction.

My own work is part of a larger critical and theoretical movement known as "unnatural narratology"; in what follows, I will use the term "unnatural" as a synonym for "antimimetic." Other theorists of unnatural narratives have rather different perspectives and provide alternative or adjacent definitions; among the most notable of these is Jan Alber's statement that unnatural narratives are those that include physically or logically impossible scenarios or events (Alber 2009; for a comparison of such definitions, see Alber, Iversen, Nielsen, and Richardson, forthcoming). Thus, not every theorist working within the domain of unnatural narratology would subscribe to the claims I develop in the pages that follow. Finally, I wish to note that while I will be focusing on Rushdie's *Midnight's Children* as my primary text, I will also allude to a wide range of even more extreme works in order to indicate the scope, extent, and significance of antimimetic strategies in texts that for too long have been dismissed or neglected as minor, marginal, or transitory.[20]

In nearly all approaches to narrative theory, past and present, there is a significant and unusual gap: a sustained neglect of antimimetic narratives and, most importantly, an absence of comprehensive theoretical formulations capable of encompassing these works. Most narrative theories are thus substantially incomplete. Nearly all are based on mimetic presuppositions and start from the position that narrators are rather like human storytellers, that characters resemble people, that the settings and events we encounter in a narrative are comparable to those we might meet up with in life, and that readers process characters and events in a work of fiction roughly in the same manner that they comprehend people and events in daily experience. This mimetic approach is useful; all authors striving for realism or verisimilitude will naturally try to reproduce the conditions of lived experience; thus, an author of a novel written in the first person will try to approximate as closely as possible the conventions of an autobiography. This is why the terms "true to life," "lifelike," "faithful," "realistic," and other synonyms have been terms of high praise for many fictional works.

Of course, not all narratives strive to be mimetic. Nonmimetic works of fantasy, for example, postulate very different worlds, entities, and behaviors. More radically, antimimetic narratives refuse to obey or openly flout mimetic conventions; instead of imitating nonfictional discourses, they traduce their conventions. *The Life and Opinions of Tristram Shandy* (1776) does not reproduce the form of an autobiography, it travesties it. Tristram begins his narrative with the story of his own conception and then devotes so many chapters to explaining the family circumstances before and during his natal state that he doesn't get around to narrating his birth until a couple of hundred pages into his story. The narrator of Salman Rushdie's *Midnight's Children* (1980), Saleem Sinai, has the same problem. More radical is Antonio Machado de Assis's *Posthumous Memoirs of Bras Cubas* (1888), a Shandean memoir written after the death of its author, and still more unnatural is E. T. A. Hoffmann's *Life and Opinions of the Tomcat Murr* (1822), which purports to be the memoirs of a cat inappropriately interspersed within the biography of a man. Most extreme is Beckett's *The Unnamable*, composed by someone who does not know who or what he is and who cannot in fact differentiate himself from others. Alain Robbe-Grillet has succinctly articulated the viewpoint of the antimimetic author. He refuses "to reproduce a pre-existing reality" (*New* 146); he chooses instead to create that which has never existed. He further notes, "I do not transcribe, I construct. This had even been the old ambition of Flaubert: to make something out of nothing, something that would stand alone, without having to lean on anything external to the work" (162). Robbe-Grillet and numerous authors like him do not wish to reproduce the world of our experience; they want instead to create original or unprecedented scenes, figures, progressions, and worlds. Their works are part of an alternative tradition that has not yet been properly accounted for by narrative theory.

Antimimetic narrative theory attempts to provide a conceptual framework for works that refuse to follow the conventions of ordinary storytelling (or conversational "natural narratives") or mimetic (realistic) forms of narrative representation. Antimimetic narratives play with, ignore, or transgress these conventions. A natural or a realistic narrative has a speaker, recognizable characters, a set of related events with a certain degree of "tellability," a consistent ontological frame, and a more or less defined audience. But antimimetic narratives challenge rather than conform to these conventions. If a natural narrative consists of someone telling someone else that something significant has happened within a recognizable storyworld, an antimimetic narrative may contest each of the terms in this statement. More specifically, it may dispense with a single, consistent, human-like speaker, using only inconsistent, nonhuman, or collapsed voices; it may represent insubstantial or inconsistent fictional artifices rather than human figures; it may recount events that seem unworthy of being narrated or that are hopelessly confused or contradictory; it may locate these events in an unrecognizable kind of world; it may project a receiver of the story that is as unusual as its narrator.

When doing narrative theory and analysis, we must recognize the central, crucial status of fiction. No matter how closely it tries to imitate nonfictional discourses, narrative fiction is always a very different kind of speech act. Its functions, intentions, and effects diverge substantially from those of nonfiction. Nonfiction is falsifiable and can be tested against other nonfictional accounts of the same events; fiction can never be falsified by real-world sources. Fiction offers narrating animals, corpses, and even machines; in the actual world, only humans can narrate. Temporal sequences that are impossible in the real world, contradictory spatial configurations, and the inversion of causal sequences where the effect precedes its cause can exist only in a work of fiction. Fictional characters can personify ideas as part of a larger allegory, they can be known more intimately than the people around us can be, and characters can even realize that they are fictional creations. The fundamental nature of the difference between fiction and nonfiction is most prominent once death appears. In fiction, characters can plead with their authors to spare their lives, temporality can be run backwards so that the dead come back to life, or a figure can die several times in fiction and miraculously be alive again in the next chapter. In life, there is only one death, and it is irreversible.

Salman Rushdie provides an excellent example of this crucial difference. Part way through *Midnight's Children,* the narrator, Saleem Sinai, realizes that he has made a mistake: "Rereading my work, I have discovered an error in chronology. The assassination of Mahatma Gandhi occurs, in these pages, on the wrong date" (189–90). Saleem, however, does not correct his text: "in my India, Gandhi will continue to die at the wrong time" (190). In a work of fiction, an author can kill off any character, even historical ones, at any time. Rushdie's deliberate reconfiguring of historical events in a work of fiction is not merely a game. Instead, it is pointedly juxtaposed with and powerfully opposed to the Pakistani government's falsification of historical facts. Thus, during the invasion of East Pakistan, we read "Shaheed and I saw many things which were not true, which were not possible, because our boys would not, could not, behave so badly; we saw men in spectacles with heads like eggs being shot in side-streets, we saw the intelligentsia of the city being massacred by the hundred, but it was not true because it could not have been true" (432). Saleem reenacts in a satirical manner the government's censorship of news of these actual atrocities. We are vividly shown the difference between altering the historical record in a work of fiction and falsifying historical facts in nonfictional discourse. The former is a serious kind of play, the latter a sordid lie.

NARRATIVE THEORY has long had a bias toward the representational aspects of narrative. At the very inception of narrative theory is the *Poetics* of Aristotle, with its pronounced focus on mimesis and lifelike representations of human behavior. Literary theory from the Renaissance to the nineteenth century continued to insist on literature's duty to "hold a mirror up to nature," and nearly all twentieth- and twenty-first-century narrative theories are likewise grounded in a mimetic conception of narrative. This is even true of a theoretical approach like structuralism that purports to sidestep questions of representation and bears no particular allegiance to mimesis. Nevertheless, it often limited itself to mimetic models. The central category of the highly influential structuralist account of narrative time, for example, is that of "order," or the way the story (*fabula*) is actually arranged in the text (*sjuzhet*). Such a conception is perfectly adequate for all nonfictional works and for most works of fiction. One event comes earlier or later in the story; it is presented either earlier or later in the text. We can say "World War I preceded World War II" or we can say "World War II was preceded by World War I"; though the order in which the events are presented (the *sjuzhet*) is different in each sentence, the sequence of events in the story (the *fabula*) remains the same. As long as we are dealing with nonfiction or fiction that imitates the conventions of nonfiction, there is no problem. However, the many works that do not have a single, recoverable story or a single, fixed presentation are necessarily omitted from this account; we will need to reconceptualize the entire nature of the representation of temporality if we are to have a complete theory that includes the unnatural and impossible chronologies that exist only in fiction. As we will see, attention to antimimetic narratives regularly demands that we extend or reconstruct basic categories of narrative theory.

Antimimetic narratives have been around since the time of Aristophanes and Petronius, and they were common in the Middle Ages (dream visions, Rabelais' *Gargantua and Pantagruel*) and the Renaissance (especially Shakespeare's more fanciful and self-conscious dramas such as *The Winter's Tale*). Antimimetic strategies inform the entire tradition of works inspired by *Tristram Shandy* and are especially prominent in postmodern fiction and the theater of the absurd. Popular narrative media are also well stocked with antimimetic series and genres, from tongue-in-cheek Broadway musicals to comic books to children's cartoons to the Bob Hope–Bing Crosby "road" movies. Even natural narrative contains its own antimimetic examples, like the "shaggy dog" story that continues endlessly or the more extreme kind of tall tale.

There are several reasons why antimimetic narratives need to be included within narrative theory. Such an inclusion will allow us to have a comprehensive theory of narrative rather than merely a theory of mimetic narratives; it will enable us to come to terms theoretically with some of the most interesting literature of our time: avant-garde, late modernist, and postmodern; it helps us understand and appreciate the distinctive nature of narrative fiction; and it provides a set of terms and concepts for the analysis of hypertext fiction.

In addition, the inclusion of antimimetic works opens up to narrative theory a vast segment of the history of literature that has until now been largely excluded. Including unnatural narratives reconnects modern experimental literature with experimental work in other genres, especially painting, whose extreme, unnatural, antirealist, impossible, and nonrepresentational works have provided inspiration for writers of prose for over a century. Finally, the goal of narrative theory is to provide a theoretical account of all narratives. A theory of narrative that excludes antimimetic works is as incomplete as a theory of art that treated all art as representational and could not discuss abstract art. The goal of my work is to expand or re-form the categories of narrative theory so that it is able to circumscribe these playful and outrageous kinds of texts.

NOTES

1. See, for example, Prince's "On a Postcolonial Narratology." [RW]

2. I am referring to Genette's many disclaimers in *Narrative Discourse: An Essay in Method.* [RW]

3. For a classic discussion of this link between experimental fiction and feminism that greatly influenced feminist narratology, see duPlessis. [RW]

4. See, for example, Aldama's *Your Brain on Latino Comics.* His corpus is made up of pointedly non-meanstream texts; in keeping with the larger project of cognitive narrative theory, however, his work is focused on the commonalties among human brains and bodies. [RW]

5. I am referring to the mid-1980s, when Susan Lanser's work and my own first began defining the term "feminist narratology." See Lanser, "Towards a Feminist Narratology," and Warhol, *Gendered Interventions.* [RW]

6. As will become clear in what follows, I use the term "referential" in a broader sense than does Dorrit Cohn in *The Distinction of Fiction,* for example. Discussing ideas also explored by theorists such as Philippe Lejeune, Lubomír Doležel (*Heterocosmica*), and Marie-Laure Ryan (*Possible Worlds*), Cohn argues that fictional narratives are non-referential because, in contrast with historiography, journalistic reports, biographies, autobiographies, and other narrative modes falling within the domain of nonfiction, fictional works are not subject to judgments of truth and falsity (15). As Cohn writes, "in fictional poetics, though the concept of reference has recently been reinstated, its qualification by such terms as *fictive, nonostensive,* or *pseudo-* sufficiently indicates its nonfactual connotations, even when it denotes components of the fictional world taken directly from the world of reality" (113). In my approaches to the present volume, however, I link worldmaking to "the referential dimension of narrative" to preserve the intuition that fictional as well as nonfictional narratives consist of *sequences of referring expressions* (see also Schiffrin), whose nature and scope will vary depending on the storytelling medium involved. Through these referring expressions, narratives prompt interpreters to co-construct a discourse model or model-world—that is, a storyworld—containing the situations, events, and entities indexed by world-evoking expressions at issue (for further discussion, see Herman, *Basic Elements* and *Story Logic*). In other words, narratives refer to model-worlds, whether they are the imagined, autonomous model-worlds of fiction or the model-worlds about which nonfictional accounts make claims that are subject to falsification. [DH]

7. With signified and signifier, compare story (*fabula*) and discourse (*sjuzhet*). [DH]

8. In *Basic Elements,* I more fully characterize narrative as a mode of representation that (a) must be interpreted in light of a specific discourse context or occasion for telling; (b) focuses on a structured time-course of particularized events; (c) concerns itself with some kind of disruption or disequilibrium in a storyworld inhabited by intelligent agents; and (d) conveys what it is like for those agents to live through the storyworld-in-flux. [DH]

9. Compare Brenner's account of how, for Wittgenstein, "[p]hilosophical investigation recollects the grammar of terms that are deeply embedded in everyday language" (7). [DH]

10. Here I am drawing on Wittgenstein's discussion, in section 122 of the *Philosophical Investigations,* of the key concept of "surveyability." Suggesting that the purpose of philosophy is to provide an overview or survey of the different ways in which uses of

words fit together in a language, Wittgenstein writes: "A main source of our failure to understand is that we don't have *an overview* of the use of our words.—Our grammar is deficient in surveyability. A surveyable representation produces precisely that kind of understanding which consists in 'seeing connections'" (54). [DH]

11. For more on the scope and aims of the project of metanarratology, see Herman, "Formal Models." [DH]

12. As Goodman puts it, "If I ask about the world, you can offer to tell me how it is under one or more frames of reference; but if I insist that you tell me how it is apart from all frames, what can you say? We are confined to ways of describing whatever is described. Our universe, so to speak, consists of these ways rather than of a world or of worlds" (2–3). Compare Merlin Donald's complementary account of the evolution and functions of mimesis or "mimetic skill." For Donald, such skill "usually incorporates both mimicry and imitation to a higher end, that of re-enacting and re-presenting an event or relationship" (169). Hence, extended to the social realm, mimetic skill "results in a collective conceptual 'model' of society" (173). See also my contribution to Part Two. [DH]

13. See chapter 5 for analogous remarks concerning the need to reassess the grammar of questions about narrative that feature the concept of "Theory of Mind." [DH]

14. In characterizing narrative texts as blueprints for building storyworlds, I am drawing on Reddy's critique of what he termed the "conduit metaphor" for communicative processes (see Green, 10–13, for a useful discussion). Reddy suggested that rather than being mere vessels or vehicles for channeling thoughts, ideas, and meanings back and forth, utterances are like blueprints, planned artifacts whose design is tailored to the goal of enabling an interlocutor to reconstruct the situations or worlds after which the blueprints are patterned. Further, in contrast with the conduit metaphor, which blames miscommunication on a poorly chosen linguistic vessel, the blueprint analogy predicts that completely successful interpretation of communicative designs will be rare—given the complexity of the processes involved in planning, executing, and making sense of the blueprints. Hence my emphasis in this volume on the *defeasibility* of inferences about story creators' intentions. [DH]

15. Relevant studies include Doležel; Duchan, Bruder, and Hewitt; Emmott; Gerrig; Herman, *Story Logic* and *Basic Elements;* Pavel; Ryan, *Possible;* and Werth. [DH]

16. Conversely, Donald explores how narrative, among other semiotic and thus cultural practices, itself contributed to the development of humans' cognitive abilities (201–68). [DH]

17. There are as yet few critical studies of this recently published text. But see Head, "Novella," and, for background on the novel's composition, Zalewski, who reports that Timothy Garton Ash's comments on an early draft caused McEwan to remove more explicit references to Florence's sexual abuse at the hands of her father (see my discussion in chapter 3). Meanwhile, Head's *Ian McEwan* provides invaluable insights into McEwan's oeuvre prior to the publication of *On Chesil Beach.* [DH]

18. Readers of *On Chesil Beach* familiar with Ford Madox Ford's 1915 novel *The Good Soldier* will recognize that the first names of McEwan's two main characters echo those of Edward Ashburnham and Florence Dowell, whose ill-fated, destructive affair is narrated ex post facto—and through a complex layering of time-frames—by Florence's perversely obtuse husband, John Dowell. [DH]

19. There are still other forms of representation as well, such as what I call the nonmimetic, that includes genres like fairy tales, animal fables, and fantasy, whose charac-

ters and events do not primarily reproduce people and situations in life. Thus, it does not make sense to say that the depiction of a particular fairy or talking pig is realistic or unrealistic. Antimimetic authors can also parody these forms as well, as we see in Angela Carter's postmodern rewrites of classical fairy tales. In my sections I will be concerned with narratives that are predominantly and, in fact, flagrantly antimimetic, since I find antimimetic texts more challenging than nonmimietic narratives in the ways they contest the conventions of nonfictional and realistic representation. [BR]

20. For further reading on these issues, see Alber and Heinze; Alber, Iversen, Nielsen, and Richardson (2010); Richardson, "Narrative Poetics"; and the Unnatural Narratology website homepage http://nordisk.au.dk/forskning/forskningscentre/nrl/unnatural/. [BR]

2

Authors, Narrators, Narration

James Phelan and Peter J. Rabinowitz

"Somebody tells." This chapter will begin to sketch out the rhetorical tangles around the apparently simple phrase that begins our definition. Reading literary narrative is typically more difficult than reading, say, physics textbooks because the "somebody" who tells is neither simple nor stable—and because the resulting complexity and instability are not weaknesses to be minimized but key components of the experience, including the particular pleasures it brings.

Most obviously, from the rhetorical perspective, in many texts (including all fictional narrative) the somebody who tells is split into at least two figures, the author and the narrator. There's little need to rehearse this distinction here: it's something pointed out in nearly every manual on narrative fiction, and it's something that children learn fairly quickly. Only the most unschooled reader doesn't understand that Huck is not Twain. But while the distinction itself is relatively unproblematic, there *are* complications with each of the terms. Furthermore, once we shift our attention to "narration," we need to recognize that authors often use the dialogue between characters to accomplish telling functions.

AUTHORS

Surprisingly, it's the concept of "author" that nowadays generates the greater theoretical wrangling. Two issues are particularly vexed. First, especially in the wake of poststructuralism's provocative proclamation of "The Death of the Author," there is serious disagreement about whether we should be talking about authors at all, especially about authors as . . . well, authorities on or even designers of texts whose designs are of any significant consequence for interpretation—if they can be recovered at all. As committed pluralists, we believe that the question ought not to be posed as an either/or: valuable critical work can be done by ignoring authors and their purposes, and just as valuable work can be done by attending to them. A purely formal description such as Vladimir Propp's account of the grammar of Russian folktales, can be highly illuminating without any discussion of authorial participation. So too can an ideologically oriented analysis such as D. A. Miller's Foucauldian account in *The Novel and the Police* of Victorian fiction's role in enforcing certain cultural prescriptions. But to the extent that you are considering narrative *as a communicative process,* then authors, and their communicative purposes, matter: there can be no rhetoric without a rhetor. Our commitment to pluralism interacts with our commitment to rhetorical theory in our claim that viewing narrative as a communicative process is *one* valuable (and widely practiced) way of thinking and that certain consequences follow from looking at narrative in this way.

In stressing the author's decisive role, however, we are not suggesting that the task of interpretation (or the goal of reading) should be reduced to the discovery of the author's conscious intentions. As we noted in the introduction, we account for the effects of narrative by reference to a feedback loop among authorial agency, textual phenomena, and reader response. Furthermore, the exercise of authorial agency entails necessary sacrifices: as Wayne C. Booth—whose 1961 book *The Rhetoric of Fiction* persuasively demonstrated the advantages of approaching narrative as rhetorical action—eloquently argues, the choice to do one thing inevitably blocks your ability to do other things. For example, once Twain decides to tie Huck's growing ethical maturity to his ability to negotiate the conflict between his feelings for Jim as a man and his sense of how whites act toward slaves, Twain has to set his novel before the Civil War, which in turn means that there are certain of his favorite themes (for instance, his criticisms of postwar economic excesses) that he cannot take up. Then, too, there can be unintended (or sometimes unanticipated) consequences of some things an author chooses to do: as Ralph Rader has pointed out, certain "indirect facts" of the text, certain aspects of a text pointed to by persistent responses to it—for example, the impression that Milton's God in *Paradise Lost* speaks like a school divine—may be "simply . . . the *unintended and unavoidable negative consequence* of the artist's positive constructive intention" (in order to justify the ways of God to men, Milton needed to have God speak, but it was inevitable that the transcendent Being would sound disappointingly human) (Rader 38).

Still, such authorial limitations do not undermine our key point: once you decide to take a rhetorical perspective, the best way to make initial sense of texts is to treat them as if they are *intended* to be made sense of—and then, once we've reconstructed that multidimensional sense, we can take the next step of evaluating the author's communication. Thus, when Huck heartlessly answers Aunt Sally's question about whether anybody was hurt by the blown-out cylinder head—"'No'm. Killed a nigger'"—and when she replies equally heartlessly—"'Well, it's lucky; because sometimes people do get hurt'"—as rhetorical theorists we can reasonably assume that Twain designed those responses as something for us to *interpret*. He didn't want us to stop at their literal meaning but wanted us to go further, to decide what they reveal about each character, how those revelations influence our ethical judgments of them, and how the exchange affects our understanding of the larger narrative. Those decisions may not be easy—is Huck reverting to his old self? is he simply playing a role for safety?—but they become either impossible or arbitrary if we don't assume that someone chose those words for a reason. Once we make those decisions about the implied Twain's reasons, we are in a good position to evaluate his choices, including the specific diction and syntax of the exchange, his placement of it at this point in the progression, and, indeed, his decision to include it at all. In contrast, deciding to censure or defend Twain's choice *before* considering his purposes typically means projecting our values onto Twain's novel—and thus forgoing our chance to understand its designs on us, much less to be influenced by them.

While our most important commitment is to the role of authorial agency in narrative communication, we also endorse the concept of the implied author that Booth introduced in *The Rhetoric of Fiction*. Booth defined the implied author as the version of himself or herself whom the actual author constructs and who communicates through the myriad choices—conscious, intuitive, or even unconscious—that he or she makes in composing and revising a narrative. The concept has subsequently been contested, with some theorists such as Gérard Genette—and our collaborator David Herman—saying that it is unnecessary and others such as Mieke Bal saying that it is too imprecise. At the same time, others have found it very valuable. We side with the last group for a number of reasons:

1. It recognizes that writing narrative is inevitably an act of self-presentation. Booth points out the often significant difference between the biographical authors we learn about from reading their biographies (or even from personal acquaintance) and the versions of those authors we come to know from encountering them in their narratives. Not all writers are self-conscious as they create their implied authors, but many—like Mark Twain—are. In his texts, Samuel Clemens constructed an image of himself (or more accurately a series of images of himself) that he believed deserved its own name. Strikingly, that name and the dominant image associated with it had effects that the biographical Clemens could not completely control: for example, many of his occasional political writings from the beginning of the twentieth century remained unpublished at the time he wrote them at least partly because they upset the image of the implied author of the popular texts.

The concept of the implied author also gives us purchase on a number of serious social and historical questions that are otherwise hard to navigate. Consider, for instance, the relations between gay writers and the images of themselves they construct when writing under conditions that make coming out dangerous. Consider, alternatively, the literature of self-justification, works by authors who are trying to present selves that counter widespread criticism of their actions (for instance, the multiple "authors" of the film *On the Waterfront,* some of whom were at least in part trying to present their decisions to testify before the House Un-American Activities Committee in a favorable light).

2. It gives us a useful way to talk about intention. A rhetorical approach is inevitably tied up with intention; yet, as many critics have rightly pointed out, the actual intentions of the actual author are often—even usually— unknowable. Furthermore, the actual author is not always the best judge of his design. Ernest Hemingway, when asked about an apparent contradiction in the attribution of dialogue to the two waiters in "A Clean, Well-Lighted Place," said that he thought the story was fine. But after his death, some Hemingway critics persuaded his publisher Scribners' that the implied Hemingway could not have intended the contradiction and so Scribners' agreed to amend the text (rightly in our view). More generally, the aim of the rhetorical approach is not to determine the conscious intention of the actual author (although, if available, that may be one piece of relevant information) but rather to discern the system of intentionality that explains why the text has this particular shape rather than some other one.

3. It helps explain why we often come to know different versions of the same actual author in different texts. The version of himself that Twain constructs in *Adventures of Tom Sawyer* is far less pessimistic than the version he constructs in "The Man That Corrupted Hadleyburg," much less "The United States of Lyncherdom." The attitudes toward women in the implied Ernest Hemingway's "The Short, Happy Life of Francis Macomber"

are markedly different from the attitudes toward women in his "Hills Like White Elephants." In these cases, we have the same actual author but distinct implied authors.

4. It gives us a way to talk about texts with problematic authorship. This includes, for instance, ghostwritten, anonymous, and fraudulent texts. It also includes collaboratively written texts (such as the one we're writing here): the two (or more) actual authors construct a hybrid version of their actual selves, and it is that hybrid version that readers come to know.

 We want to stress that in our view the implied author, though knowable through the text, is not a textual construct equivalent to one of the characters but rather the agent who constructs the text. In other words, in the light of our main commitment, to authorial agency, we are less invested in the distinction between actual and implied author than we are in the view that texts are not collections of free-floating signifiers but purposive communicative actions designed by some authorial agent. At the same time, as we noted in our introduction, *we* are interested in analytic categories only to the extent that they have some significant payoff—and we recognize that in many critical discussions the key distinction is between authorial agency and textual free play rather than between the actual and the implied author. In those cases, we will often use the name of the author to cover both the real author and the implied author.[1]

NARRATORS

One of the most important choices an author makes is about the *kind* of narrator to employ. Working in a specific context—in particular, trying to counter the prevalent orthodoxy that placed "showing" in a position over "telling," and trying to get beyond the easy, but misleading, distinction between first- and third-person narration—Booth was especially concerned with the distinction between dramatized and undramatized narrators. His most durable contribution, though, was his development of the concept of the "unreliable narrator."

Booth's initial conception was relatively simple: a narrator is "reliable when he or she speaks for or acts in accordance with the norms of the work (which is to say, the implied author's norms), unreliable when he does not" (158–59). Since then, however, rhetorical narrative theorists have introduced a number of refinements. For instance, Jim has developed a distinction between restricted narration and unreliable narration[2] and a taxonomy of six types of unreliability. Both developments arise from his observation that narrators perform three primary tasks: they report (along the axis of facts, characters, and events), interpret (along the axis of knowledge or perception), and evaluate (along the axis of ethics). When a narrator performs only one of the three tasks and the author uses that restriction to communicate something that the narrator is unaware of, the implied author is using restricted narration. In the most common kind of restricted narration, the implied author will have a naïve narrator reliably report the events but not attempt to interpret or evaluate them, and in so doing communicate an interpretation or evaluation that is beyond the capacity of the naïve narrator. Here's an example from *Huckleberry Finn:* "Tom Sawyer, he hunted me up, and said he was going to start a band of robbers, and I might join if I would go back to the widow and be respectable. So I went back" (32). Twain restricts Huck to the task of reliably reporting events, thereby implying that Huck fails to grasp the irony of what he reports: the contradiction in Tom's logic that allows him to use respectability as an eligibility condition for joining a band of robbers.

When a narrator performs any of the three tasks inadequately (as measured against how the implied author would perform it), then we have unreliable narration. But narrators can be inadequate in two main ways: by distorting things or by failing to go far enough. Consequently, narrators can be unreliable by misreporting, misinterpreting, and misevaluating (in these cases readers need to reject the narrator's version and, if possible, replace it with another one) and by underreporting, underreading, and underevaluating (in these cases readers need to supplement the narrator's version).

Just as significant is Jim's more recent distinction between estranging unreliability ("unreliable narration that underlines or increases the distance between the narrator and the reader") and bonding unreliability ("unreliable narration that reduces the distance between the narrator and the reader") (Phelan, "Estranging" 222–23). In the wake of Booth's work, the default position was that unreliability served to distance us from the narrator—to be an unreliable narrator was, ipso facto, to be somehow deficient (in particular, given Booth's ethical emphases, morally deficient). But in fact our relations to unreliable narrators, like our relations to other people, are more complex than this kind of judgmental clarity would suggest, and authors use this complexity to create a range of emotional and ethical effects. The bonding/estranging distinction recognizes that with unreliable narration, this range extends from affective and ethical repulsion at one end to affective sympathy and ethical admiration at the other. Booth's original conception privileged the relationship of reader and implied author: "the emotions and judgments of the implied author are . . . the very stuff out of which great fiction is made" (86)—and Booth eloquently demonstrated how sharing those emotions and judgments often involves our communion with the implied author either through her surrogate, the reliable narrator (as in Jane Austen's *Emma*) or "behind [the] back" (*Rhetoric* 159) of the unreliable narrator (as in Ring Lardner's "Haircut"). Recognizing bonding effects illuminates the importance of a different kind of communion accompanying the behind-the-back connection of unreliability: a communion between readers and a *narrator* who could never be mistaken for the implied author's surrogate. In this way, the bonding/estranging distinction adds an important dimension to our understanding of the workings of narrative communication.

We can clarify these theoretical points by exploring the varying nature and effects of unreliable narration in *Huckleberry Finn*. First, a fairly simple example: Huck describes the widow Douglas's response to his return to her home this way: "The widow she cried over me, and called me a poor lost lamb, and she called me a lot of other names, too, but, she never meant no harm by it" (32). This passage uses a combination of reliable reporting, misinterpreting, and underevaluating in the service of bonding effects. Huck misinterprets the widow's joyous religious references as name-calling because he doesn't recognize the New Testament source—and that misinterpreting leads him to undervalue the ethical quality of her response. Yet this comic failure of understanding simultaneously reveals a moral strength. Although Huck's ignorance means that he fails to grasp both the extent of the widow's joy and her beliefs about what his return means, Twain demonstrates that Huck's ethical compass is sufficiently sensitive for him to appreciate that she "never meant no harm." Again, the overall effects are to bring us affectively and ethically closer to Huck even as we continue to register our interpretive distance from him. Simply to call him an "unreliable narrator" fails to capture these effects and, consequently, is itself a kind of underinterpreting.

The same kind of interplay—with more subtlety and greater consequences—marks Huck's self-examination in Chapter XXXI, which leads to his famous decision to go to hell rather than inform Miss Watson of Jim's whereabouts.

> I know very well why [the words of my prayer] wouldn't come. It was because my heart warn't right; it was because I warn't square; it was because I was playing double. I was letting *on* to give up sin, but away inside me I was holding on to the biggest one of all. I was trying to make my mouth *say* I would do the right thing and the clean thing, and go and write to that nigger's owner and tell where he was; but deep down in me I knowed it was a lie—and He knowed it. You can't pray a lie—I found that out. (200)

Here we have a case of misevaluating being used for bonding effects. Huck judges himself to be ethically deficient, while the implied Twain guides us to judge Huck's inability to act against Jim's interest as a sign that he is acting according to a higher ethical standard.

Huck then writes the letter to Miss Watson, revealing Jim's location, so that he'll be able to pray for help to stop sinning. He immediately feels better; but before he prays, he starts thinking about the River trip:

> And I got to thinking over our trip down the River; and I see Jim before me, all the time, in the day, and in the night-time, sometimes moonlight, sometimes storms, and we a floating along, talking, and singing, and laughing. But somehow I couldn't seem to strike no places to harden me against him, but only the other kind. . . . and at last I struck the time I saved him by telling the men we had small-pox aboard, and he was so grateful, and said I was the best friend old Jim ever had in the world, and the *only* one he's got now; and then I happened to see to look around, and see that paper. (200–201)

At this moment, Huck is reliable as reporter, interpreter, and evaluator—and this burst of insight serves to reinforce the previous bonding unreliability. It does so by revealing the ethical heart of Huck's previous misevaluating, showing us that it applies not to his judgments of Jim but to his conception of "the right thing and the clean thing" in this situation. To send the letter would be to follow the dictates of conventional Christianity, but it would simultaneously follow the dictates of a slave society that has used Christianity as one of its buttresses. Huck intuitively recognizes that by following both sets of dictates, he would be going against everything his experience of Jim has taught him about the right and clean thing to do. Thus, when Huck makes his decision to tear up that paper and—in a return to unreliability—evaluates his action most negatively, we feel our strongest sympathy and our greatest ethical approval of his actions.

> "All right, then, I'll go to hell"—and tore it up.
> It was awful thoughts, and awful words, but they was said. And I let them stay said; and never thought no more about reforming. I shoved the whole thing out of my head, and said I would take up wickedness again, which was in my line, being brung up to it, and the other warn't. (201)

With this climactic misevaluation, the bonding unreliability reaches its apex. In particular, having trained us with comic passages about religion, including the one discussed earlier, Twain is now asking us to work through something far deeper. On the one hand, there's still a level of broad comedy, since, for Twain and his authorial audience, Huck's fear of going to hell is just as much a superstition as Jim's fear of taking up a snakeskin in his hand. At the same time, we transcend Huck's misinterpretation and admire the courage that his choice reveals. While Huck is sure that he's damned, Twain's audience is even more certain that he is making the right ethical choice.

As our tone suggests, we greatly admire Twain's handling of the relationships among author, narrator, and audience in this passage, and we extend our admiration for his craft to the whole first two-thirds of the narrative. In chapter 7, which explicitly takes up the question of evaluation, we will discuss what we regard as Twain's far less successful narration in the last third of the novel, the infamous Evasion section.

CONVERSATION AS NARRATION

One consequence of viewing narrative primarily as a communicative event rather than primarily a textual structure is that we are less beholden to the distinction between story and discourse than many other theorists. That distinction neatly separates elements of story (events and existents, including settings and characters) from elements of discourse (structure and modes of narration) in the interests of analytical precision. In this view, scenes of character–character dialogue are part of story, since they are events involving characters, while any narratorial commentary on the dialogue is part of discourse. But from the perspective of rhetorical theory, such analytical precision comes at the cost of explanatory power, since authors can use character–character dialogue both as events and as modes of narration. Thus, scenes of character–character dialogue with interspersed narratorial commentary often show an author using different resources of narrative (characters, the narrator, the occasion of the dialogue) in order to combine the representation of an event with reporting, interpreting, and evaluating.

At the end of Chapter XII, Twain tells about a climactic moment in Huck and Jim's experience on board the wrecked steamboat *The Walter Scott*. Huck has been reporting the conversation he overhears between Jake Packard and Bill about whether they should kill Jim Turner, which ends with Packard convincing Bill that they can leave the wreck by using its small boat and then watch to make sure he drowns when the wreck breaks up. That dialogue itself is obviously full of reporting, interpreting, and evaluating, but even more salient are the narrative functions of the dialogue between Huck and Jim about what they need to do in light of what Huck has overheard. Huck has just heard Jim moan, when Twain gives us the following exchange:

> "Quick, Jim, it ain't no time for fooling around and moaning; there's a gang of murderers in yonder, and if we don't hunt up their boat and set her drift-ing down the river so these fellows can't get away from the wreck, there's one of 'em going to be in a bad fix. But if we find their boat we can put *all* of 'em in a bad fix—for the Sheriff'll get 'em. Quick—hurry! I'll hunt the labbard side, you hunt the stabbard. You start at the raft, and—
>
>   "Oh, my lordy, lordy! *Raf*'? Dey ain' no raf' no mo', she done broke loose en gone!—en here we is!" (86–87)

In Huck's portion of this dialogue, Twain shows him offering to Jim—and by extension to Twain's actual audience—ethical judgments about "these fel-lows" as well as interpretive judgments about what he and Jim need to do. These judgments are as clear and significant as they would be if Twain had switched the mode to Huck's telling his narratee about how he'd sized up the situation. However, by conveying Huck's judgments in his address to Jim, Twain also tells us about the way Huck implicitly trusts Jim even as he shows Huck's instinctively clear ethical judgments and his shrewd strategy for deal-ing with the situation. Jim's line in turn reports a significant new event, which is itself a serious local complication of the instabilities, along with his affec-tive response. Twain also invites us to infer the significance of what Jim does not say, namely, "I told you so," since Jim had advised against leaving the raft to board *The Walter Scott*. The larger point here is that Twain is using the resources of character-character dialogue as narration by other means.[3]

Robyn Warhol

Who is speaking? To whom? In what circumstances? These most basic questions of classical narrative theory provide the starting place for a feminist narratological study of narration. For a gender-centered analysis, the personification of narrator and narratee implied in the usage "who?" and "to whom?" is entirely appropriate, because feminist narratology so often treats a text's situation of enunciation as if it were an exchange between embodied persons. "Who is speaking?" refers not just to the narrator(s) but also to the author; "To whom?" asks about actual audience, as well as narratee. And for the feminist narratologist "In what circumstances?" means "At what moment in history?" as well as "At which diegetic level?" or "With what degree of focalization?" A text has its origin in the material world, a world where gender shapes perceptions and realities that go into the writing and reading of books. Therefore the identity, experience, and socio-cultural-historical circumstances of the author—not to mention the reader—are important in understanding the ways that narrative participates in the politics of gender.

In this belief, feminist narratology departs radically from its classical roots. For Gérard Genette, Gerald Prince, and Dorrit Cohn—the three most influential of the theorists whose narratological models served as the jumping-off point for the first generation of feminist narratologists—narrative discourse is an abstract structure, to be rigorously distinguished from its real-world creator or receivers. Feminist critics from Virginia Woolf forward have regarded abstractions suspiciously, however, constantly aware of the gendered body that writes or reads every text. For this reason, the person who wrote the text is a living presence in feminist narratology. Too deeply invested in poststructuralism to place much value on "authorial intention," feminist narratology nevertheless asks how the author's gendered experiences of a particular time in a particular place affect the structures he or she employs in putting together the story and discourse that comprise narrative. Unlike classical narratologists, critics who use feminist narrative theory tend to be as interested in the interpretation and evaluation of texts as in the description of how texts work. In asking "What does this narrative mean?" or "Is this text any good—in terms of aesthetics, ethics, or politics?" the feminist narratologist is not barred, as are her classical forebears, from consulting what is known about the Author herself.

Jane Austen's history, then, as a genteel clergyman's daughter writing in England during the early nineteenth century colors the feminist narratologist's analysis of *Persuasion*. Because she has become a cult figure both inside and outside academia, Austen is particularly present in most analyses of her work. Often, author and narrator are elided in what is understood as "Austen's voice," a distinctive blend of ironic hyperbole, orderly syntax, parallel phrasing, free indirect discourse, and periodic sentences. From the beginning many critics have tended to regard that voice as a representation of Austen herself. Departing from the sentimentalized Victorian image of "gentle Jane" disseminated by her nephew J. E. Austen-Leigh's biography of Austen, and taking a cue from the mid-twentieth-century belief, articulated by D. W. Harding, that Austen's voice speaks with "regulated hatred" about characters "she herself detests and fears" (12), many feminist critics identify the novelist's persona with Cassandra Austen's one surviving sketch of her sister: critical, quizzical, sharp, humorous, impatient, penetrating, active.[4] Austen's evident authorial investment in the conventional marriage plot posed a stumbling block for some second-wave feminist critics, but the kind of gender-centered narrative criticism I practice finds Austen's feminist message less in the details of her stories than in her handling of narration.[5]

Austen's famous irony provides a classic example of what feminist narratologists have called "double-voicing," in that her narrator characteristically makes utterances that appear to mean something other than precisely what is said. Thus, one voice speaks the literal meaning of the utterance, and a second, implicit voice ironizes that literal meaning. But sometimes the narrator will set up the double-voicing by straightforwardly describing characters or situations as the narrator of *Persuasion* does in this early pronouncement on Anne's father: "Vanity was the beginning and the end of Sir Walter Elliot's character; vanity of person and of situation" (10). In the beginning of *Persuasion,* as in her other novels, Austen's narrator lays out the basic characteristics as well as the familial and financial situations of all her principal characters, thus setting up the range of possibilities for ways the story might develop. Having made so clear a statement of "the beginning and end" of Sir Walter's character, the narrator thereafter freely exercises her penchant for explaining Sir Walter's thoughts and actions as though they were perfectly sensible, while silently communicating the ludicrousness of what the character says and does. For instance, once Lady Russell has persuaded Sir Walter that his straitened financial circumstances require him to rent out Kellynch Hall, the narrator deadpans her description of his attitude, a deadpan that depends on our recognizing her mingling of Sir Walter's voice with the narrator's in free indirect discourse:

> Sir Walter could not have borne the degradation of being known to design letting his house.—Mr. Shepherd had once mentioned the word "advertise;"—but never dared approach it again; Sir Walter spurned the idea of its

being offered in any manner; forbad the slightest hint being dropped of his having such an intention; and it was only on the supposition of his being spontaneously solicited by some most unexceptionable applicant, on his own terms, and as a great favour, that he would let it at all. (19)

Austen's narrator thus exposes Sir Walter's silliness without directly criticizing it. One way to think about how her irony works is to realize that if Sir Walter could read this passage, he would recognize what the narrator is overtly saying as "quite right." This realization, in turn, opens up the presence of Sir Walter's voice and the beliefs associated with it in this passage, especially in "degradation," "spurned," "forbad," "most unexceptionable applicant" and "great favour." Austen's narrator—or rather the implied author informing that figure—counts on the authorial audience to recognize the vainglorious overstatement in Sir Walter's language, especially when juxtaposed with such plain speaking as "advertise," and thus get the joke. This is classic feminist "double-voicing": in this paragraph Austen's narrator takes the patriarch down without uttering a single word against him.

As this passage indicates, Austen's ironic, double-voiced narration is intimately tied to her trademark use of free indirect discourse. Moving seamlessly between the narrator's opinions and the characters' thoughts or utterances, the narrator uses the characters' own words against them. In *Persuasion* Austen uses this technique not only when representing characters who are being satirized—Sir Walter, Lady Russell, Anne's sisters Elizabeth and Mary, the Musgrove girls, Mrs. Clay, Mr. William Walter Elliot, to mention just a few—but also when representing the heroine herself. Frequently the narrator renders Anne's thoughts as Anne might have voiced them had she spoken, seldom shielding the heroine from the narrator's usual ironic practice. For example, in one of the scenes where Anne anticipates seeing Frederick Wentworth eight years after the rupture of their love affair, the narrator writes, "What was it to her, if Frederick Wentworth were only half a mile distant, making himself agreeable to others!" (51). The exclamation point expresses the energy Anne must exert to convince herself that Wentworth's whereabouts are nothing to her, at the same time that it indicates the narrator's ironic take on Anne's thoughts. When Anne hears from her sister Mary what Wentworth has said upon seeing Anne again, the free indirect discourse with which the narrator renders the heroine's thoughts again gives the heroine the lie:

"So altered that he should not have known her again!" These were words which could not but dwell with her. Yet she soon began to rejoice that she had heard them. They were of sobering tendency; they allayed agitation; they composed, and consequently must make her happier." (54)

Succeeding events—not to mention the state of anxiety that persists for her throughout the rest of the novel—show the momentary self-delusion Anne indulges during this burst of rationalization. Even this most admirable of Austen's heroines is not immune from the narrator's ironic double-voiced discourse.

Austen's narrators speak from the position that used to be called by the oxymoronic term "limited omniscience," more properly described as het-erodiegetic narration focalized almost exclusively through the protagonist. What the narrator "knows" is a question I will take up later, when discussing perspective below; who the narrator "is" can be understood as a separate question. For the most part a disembodied voice, Austen's narrator only rarely uses the first person, most often near the end of her novels. *Persuasion* is no exception, as the narrator's rare "I" appears in the first paragraph of the novel's final chapter. Because Austen's narrator is never a character within the diegetic world, the brief appearances of her "I" make for moments of metalepsis, reminders that the diegesis hangs by the thread of the narrator's words and, in turn, by the novelist's invention. Significantly, these metalepses frequently coincide, as in *Persuasion,* with the much-longed-for resolution of the marriage plot. Just when she comes to an opportunity to give juicy details about the heroine's blissful union with the hero, Austen's narrator pops up with a self-reference, explicitly refusing, in Austen's characteristic way, to narrate those very details. In *Persuasion,* the narrator's "I" appears in a moment of unnarration, relegating romantic details to rhetorical questions and declining to draw a conventional moral:

> Who can be in doubt of what followed? When any two young people take it into their heads to marry, they are pretty sure by perseverance to carry their point, be they ever so poor, or ever so imprudent, or ever so little likely to be necessary to each other's ultimate comfort. This may be bad morality to conclude with, but I believe it to be truth; and if such parties succeed, how should a Captain Wentworth and an Anne Elliot, with the advantage of maturity of mind, consciousness of right, and one independent fortune between them, fail of bearing down every opposition? (199)

The moral of a story is attributable to the author, as Austen's narrator is well aware; and *Persuasion* is not the only one of Austen's novels that ends on a moral the narrator declares to be questionable. *Northanger Abbey,* published posthumously together with *Persuasion,* comes to a similarly open conclusion:

> To begin perfect happiness at the respective ages of twenty-six and eighteen is to do pretty well; and professing myself moreover convinced that [his father's] unjust interference, so far from being really injurious to their felicity, was perhaps rather conducive to it, by improving their knowledge of each other, and adding strength to their attachment, I leave it to be settled, by whomsoever it may concern, whether the tendency of this work be altogether to recommend parental tyranny, or reward filial disobedience. (240)

"Professing [her]self convinced" that Henry and Catherine's relationship has benefited from adversity, the narrator refers to them as though the characters inhabited the same plane as the narrator. Referring in the same sentence to their status as creatures of a narrative creation (by mentioning "this work"), she immediately undermines the suggestion that Henry and Catherine have any substance beyond the fictitious world. That the narrator steps into the diegetic frame to draw attention to herself by making jokes about the morals of her marriage-plot conclusions should come as a surprise. These metaleptic moments are serving a feminist purpose, destabilizing what is supposed to be the conventional resolution of the happy ending. What is the moral of the story, or what should the moral of the story be? Austen's narrator isn't telling.

David Herman

In this chapter I focus on narration as a mode of situated communicative action, which can be analyzed, on the basis of textual performances, in the same way that other sorts of action are—namely, in terms of *reasons for acting*. We can think of a nested structure of actions in this connection: local textual choices subserve the more global purposes of narrative worldmaking, which are nested in turn in a still broader ecology of representational goals. In everyday discourse I can recruit from words, gestures, and other communicative resources to construct a narrative that I use in turn to account for (or repudiate) someone's conduct, for example, or to justify the attachment I feel for a particular place. Likewise, written, literary narratives like McEwan's can be characterized as a form of communicative action, for the uptake of which inferences about authors' (and sometimes narrators') reasons for acting are not only pertinent but necessary.

NARRATIONAL ACTS AND REASONS FOR THEM

What distinguishes actions from mere behaviors is that whereas both are the effects of *causes* that can be described in physical or material terms, only in the case of actions does it make sense to ask, too, about *reasons*—that is, about why an agent has chosen to act in a particular way instead of in other possible ways (Brockmeier; Malle).[6] For example, anatomical structures and physiological mechanisms provide the causal basis for my ability to extend my index finger outward while curling my other fingers in against the palm of my hand. But when it is situated in the frame of (communicative) action, this bodily movement or behavior can also be parsed as a pointing gesture, which I perform for reasons that you provisionally ascribe to me as part of the process of interpreting my behavior *as* a gesture, rather than an uncontrolled reflex or unintentional tic. Reasons for acting can be analyzed, in turn, into interlocking sets of beliefs and desires (or, more generally, propositional and motivational attitudes), as when you interpret my bodily movement as a pointing gesture by ascribing to me the belief that there is something in our shared environment that is worth calling to your attention, as well as the desire to elicit your attention by pointing at the object in question.[7]

Narrational acts do stem in part from causes—for example, the movement of vocal cords or of fingers on a computer keyboard. But beyond this they result in textual performances on the basis of which reasons for acting—reasons for producing a narrative that has a particular plot structure, mode of temporal sequencing, thematic focus, etc.—can be ascribed to those who engage in narrational conduct. Narration, in other words, does involve behavior that is explicable in causal terms; yet it cannot be exhaustively described as behavior but rather falls in the subcategory of behaviors that constitute actions and that are engaged in for reasons. Interpreters impute these reasons to narrating agents to make sense of their behaviors as communicative actions in the first place.

Thus, though it is of course possible to explore what physical mechanisms and processes may have caused a writer's behavior, when one moves to the domain of narrational action *why*-questions, or questions about reasons, become pertinent. Why does McEwan use analepses or flashbacks to Florence's and Edward's courtship and earlier family histories, instead of a more straightforwardly chronological presentation of events? Likewise, what is the reason for the text's periodic shifts between Florence's and Edward's vantage points over the course of the story, when in principle McEwan could have used a distanced, authorial mode of narration throughout or, alternatively, a single reflector or center of consciousness for the duration of the novel (Stanzel)? In connection with the novel's non-chronological narration, to be discussed in more detail in chapter 3, I impute to McEwan the belief that (in the context of this fictional world) Florence and Edward act the way they do in the present moment in part because of how they have been shaped by past situations and events; I also impute to the author the desire to foreground the impact of those earlier contexts on the newlyweds' current choices and experiences. Similarly, to anticipate issues discussed more fully in chapter 4, in connection with the text's use of what Genette would term "variable focalization" (*Narrative Discourse* 191), or the adoption of shifting perspectives on the world of the narrative, I impute to McEwan the aim of underscoring the very different profiles that events can assume depending on one's background assumptions, life history, and gender identity—as well as the importance of facing such differences squarely and negotiating them carefully.

Clearly, these are only initial, rough characterizations of the sorts of reasons for narrational acts that interpreters might ascribe to McEwan on the basis of the text. A fuller account would need to specify more precisely the procedures for ascription, the textual designs that motivate those ascriptions, and the pairings of propositional attitudes (believing, doubting, or imagining x) and motivational attitudes (desiring, loathing, or feeling indifferent toward y) that help constitute the reasons being ascribed. Along these lines, the technical concepts and nomenclatures developed by theorists of narrative can be viewed as frameworks for categorizing and differentiating among textual features in ways that bring to light their functions as story-conveying elements within larger narrative designs. Such analytic schemes make those features more amenable to being analyzed via reasons for (narrational) action that help explain their use in a given context. In this respect, narrative theory can be compared with a science; but it is a science of reasons rather than causes. Whereas sciences such as anatomy and physiology explore the causal basis for bodily behaviors, by identifying various physical structures, mechanisms, and processes, narrative research aims for increasingly precise characterizations of reasons for acts of narration, by focusing on the textual structures that provide warrant for inferences about those reasons.

AGENTS OF NARRATION

Up to now, I have focused on the process of narration rather than on the agent or agents who carry it out, or the (more or less direct or oblique) inferential pathways that lead from acts of narration to performers of those acts. Granted, along with any previous familiarity that a reader may have with a given writer's work, paratextual features of novels like McEwan's—for example, a title page that includes the phrase "A Novel" under the main title—already help channel and delimit inferences about the reasons for acting that can be assumed to underpin specific textual choices in the narrative. But though paratextual cues and prior knowledge help mold one's general or global approach to narrational acts, making sense of those acts on a local, moment-by-moment basis entails grounding them in reasons for acting, which in turn entails moving along an inferential route that points in the opposite direction—from the act to the agent of narration. To sketch out how one might begin describing this pathway and some of the implications of pursuing it, I turn now to broader issues that arise when one approaches the telling of stories as a form of communicative action whose uptake requires reasoning about tellers' reasons.

Two key concerns can be singled out. For one thing, a focus on narration as action exposes the limitations of anti-intentionalism in narrative study, bringing to the fore how ascriptions of communicative intentions lie at the foundation of narrative experiences. But to what agent or agents can (or should) these intentions be ascribed? Here emerges a second set of issues, concerning the notions of author and narrator and the relation between them. In an approach that openly acknowledges the need to ascribe intentions to narrating agents, I argue, authors or story creators become centrally important, while the category of "narrator" will be more or less salient depending on the profile of a given narrational act. Furthermore, I suggest that an approach to narration as action removes the basis for appeals to an implied author as the source of intentions projected in or assumed by a narrative.

1. Reclaiming intentions: The approach to narration being sketched here develops further the critique of anti-intentionalist assumptions that I outlined in a previous study (Herman, "Intentional"). Characterizing narration as a form of communicative action whose interpretation involves—indeed, requires—ascriptions of reasons for acting is a manifestly intentionalist line of inquiry.[8] Hence my approach contrasts starkly with W. K. Wimsatt and Monroe Beardsley's discipline-shaping essay "The Intentional Fallacy" (originally published in 1946), which argued that using an author's intentions as a yardstick for literary interpretation is neither possible nor desirable. More specifically, Wimsatt and Beardsley argued against confusing the author's designing intellect, which they admit to be the cause of the poem, with a standard for judging or interpreting the poem; this is the broader "genetic fallacy" (confusing the nature of a thing with its origin) of which for Wimsatt and Beardsley the intentional fallacy is a special case. As the previous discussion indicates, however, origins can be subdivided into reasons and causes, depending on whether one is examining actions or behaviors, respectively. To reiterate: construing people's doings in terms of reasons for acting is the basis for understanding those doings *as* actions in the first place.

Thus Wimsatt and Beardsley begged the question, arguably, when they equated (a) an interpretive practice based on ascriptions of intention with (b) commission of the genetic fallacy. Interpreting an act of narration by ascribing reasons for it is no more a confusion of the act with its causal origins than is interpreting someone's rude behavior by appealing to reasons why he or she is acting that way. To the contrary, it is indeed part of the nature of an action for it to be explicable through an account of how it arises from or originates in a reason (or set of reasons) that involves intentions and other motivational and propositional attitudes. In this same connection, note that Booth developed the concept of the implied author to be able to factor in readers' inferences about the communicative intentions and purposes manifested in narrative texts, but at the same time avoid running afoul of the anti-intentionalist strictures set out by Wimsatt and Beardsley. The better solution, I argue in my next subsection, is to dispute the anti-intentionalist's premises from the start, anchoring the process of narrative interpretation in defeasible or possibly wrong inferences concerning authors', not implied authors', communicative intentions.

2. Authors and narrators: But shouldn't reasons for telling be ascribed to narrators rather than authors? There is no one-size-fits-all answer to this question; rather, the structure of a given narrational act, the profile it mani-

fests as it unfolds in a particular context of storytelling and story interpretation, determines the nature of the inferential pathway that leads back to the
agent or agents who performs/perform it. The pathway may be relatively
direct, as in (some) autobiographical narration, or relatively indirect, as in
first-person or homodiegetic narratives that feature unreliable tellers—with
an intermediate position being occupied by texts that, like McEwan's, are
narrated heterodiegetically. The pertinence of the concept of "narrator" varies across these and other storytelling situations. In *On Chesil Beach,* the narration is conducted in a way that suggests the presence of a teller arranging
the sequence in which events are recounted, filtered through Edward's and
Florence's perspectives, and so on. But this teller remains nonpersonified,
uncharacterized, all but obviating the need to draw inferences concerning
the teller's (in contradistinction to the author's) reasons for narrating events
in the way they are presented (compare Walsh 69–85).

By contrast, McEwan's 1978 novel *The Cement Garden* is recounted by
Jack, one of the family members whose responses to the death of their parents constitute the subject of the narrative. Here two levels of narrational
action (and the reasons that respectively underpin them) need to be considered: that by means of which the author evokes Jack as a character who tells
about his efforts to bury his dead mother in concrete, his incestuous relationship with his sister, and so forth; and that by means of which Jack produces
the narrative that details these same events, with Jack's own reasons for telling his story in the way that he tells it now coming into question. Drawing
inferences about the motivational and propositional attitudes that account
for Jack's narration thus requires navigating a nested structure of reasons
within reasons, whereby readers frame inferences about Jack's intentions and
other attitudes by grounding them in inferences about McEwan's reasons for
creating Jack as a fictional person who has such attitudes.[9]

This nested structure assumes a different shape in the 1993 film version
of *The Cement Garden.* In this case there is a diversified set of narrating
agents, including cinematographers, the film's director (Andrew Birkin), and
its editors, among other story creators, who collaborate on the production
of what viewers construe as a more or less unified narrational action (Bordwell). In this complex, collaborative act of narration the characters' own
reasons for acting once again figure, at the diegetic level, as key targets for
interpretation. But arguably the inferential processes activated by the film,
like those triggered by a ghostwritten text or a hoax such as James Frey's *A
Million Little Pieces,* are of the same basic kind as the inferences prompted by
third-person "authorial" narration or first-person narration, whether reliable
or unreliable. Thus, whereas Genette in using Occam's razor to critique the

concept of the implied author made an exception for ghostwritten narratives and hoaxes (*Revisited* 146–47), I suggest that in these cases too an intentionalist approach grounded in the logic of narrative worldmaking warrants greater parsimony.

Here I target for critique ideas associated with what has become known as the narrative communication diagram, which features not only authors and readers but also implied authors and implied readers, as well as narrators and narratees. My argument is that this diagram, precisely by hedging against intentionalism, opens the door to what Alfred North Whitehead (58–59) once described as the problem of "misplaced concreteness." This problem comes into play when the heuristic status of models for inquiry becomes obscured or forgotten. In direct proportion with the force of its ban against ascriptions of intentions to authors, the diagram invests the construct of implied author with operative power, that is, knowable reasons for acting; and an entity originally designed to serve heuristic purposes thus becomes reified as the basis for interpretations of a text. But an openly intentionalist approach to worldmaking avoids such misplaced concreteness. From the perspective afforded by this approach, hoaxes and collaboratively authored texts (like other narrational acts) cue interpreters to frame defeasible or possibly wrong inferences about story creators' reasons for narrating. Accordingly, rather than distinguishing between the actual Frey and an implied author projected by his text, I can more parsimoniously characterize the text as one that, like all other narratives, was designed as a blueprint for world building. If I do not know about the controversy surrounding the text and Frey's eventual confession that he fabricated key elements of his narrative, I will assume that the storyworld evoked by the text is capable of being disconfirmed through triangulation with other accounts of the events at issue. Once I know that James Frey concocted incidents in his putatively nonfictional account, however, I will use different strategies for world-construction, modifying the inferences I initially drew concerning Frey's reasons for narrating in the way that he did the events associated with his addiction and recovery. Specifically, I will interpret the text as one purposely—intentionally—designed by its author to prompt infelicitous modes of world-building; in other words, I will factor this additional assumption into the broader context that allows me to situate Frey's narrating act and explicate it in terms of reasons. And the same goes for collaboratively created narratives like movies. Once I have been schooled in how movies are actually made, I will be able to situate Birkin's version of *The Cement Garden* in a different context. I can now see the film as the result of a sustained effort on the part of the movie's multiple creators to coordinate local feats of story-elaboration, cobbled together more or less seamlessly, to produce the effect of a single act of narration.

I am advancing, then, a two-part argument against models based on the notion of the implied author. The first part of the argument is that the idea of the implied author arises from efforts to accommodate an anti-intentionalist position that I believe it is preferable to dispute from the start, by grounding the worldmaking process in defeasible ascriptions, to authors or story creators, of reasons for performing acts of narration. The second, related part of the argument is that talk of implied authors entails a reification or hypostatization of what is better characterized as a stage in an inferential process (see also my contributions to chapter 6 and to Part Two of this volume). At issue is the process by which interpreters, by ascribing to story creators reasons for performing acts of narration, build and rebuild narrative worlds whose contours may change in light of ongoing attempts to factor in textual as well as contextual information. If, for instance, it emerged that the details of Edward Mayhew's life history exactly paralleled McEwan's own (in a kind of reverse-Frey scenario), then I would have to alter my understanding of the relation between the author and the narrator, the actual world and the storyworld. But instead of trying to account for this change by multiplying explanatory entities, and by distinguishing between an author implied in or by the text and an author who actually created it, in my approach I assume that there are only authors or story creators whose reasons for producing a given narrative I may well need to recontextualize and thus interpret differently over time.

In turn—to anticipate issues discussed in chapter 6—an intentionalist approach to worldmaking has major consequences for accounts of the role of the reader in narrative contexts. Suffice it to say for now that the approach I sketch out in this volume is premised on an intentionalism without implied authors—and thus without implied readers. In place of the narrative communication diagram, my approach to narrative world-building grows out of a rigorously intentionalist but more minimal explanatory model that I abbreviate as CAPA. This model encompasses Contexts for interpretation (including contexts afforded by knowledge about narrative genres, an author's previous works, or Frey-like confessions); storytelling Actions performed within those contexts, and resulting in texts that function as blueprints for worldmaking; Persons[10] who perform acts of telling as well as acts of interpretation; and defeasible Ascriptions of communicative and other intentions to performers of narrative acts—given the contexts in which the persons at issue perform those acts and the structure that their resulting narratives take on. I provide more details about the CAPA model, and its advantages over the narrative communication diagram, in my contribution to Part Two.

Brian Richardson

I will start with a standard account of author-narrator relations and then go on to see how antimimetic writers play with these boundaries. The author is the human being who actually puts pen to paper (or fingers to the keyboard) and puts his or her royalties in the bank; the implied author is the figure or sensibility we imagine the author to be, based primarily on our reading of the work; and the narrator is the fictional person (or persons) who is responsible for transmitting the narrative. Or, in the useful formulation of William Nelles: "The historical author writes, the implied author means, and the narrator speaks" (22). As the classic example has it, in *Huckleberry Finn,* the author is Samuel Clemens, the implied author or sensibility is that of "Mark Twain," and the narrator who relates the story is Huck Finn. The concept of an implied author is especially important when discussing co-written, ghost-written, or anonymous works: political speechwriters all want to sound like the candidate who will speak their words; the multiple authors of a religious work, modern novel, or Hollywood movie want the material to sound as if it came from the same person; and the concept is essential when we ascribe anonymous works to a historical author or construct a single figure on the basis of a style that is repeated (e.g., "the 'Pearl' Poet" or "the Wakefield Master"). Two historical authors may also combine to provide a single authorial voice, as Conrad and Ford do in *Romance.* The concept of the narrator has been important historically for correctly dissuading readers from simplistically equating the author of a text with its speaker: T. S. Eliot is not J. Alfred Prufrock, and Vladimir Nabokov is not to be equated with the narrator of *Lolita:* "my creature Humbert is a foreigner and an anarchist, and there are many things, besides nymphets, in which I disagree with him," explained the author (317). It is also possible for us to detect the views of an actual author in the mouth of a narrator or other character, including an unlikely one. I call this "transparent narration," a more direct and even nonillusionistic type of narratorial communication than what James Phelan has called "mask narration" (*Living* 201–4). For Phelan, mask narration occurs when an author uses a character narrator to express the author's beliefs; the masking can be subtly or sloppily done. By contrast, transparent narration breaks the frame of fictionality by making nonfictional statements in the narrative. There is no pretense of hiding; the mask is simply discarded as the line between author and narrator is erased. Thus, in Kurt Vonnegut's *Slaughterhouse Five,* the narrator identifies himself as a character in the novel's storyworld and simultaneously affirms the reality of the novel's historical testimony of the Allied firebombing of Dresden: "That was me. That was the author of this book" (125).

The concept of an implied author is particularly useful for discussing the variously unreliable narrators of modernist fiction; a fallible narrator presupposes a cunning implied author who wants the intended reader to perceive the strategy of unreliability and thereby "get the joke." Postmodern and other antimimetic authors, however, delight in collapsing established categories, and the triad of author, implied author, and narrator too has been a source of that delight, as the distinctions essential to modernism are exploded by postmodernism. Kurt Vonnegut, Paul Auster, and Richard Powers all have written works of fiction that include characters bearing the author's name and some of his characteristics; they deliberately conflate these different versions of themselves. Nabokov is especially cunning in hiding figures of himself within his fictional texts, even to the point of including anagrammatic forms of his name ("Vivian Darkbloom"). In some instances ("First Love," "Mademoiselle O"), Nabokov has published essentially the same text both as fiction and as autobiography, while *Bend Sinister* (1947) ends with by the protagonist's metafictional intuition that he is returning to the bosom of his creator (see Richardson, "Nabokov's"). Such interpenetrations point to the inherent constructedness of our notions of the author or implied author as well as all notions of the self. They also identify and reaffirm fiction's status as fiction.

The last half of the twentieth century has seen an explosion of experiments with narrators and narration. Although many of these experiments have been tried before, postmodernism has returned to them and explored their capacity for defamiliarizing our perceptions and otherwise responding to our contemporary world. Modern authors have employed first-person plural ("we" narration), third-person plural (where the persons depicted are nearly always multiple and referred to as "they" or "them"), passive voice narration in which the speaker and/or agent remains anonymous and unidentified, and multiple kinds of narration within the same text. All of the forms just mentioned appear in Joseph Conrad's *The Nigger of the 'Narcissus'* (1899), including the regular juxtaposition of first- and third-person plural accounts, as a position of objectivity does battle with the fact of human subjectivity. Other works start in one form and end up in the other, as what seems to be an omniscient third-person perspective turns out to be the voice of a single individual, as in Iris Murdoch's *The Philosopher's Pupil* (1983). In the contemporary novel, Carlos Fuentes alternates among first-, second-, and third-person narration in *The Death of Artemio Cruz* (1962), as does Nuruddin Farah in *Maps* (1986). This kind of multiperson narration forces together opposed narrative perspectives that mimetic authors rigorously keep separate. Another compelling modern narrative stance is second-person narration, where the protagonist is referred to in the second person. In Mary McCarthy's "The Genial Host" (1942), we read: "Now you hesitated, weighing the invitation. Sooner or later you would break with him, you knew. But not yet, not while you were still so poor, so loverless, so lonely" (163). Second-person fiction cannot easily be reduced to either homodiegetic or heterodiegetic status, but hovers ambiguously between these two conventional positions. Narrative theory needs a more capacious and flexible model of narration in order to circumscribe the full range of modern and contemporary practices.

The practice of unreliable narration, in which it is apparent that the narrator is deficient in factual knowledge, interpretation, or judgment, has been clearly set forth by Phelan and Rabinowitz. These categories, however, are all based on a mimetic model of narration, that is, of human-like narrators making typically human distortions as they narrate. What happens when an antimimetic author employs this strategy? Here is Saleem critiquing his own reliability: "Why did Saleem need an accident to acquire his powers? Most of the other children [born the same day] didn't." He points out that sometimes "Saleem appears to have known too little, at other times, too much" (530)—this formula is a good description of antimimetic unreliability, by the way. Postmodernism produces still more extreme kinds of unreliability. We have a "fraudulent" narrator when the stated narrative situation is impossible, as when a child displays verbal powers available to only a few adults. A "contradictory" narrator presides over a text that is a mass of contradictions (Robbe-Grillet's *Jealousy* [1957]), and a "permeable" narrator has a mind that, like Saleem Sinai's in *Midnight's Children,* can be invaded by the private thoughts of others. A "dis-framed" narrator is one whose discourse violates the narrative frame that is supposed to contain it, as when a character narrator claims to have written other books by the author that created him. Each of these possibilities can be seen as radical extensions of the practice of the unreliable narrators of romantic and modernist narratives, but in each case these practices are pushed into the realm of the impossible. The reader is thus shown the fabricated nature of the fictional narrator and, by extension, the artificiality of mimetic limitations that realism imposes on his or her narration. Fictional narrators can do virtually anything, and it is the goal of antimimetic fiction to radically extend practices far beyond what has been expected, imagined, or considered possible.

Antimimetic narrators often include unusual, unnatural, or nonhuman speakers. These include the deranged narrators of Beckett and Nabokov, the mute narrators of Calvino's *The Castle of Crossed Destinies* (1969), the dead narrator of Beckett's "The Calmative" (1946), a narrating horse in John

Fowles's *Sweet William* (1993), and story-telling machines in Stanisław Lem's *The Cyberiad* (1967). Postmodern narration can become even more unstable as it presents divergent or disparate textual fragments that seem impossible for a single human individual to have composed. Beckett's "Unnamable" is an especially antihuman narrator: its identity is constantly fluctuating, inconsistent, and self-contradictory. We can conclude that the death of the traditional narrator is a key precondition for the creation of new forms with other, disparate, decentered voices. A simple humanistic framework cannot begin to encompass such acts of narration.

Rushdie plays impressively with the conventions of ordinary narration in *Midnight's Children*. On the last page of the book, Saleem wishes for grammatical options that exceed the normal three persons: "I have been so-many too-many persons, life unlike syntax allows one more than three" (533). But this limitation is hardly a problem for this narrator. He is, after all, able to read the minds of other individuals born on the same day, a possibility normally reserved for omniscient novelists. His mother, it might be noted, seemed to have similar powers and was said to be able to eavesdrop on her daughter's dreams (58). At one point in his narrating, he is so ashamed of his actions that he refuses the first-person pronoun: "'I am glad,' my Padma says, 'I am happy you ran away.' But I insist: not I. He. He, the Buddha. Who . . . would remain not-Saleem" (414). At other times, he narrates as if his novel were a film: "Close-up of my grandfather's right hand: nails knuckles fingers all somehow bigger than you'd expect" (30). Throughout the text, Rushdie both evokes and transgresses the possible knowledge of a human narrator and often winds up with extrahuman powers. Once again we see a refusal of conventional parameters, an insistence on creating new, unusual forms, an underscoring of the artificiality of all narrative construction, and an assertion of the power of fictions in human existence.[11]

NOTES

1. For additional discussion of our views of the implied author, see Peter's "'The Absence of Her Voice from that Concord': The Value of the Implied Author" and Jim's "The Implied Author, Deficient Narration, and Nonfiction Narrative: Or, What's Off-Kilter in *The Year of Magical Thinking* and *The Diving Bell and the Butterfly*?" [JP/PJR]

2. The distinction is not a binary one, since the criteria for determining unreliable narration are of a different order from those for determining restricted narration. Unreliable narration is a function of distance between implied author and narrator, while restricted narration is a limitation on the narrator's activity. Thus, restricted narration can be either reliable or unreliable. [JP/PJR]

3. For a fuller discussion of conversation as narration see Jim's "Rhetoric, Ethics, and Narrative Communication; Or from Story and Discourse to Authors, Resources, and Audiences." [JP/PJR]

4. A docent at the Jane Austen Centre in Bath recently showed museum visitors both Cassandra's portrait and the prettied-up Victorian revision of it, explaining that the latter circulates more widely because "the family always thought Cassandra's portrait of Jane didn't look very flattering, or very feminine" (July 7, 2009). That is precisely the quality of Cassandra's drawing that has attracted feminist critics, for reasons well laid out by Margaret Kirkham. [RW]

5. Elsewhere I have developed an extended argument about the relationship between Anne's placement as focal character and the agitated state of her body. See "The Look, the Body, and the Heroine of *Persuasion*." [RW]

6. Here it should be noted that, for his part, Davidson (3–19) characterized explanations that appeal to reasons as a species of causal explanation. [DH]

7. The situation is more complicated than this brief characterization would suggest. As Tomasello stresses, when one performs a communicative action, one intends for someone to recognize not only what one is trying to communicate but also one's intention to perform that communicative act (94–133). See also H. Clark (129–32) and Grice (217), as well as my contribution to Part Two of this volume. [DH]

8. Abbott (*Introduction* 100–111) places intentional interpretations on the same footing as symptomatic and adaptive interpretations, which involve reading texts as symptoms of the conditions (social, ideological, or other) out of which they arise or as the starting point for radically transformative retellings, respectively. However, I would argue that intentional readings are more basic or fundamental than the other two types. You can interpret a text as a narrative without reading it symptomatically or adaptively; but you cannot read a story symptomatically or adaptively without having first established that it is a narrative produced for particular reasons—reasons that you then work to background, or bracket, in order to read for symptoms or else engage in transformative adaptations. [DH]

9. In my response in Part Two, I argue that in order to characterize the world-building activities cued by such nested communicative situations, one need not appeal to the multiple reading positions described—and I would suggest reified—by theorists who draw on the narrative communication diagram. [DH]

10. I discuss the concept of "person" in more detail in chapter 5, in connection with issues of character and characterization. As I note there, work by Peter Hobson, P. F. Strawson, and others suggests that part of what it means to be a person is to have a mind as well as a body, that is, a constellation of mental and material predicates. More

than this, the idea of person entails that mental predicates will be self-ascribable in one's own case and other-ascribable in the case of others. In turn, because narrative texts result from actions performed by that subclass of persons known as authors, it is arguably built into the experience of narrative to engage in (defeasible) ascriptions of mental predicates to story creators—that is, to other-ascribe to authors reasons for their textual performances. [DH]

11. For further reading on these issues, see Hansen, Iversen, Nielsen, and Reitan; Heinze; Nielsen; Mäkelä; and Richardson, *Unnatural Voices.* [BR]

3

Time, Plot, Progression

James Phelan and Peter J. Rabinowitz

In the introduction we identified attention to narrative progression as one of the core elements of the rhetorical approach, noting that we regard the progression of a narrative—its synthesis of textual and readerly dynamics—as the key means by which an author achieves his or her communicative purposes and the study of progression as a key source of insights into understanding how a narrative creates its effects. As we elaborate on these points and analyze the progression of *Huckleberry Finn,* we also seek to contribute to the long-standing debate about Twain's treatment of race in the novel. We begin with an explanation of why we prefer the term *progression* to the traditional term *plot.*

PROGRESSION VS. PLOT

Definitions of plot range from minimalist ones that make it synonymous with *fabula*—the chronological sequence of events in a narrative—to maximalist ones that characterize it as the larger principle of organization of a narrative (see, for example, Crane; Peter Brooks; and Ricoeur). But even the maximalist definitions give pride of place among the elements of narrative to events, their ordering, and their interconnections (causal, accidental, analogical, etc.) Our concept of progression arises from a different way of thinking about the larger principle of organization of a narrative, one grounded in the link between the logic of the text's movement from beginning to middle through ending (what we call textual dynamics) and the audience's temporal experience (readerly dynamics) of that movement. The logic of the text's movement encompasses not only the interconnections among events but also the interaction of those story-level dynamics with the discourse-level dynamics arising from the interrelations of implied author, narrator, and audience. The audience's temporal experience consists of its evolving (or shifting) understandings, judgments, emotions (including desires), and expectations as it follows the textual dynamics. Furthermore, it is the author's desire to create this experience—the authorial purpose in the broadest sense—that determines the author's choices for the textual dynamics. Thus, like other narrative theorists, we are interested in a given narrative's handling of the relation between story-time and discourse-time, and, like Genette, we find it useful to attend to order, duration, and frequency of narration. But we approach those relationships in terms of their consequences for textual and readerly dynamics. Ultimately, it is by studying the complex interplay between authorial choices and their consequences that we can come to a better understanding of how a given narrative works as a communicative act, an understanding in which events and their interconnections are only one part of the totality.

Our concept of progression both subsumes and revises the maximalist definitions of plot by acknowledging the importance of events and their interconnections (the "something happened" that anchors our rhetorical definition) in the overall shape of a narrative but also reconceiving their role in the achievement of that shape. First, our concept explicitly reconceptualizes the notion of a narrative's "shape" so that it includes not only the events and their interconnections (plot dynamics) but also the trajectory of the authorial audience's judgments, interests, and responses, including the various interactions among them (readerly dynamics). This position means not only that we regard the plot dynamics as having a significant influence on audience response but also that we regard the implied author's interest in guiding the audience's response as having a significant influence on the construction of the plot dynamics.

For example, before Twain has Huck tell us about being kidnapped by Pap Finn, Twain has Huck narrate the episode of Pap's experience with the new judge in town. In this episode the judge preaches temperance to Pap, Pap vows to reform, and the judge gives Pap a room in his own house. But Pap sneaks out, trades the new coat the judge has given him for "a jug of forty-rod" (49), and ends up destroying the room, rolling off the porch roof, and breaking his arm. The judge concludes that "a body could reform the ole man with a shot gun, maybe, but he didn't know no other way" (49). If we ask why Twain includes the episode and why he places it before Pap's kidnapping of Huck, we get better answers by focusing more on readerly dynamics than on plot dynamics. Since the episode is self-contained—once it is over, the Huck–Pap relationship returns to the status quo ante—it is, from the perspective of plot dynamics, extraneous: if Twain excised it, we wouldn't say that there was a connection missing between events. But from the perspective of readerly dynamics, the episode is well motivated. Twain uses it to guide our interpretive and ethical judgments of Pap so that even as we register the comedy, we also register that Pap is both incorrigible and a serious threat to himself and others, especially Huck. Among other things, this revelation means that we recognize the woeful inadequacy of Huck's judgment of his situation after the kidnapping when he says, "it warn't long . . . till I was used to being where I was, and liked it, all but the cowhide part" (50). This recognition in turn influences our positive ethical judgment of Huck's later decision to fake his own murder.

The second way our concept of progression both subsumes and revises general understandings of plot is by combining the category of plot dynamics with the category of *narratorial dynamics* into the larger category of textual dynamics. Plot dynamics, as we've suggested, refer to the *instabilities* and complications related to characters, events, and their interconnections (in the terms of the traditional story/discourse distinction, plot dynamics involve elements of story). Narratorial dynamics refer both to what we call *tensions* arising from discrepancies of knowledge, understanding, and values among author, narrator, narrative audience, and authorial audience (elements of discourse) and to the ongoing relationships established by the author's use of the resources of narration (narrator–narratee relationships, character–character dialogue, etc.). We locate narratorial dynamics as part of textual dynamics (rather than readerly dynamics) because, like instabilities, they are encoded in the text. As we have argued in chapter 2, for example, Twain uses multiple textual signals to mark Huck's declaration, "All right, then, I'll go to hell," as unreliable narration. Just as instabilities and their complications generate readerly responses (and vice versa) as we make interpretive, ethical, and aesthetic judgments of them, so too do tensions. As we have seen, Huck's unreliable declaration actually increases our admiration of his own ultimate ethical judgment and that in turn heightens our sympathy and affection for him.

BEGINNINGS, MIDDLES, ENDINGS

Since we view progression as a synthesis of textual and readerly dynamics, we include aspects of both kinds of dynamics in our understandings of beginnings, middles, and endings. In *Experiencing Fiction,* Jim proposes the following model (with the single difference that what we here call "Completion/Coherence" he previously called only "Completion").

Beginning	Middle	Ending
Exposition	Exposition	Exposition/Closure
Launch	Voyage	Arrival
Initiation	Interaction	Farewell
Entrance	Intermediate Configuration	Completion/Coherence

The items in the first two rows are aspects of plot dynamics (instabilities and their contexts); those in the third are aspects of narratorial dynamics. The items in all three rows have consequences for readerly dynamics, consequences rooted in our interpretive, ethical, and aesthetic judgments and that influence the larger movements of readerly dynamics identified in the fourth row.

Exposition includes everything that provides information about the narrative or narration, including the occasion of the telling (sometimes the author's occasion as well as the narrator's), the characters (listings of traits, past history, etc.), the setting of the action (time and place), and the events of the narrative. In beginnings, this exposition can include such things as front matter, prefaces, illustrations, notices (as in *Huck*), and epigraphs. In endings, this exposition can include such things as afterwords and epilogues. In addition, sometimes this ending exposition can include a signal that the narrative is coming to an end (e.g., Huck's "so there ain't nothing more to write about" [263]), and in that way it contributes to the audience's sense of closure.

Launch, voyage, and arrival signify respectively the introduction, complication, and resolution (in whole or in part) of the global instabilities or tensions. We adopt the travel metaphor to signal that progression in narrative involves the representation of change over time.[1] Beyond that general point, accepting this model does not commit us to a preference for any particular trajectory of the instabilities: the initial ones may be introduced before or after the initial exposition, the complications in the voyage may arise out of tight causal links between events or from relatively discrete episodes, and the arrival may signal strong or weak resolution.

60

Initiation, interaction, and farewell signify respectively the initial narratorial dynamics, the continuation, alteration, or other development of them over the course of the narrative, and their final stage. To name just one of countless possibilities, in *A Farewell to Arms* the implied Hemingway initially establishes Frederic Henry as an unreliable interpreter and evaluator of his situation and then traces Frederic's gradual movement toward nearly complete reliability.

(3) Entrance, intermediate configuration, and completion/coherence designate the general readerly decisions, at each stage of the narrative, that follow from the interaction of the textual and readerly dynamics. More specifically, entrance identifies both the imaginative movement of the actual reader into the storyworld at the moment of launch and the authorial audience's initial hypothesis (often inchoate) about the overall direction and shape of the narrative as it is experienced during the time of reading, what we call its configuration. Intermediate configuration, then, identifies the ways in which that hypothesis gets confirmed, revised, or otherwise complicated throughout the middle. For instance, our hypotheses about the future direction of *Huckleberry Finn* change dramatically when the King and the Duke join Huck and Jim in their journey. Most progressions involve a series of intermediate configurations as the textual dynamics develop.

Completion/coherence refers to the authorial audience's final and retrospective sense of the shape and purposes of the narrative as a whole, which may or may not require a significant reconsideration of earlier hypotheses about configuration—as when Tom's revelation that Jim had been freed changes our understanding of the final section's shape by altering our interpretive and ethical judgments of Tom's motives for wanting to set Jim free. Completion/coherence includes the authorial audience's interpretive, ethical, and aesthetic judgments of the whole narrative. We may, for example, make the interpretive judgment that the arrival provides a very weak resolution to the global instabilities and tensions and then go on to make the ethical and aesthetic judgments that such a weak resolution is appropriate (or inappropriate) given the progression of the beginning and middle and what they suggest about the overall purposes of the narrative.

THE PROGRESSION OF *ADVENTURES OF HUCKLEBERRY FINN*

We have touched on aspects of the progression in chapter 2, but here we offer a synoptic view of the whole. We identify the beginning as Chapters I through VII. When Huck escapes to Jackson's Island in Chapter VII after faking his murder, Twain completes the launch. These first seven chapters activate not only our mimetic interest in Huck through his vernacular narration and initial characterization but also our thematic interest in him as an outsider who does not fit comfortably anywhere in his world. Huck, the lower-class Irish-American, is clearly out of place among the genteel English-American women, Douglas and Watson, and in their extremely conventional Christian household. Furthermore, though he likes and looks up to that other British-American Tom Sawyer, Huck finds much of Tom's behavior incomprehensible. And Tom, for all his adolescent shenanigans, is ultimately a conventional boy (the equivalent of Tom in our contemporary world would be using social media for practical jokes one day and figuring out how to get into Harvard Law School the next). Huck's life with Pap represents an alternative to "sivilized" society, but, as we see right away and as Huck eventually realizes, it's a constricting and dangerous alternative. By faking his murder, Huck launches himself into the unknown—and Twain launches a narrative that implicitly promises to resolve the global instability of Huck's relation to his society.

The initiation provided by these first seven chapters is crucial to our affective and ethical responses to Huck and his situation. Twain uses Huck as a reliable reporter (for the most part) but varies Huck's reliability as an interpreter and an evaluator. When Huck is unreliable, his unreliability almost always has bonding effects: his naïveté often provides an insightful, defamiliarizing look at aspects of conventional society, and his instinctive ethical judgments—for example, that he doesn't want to go to the "good place" if Miss Watson will be there—are often not only funny but apt. Consequently, at the moment of entrance we are sympathetic to Huck and his situation and strongly desire that he will find his way in the world, even as we have no clear expectation about how the global instability will be resolved.

We identify the middle of the narrative as Chapters VIII through the middle of Chapter XXXI, that is, from Huck's finding his way to Jackson's Island through the episodes on the raft and along the Mississippi shore right up until Huck faces his crisis of conscience about helping Jim run away. Huck's decision to resolve the crisis by deciding to go to hell is actually the first part of the arrival and, thus, ought to be part of the novel's ending. But the novel famously does not end for another twelve chapters. An analysis of the middle can help explain both why Huck's decision is part of the arrival and why the Evasion serves to destabilize it.

The first major complication of the initial global instability is Huck's discovering Jim on Jackson's Island. Huck now has the companionship of a fellow outsider and of an adult who, by virtue of his slave status and his personality, is completely different from any other significant adult figure in his life to this point. Nevertheless, because Jim is a slave, neither he nor Huck recognizes that his greater age and life experience should give him a greater authority, and so sometimes Huck will be guided by Jim, as when Jim advises him not to look at the dead man on the *Lallah Rook,* and at other times Huck is sure that he knows better, as when he decides to board *The Walter Scott,* despite Jim's objections. In this way, Huck's relationship to Jim becomes another ongoing instability, one that deepens the novel's mimetic interests and adds to its thematic component. The principals are not just Huck and Jim but also a white boy and a black man.

Just as significantly for the overall progression, Twain ties this complication in Huck's trajectory to a second global instability in the narrative as a whole: Jim's decision to become a fugitive and seek his freedom and a reunion with his family rather than to stay with Miss Watson and allow her to sell him "down to Orleans." This dual function of Jim's flight—global instability in his own trajectory, complication in Huck's—initially works very well for both the textual and readerly dynamics, but it eventually sets Twain up for his flawed ending and leads to questions about his attitudes toward race.

With respect to readerly dynamics, the dual function of Jim's flight initially works well for two reasons: (1) Jim's presence adds another layer to our affective and ethical responses, as we sympathize with Jim's plight, endorse his ethical judgments, and desire his reunion with his family. (2) Huck's interactions with Jim deepen and add nuance to our readerly responses to both characters. Take, for example, Huck's decision to play a practical joke on Jim by putting the rattlesnake skin in his blanket, a forerunner of Huck's joke about Jim's dreaming that he got lost in the fog, a joke we will examine in the next chapter. Huck is careless about Jim throughout the episode—so careless that he forgets not only that he'd planted the snakeskin but also that, according to the lore that governs his beliefs, a dead rattler will attract its mate. Huck acts promptly to kill the mate after it bites Jim, and he is genuinely remorseful, but he is also not about to "let Jim find out it was all [his] fault" (73). The episode not only increases our sympathy for Jim as the innocent victim of Huck's failed joke but also leads us to make negative ethical judgments of Huck for his disregard for Jim and his failure to own up. Twain ensures that we will stop short of fully condemning Huck, however, by representing Huck's quick response and his clear (if secretive) regret.

With respect to the plot dynamics, the dual function of Jim's flight generates the rest of the events of the voyage. It is the threat of Jim's being discovered by Judith Loftus's husband that propels both Huck and Jim ("They're after us!" Huck shouts) off the island, onto the raft, and into their adventures on the River and along the shore, the adventures that comprise the rest of the middle.

After Huck and Jim pass Cairo in the fog, the general pattern of the progression involves the juxtaposition of Huck's experiences of life on shore (which get the bulk of the narrative's attention) with his time on the raft with Jim (time that becomes rarer once the King and the Duke take over in Chapter XIX). The exact sequence and the exact number of the adventures do not matter a great deal—though the Wilks episode, in which Huck's ethical judgment leads him to betray the King and the Duke, needs to follow episodes in which Huck's judgment does *not* spur him to act against them—as long as Twain has enough adventures to accomplish his thematic purpose of exposing the deficiencies of shore society. Huck's experiences then provide the backdrop for his arrival in his decision to go to hell. Since we've already analyzed this scene in detail in chapter 2, we will not go over it again but simply add here that it takes on additional affective and ethical force precisely because it comes after the middle's exposure of the deficiencies of a slave-owning society.

Huck's decision constitutes his arrival because Twain represents it as a final decision: Huck says that he "never thought no more about reforming" (201), and the rest of the book bears him out. Huck doesn't exactly choose to reject the beliefs of civilized society (after all, he still believes that he will be damned). Rather, he refuses to let those social values and beliefs govern his ethical decisions about Jim. Instead he will live according to his own intuitive values as they've been reinforced—and even to some extent shaped—by his friendship and shared experiences with Jim. Huck's understanding, in a sense, is another instance of bonding unreliability: Huck's false belief in the consequences of his decision, and his willingness to accept those consequences, only serves to enhance our sense of his ethical strength. From this perspective, Huck's report at the end of his telling that he plans to "light out for the Territory" rather than to stay and be "sivilized" by Aunt Sally follows logically from this arrival, and we can imagine his going to the Territory as the launch for his next set of adventures. Thus, we can conclude that a significant part of Twain's purpose is to give his audience this multilayered experience of participating in Huck's gradual evolution to this point, an experience that includes our multiple judgments of Huck, of Jim, of shore society, and our corresponding thematic conclusions.

The problem in Twain's successful execution of this part of his purpose is that the Evasion intervenes between Huck's arrival and his decision to light out for the Territory—and that its textual and readerly dynamics erode the sense of resolution accompanying his arrival because they erode our sense of the finality of Huck's ethical decision about Jim. Indeed, the dynamics of the Evasion erode our confidence that Twain himself took the global instability about Jim all that seriously.

Note that in working out Huck's arrival, Twain subordinates Jim's storyline to Huck's. Once the King and the Duke enter, Jim's instability and its complications get put on the back burner—they barely affect the forward movement of the narrative. At first, this decision in itself seems defensible, since Twain offers us such a rich experience as we follow Huck. At worst, Twain's subordinating Jim to Huck during the shore episodes is a sacrifice or perhaps what Rader would call an unintended negative consequence of Twain's positive constructive intention. But such defenses are contingent on what Twain will do with Jim's storyline after Huck's arrival—and given what Twain does, the defenses seem less persuasive than the hypothesis that Twain never regarded Jim's storyline as especially worth his attention.

One consequence of the positive focus on Huck is that when Twain returns to Jim's situation, he has to deal with the additional complication that the journey into the slave states puts Jim further away from freedom than he was on Jackson's Island. Twain faces the difficult challenge of constructing a plausible and efficient means to resolve Jim's storyline, a means that would also include a role for Huck consistent with his decision in Chapter XXXI.[2] Unfortunately, in writing the Evasion, Twain falls into implausibility (Tom Sawyer turns out to be the Phelps's nephew; Miss Watson conveniently dies and frees Jim in her will) and extreme inefficiency (the seemingly endless series of steps Tom insists on). What's worse, Huck's role involves giving way to Tom Sawyer and becoming complicit in Tom's demeaning treatment of Jim, a complicity that threatens our ethical admiration for Huck. (In chapter 7 we discuss how even Huck's narration alters for the worse during the Evasion.) In so doing, Twain betrays the implicit promise about Huck's ongoing behavior that accompanies the arrival in Chapter XXXI and fails to resolve Jim's storyline in a way that maintains the dignity Jim displays when he calls Huck out for making fun of his dream interpretation when they reunite after getting separated in the fog. In other words, although Twain in the first two-thirds of the progression uses Huck's relation to Jim as the crucial measure of Huck's progress, Twain also reneges on the ethical-aesthetic obligations to Jim's storyline that his construction of the progression implicitly promises. We submit that any discussion of Twain's treatment of race in the novel would do well to pay attention to both of these central aspects of the progression.

Robyn Warhol

Story-time in Jane Austen's novels covers a single period in a heroine's life, from the point in her life when she is eligible for marriage to the event of her wedding. Everything else that has happened to the heroine gets summarized in the expository passages at the novel's beginning, and everything that is to happen after her engagement—including the wedding itself—is summed up even more briefly. With the exception of *Mansfield Park,* the dramatized action always unfolds over a period of just a few months, from the introduction of a potential hero onto the heroine's scene to the time when she and her true love (not always the man who was the initial candidate) declare their mutual affection. Sometimes—as in *Pride and Prejudice* as well as *Persuasion*—the hero and heroine have one or two conversations at the end about the events that have led to their union, but (as in *Mansfield Park* and *Northanger Abbey*), this is not obligatory. For Austen, as for many British authors writing novels about heroines in her period, these months are the only part of a woman's life that meets the threshold of narratability. As D. A. Miller has observed, narratability comes to closure in Austen's novels when "the ending of the marriage plot disarms the threat of frustration and suspense, and the narrative of circumstance is concomitantly abridged under an 'etc. principle'" (*Narrative and its Discontents,* 43). In other words, the future life of the heroine is assumed to be so obvious as to be boring. The marriage plot has reached its climax and its closure, and there is nothing left to tell.

In terms of deep structure, one can outline the Austen plot with that improbably unshakable confidence Vladimir Propp exhibited in his analyses of folk tales. Resembling nothing so much as a theme and variations in classical music, the pattern of her plots follows a feminine inversion of the ancient "boy meets girl" romance plot: girl meets boy, girl loses boy, girl and boy are united in the end. With equal consistency Austen introduces a good suitor (Colonel Brandon, Mr. Darcy, Edgar Bertram, Mr. Knightley, Henry Tilney, Captain Wentworth) and a bad suitor (Willoughby, Wickham, Henry Crawford, Frank Churchill, John Thorpe, William Walter Elliot). As so often happens with musical variations, the final one—*Persuasion*—appears most different from the announced theme, not just because the good suitor's name begins with "W" (usually a dead giveaway for the wrong choice), but more importantly because Anne Elliot's original marriage plot is behind her, having gone wrong "more than seven years" before the novel's opening (28). *Persuasion*'s marriage plot begins when the heroine's former suitor comes back; their history together is backstory. Arguably, Anne Elliot at nineteen was not yet really eligible for the Austenian happy ending. "Young and gentle as she was" (28), she had found that the feelings Lady Russell's opposition to her engagement had produced were "more than Anne could combat" (27). In retrospect Anne tells Frederick she believes she was "perfectly right in being guided by" Lady Russell at nineteen (198), but when he asks whether she would have renewed the engagement if he had contacted her again when he returned to England two years later, her reply is an energetic (and very modern-sounding) "Would I!" (199). In other words, Anne Elliot at twenty-one was eligible in a way that her teenaged self had not yet been; by the time she is twenty-six she is more than ready to play her role in Austen's typical plot.

Given the predictability of the outlines of Austen's plots, the interest is of course all in the details, the subtle renditions of conversations and situations adding up to the powerful illusion that these figures are people (I'll say more about this in the section titled "Character"). The closure is always the same—girl and boy are united in the end—but *Persuasion* presents an interesting case in that the novelist drafted two endings, two different paths to the consummation of the heroine's desire. Both endings are extant, and though the revised ending appears within the text of all editions of the novel, many editors include the "Cancelled Chapters" as an appendix. The alterations in plot that Austen introduced in her revision make profound changes in the novel's thematics. Most significant is an alteration in the degree of the heroine's agency, an important consideration for feminist critics. A passive and unwilling participant in an awkward encounter during the original ending, Anne in the revision takes independent action toward her desired end.

In the canceled chapters, Anne encounters Admiral Croft on the street, and he ushers her into his house to visit his wife, assuring her all the while that there is no one with Mrs. Croft except the mantua-maker. Not wanting to intrude, Anne holds back, but the Admiral almost drags her into his drawing room, mentioning just by the way that Anne "will find nobody to disturb [her]—there is nobody but Frederick here," shocking Anne with this offhand reference to his brother-in-law. Before leaving them together, the Admiral privately commissions Wentworth to ask Anne whether rumors of her engagement to Mr. Elliot are true, as their marriage would have implications for the Crofts' remaining in Kellynch Hall. This leads to an exchange in which Wentworth hesitantly asks her about the rumor, and Anne blushingly denies it. On hearing there is no truth in the report, Wentworth

> now sat down—drew [his chair] a little nearer to her—& looked, with an expression which had something more than penetration in it, something softer;—Her Countenance did not discourage.—It was a silent, but a very

> powerful Dialogue;—on his side, Supplication, on her's acceptance.—Still,
> a little nearer—and a hand taken and pressed—and "Anne, my own dear
> Anne!"—bursting forth in the fullness of exquisite feeling—and all Sus-
> pense & Indecision were over.—They were re-united. (207)

"A silent . . . Dialogue" leaves the heroine nothing to say; "a hand taken and
pressed," in its disembodied grammatical passivity, leaves her no action to
take. All Anne has to do is to sit and meet the hero's gaze, and she gets her
happy ending.

Anne's meek passivity in this episode departs from the gradually increasing actions she has been taking to let Wentworth know how she feels.
Uncharacteristically bold, she steps forward to greet him on his entrance
to the Octagon Room assembly: "He was preparing only to bow and pass
on, but her gentle 'How do you do?' brought him out of the straight line to
stand near her, and make enquiries in return" (146). Anne's action precipi-
tates her learning from him that he has no lingering attachment to Louisa,
and furthermore she feels that "[h]is choice of subjects, his expressions, and
still more his manner and look, had been such as she could see in only one
light" (150), favorable to her wishes. They are divided by the flow of people,
and Anne ends up seated at the concert next to Mr. Elliot, though she is
thoroughly distracted by looking around for Captain Wentworth. When the
group she is with shift their places on the benches, Anne contrives to "place
herself much nearer the end of the bench than she had been before, much
more within reach of a passer-by" (153) so that Wentworth, when he finally
walks through that part of the room, has the opportunity to speak to her
again.

Anne's comparative forwardness at the Assembly Rooms disappears in
the canceled chapters, but in the revision Anne takes even bolder steps.
Instead of a chance encounter with Admiral Croft, the novelist introduces
a gathering at the Musgroves' apartment in Bath's White Hart Inn, at which
Wentworth and his friend Captain Harville are present. Here Anne famously
debates with Captain Harville the question of women's constancy in love,
making some observations worthy of Mary Wollstonecraft in their feminist
thrust. She argues that women's focus on romantic love arises from their rel-
egation to the domestic sphere: "We live at home, quiet, confined, and our
feelings prey upon us. You are forced on exertion. You have always a profession, pursuits, business of some sort or other, to take you back into the world
immediately" (187). When Captain Harville supports his case with literary
references ("I do not think I ever opened a book in my life which had not
something to say upon woman's inconstancy. Songs and proverbs, all talk

of women's fickleness" (188), he anticipates Anne's response: "But perhaps you will say, these were all written by men" (188). Aware by now that Wentworth is probably straining to hear their conversation, Anne seizes the point, outlining what would, a hundred years later, become a central argument in Virginia Woolf's *A Room of One's Own:* "Yes, yes, if you please, no reference to examples in books. Men have had every advantage of us in telling their own story. Education has been theirs in so much higher a degree; the pen has been in their hands. I will not allow books to prove anything" (188). What makes Anne's assertiveness important for the plot is her consciousness that Wentworth is seated at a desk nearby, listening to what she says. Her spirited defense is another Austenian example of feminist double-voicing, as she carries on her side of the debate with Captain Harville while communicating to her other audience, Captain Wentworth, her own continuing devotion. For someone as shy as Anne, the exertion is heroic. And it works—the letter Wentworth composes while listening to her argument brings her the "overpowering happiness" every Austen heroine deserves (191).

Having two possible endings, then, highlights the importance of plot in interpretation of the novel's themes. The only really startling action in *Persuasion* is Louisa's accident on the Cobb. The rest of what happens hinges for its interest on what someone says (or doesn't say) to someone else or on how he or she looks or seems to feel while saying it. Narrative progression proceeds through dialogue and the heroine's reflections on the utterances of others; in *Persuasion,* action is consistently precipitated by words. For this reason, too, the revised ending improves on the canceled chapters in that its resolution of the action depends not on "a silent, but very powerful Dialogue" but on something the heroine says aloud, as if she were self-conscious about the power that language wields in this narrative world.

Persuasion's two endings leave the resolution of its plot to the taste of individual readers, who might or might not share the feminist agenda that my preference for the revised ending reveals. But the alternate endings also gesture toward a propensity shared by many Austen enthusiasts for being impatient with the hasty closure of her novels, wanting the plots to continue into the details of the heroines' marriages and beyond. The proliferation of sequels to Austen novels—going back as far as 1850 and increasing in numbers through the beginning of the present century—suggests that many readers can't resist filling in the blank left by the "etc. principle."[3] According to her nephew's biography, Austen herself imagined futures for her characters that she did not include in the narration of her books but shared with friends and family members.[4] Jane Austen was already thirty-six when she published her first novel, and she completed five more before dying at the age of forty-one.

Her too-short career as a professional author partly accounts for the apparently insatiable public appetite for more Austen plots than she was able to produce, even at the astonishing rate she achieved in those last five years of her life.[5] But I think the restlessness inspired by Austen's endings has as much to do with the instability of her plots' closure as with the scarcity of Austen texts. Gestures like the unnarration at the end of *Persuasion* (which I have detailed in Part One) suggest that the texts themselves resist the implication that the novel has really been "about" the marriage plot. According to my feminist narratological reading, *Persuasion* is less about Anne Elliot's quest for marriage to Frederic Wentworth than it is about the subtle but crucial ways in which the heroine achieves agency in circumstances calculated in every way to oppress her. The perfunctoriness of the way Austen ends her plots lets all the air out of the marriage plot, the machine that only *seems* to propel her novels forward.

David Herman

There is of course an extensive tradition of research on the temporal structure of stories, ranging from Viktor Shklovskii's work on plot as a structuring device, which established the foundational distinction between the chronological sequence of events told about (*fabula*) and the sequence in which they are told (*sjuzhet*); to Genette's systematization of the temporal relationships that can obtain between these two sequences (*Narrative Discourse* 33–160; see also Herman, *Story Logic* 211–61); to Meir Sternberg's analysis of strategies for sequencing expositional material in the telling of a story, as well as those strategies' effects on narrative processing (*Expositional*). Key ideas from this research tradition can be harnessed for an approach centering on the co-construction of storyworlds, and can be used to throw light on what I've characterized as the WHEN aspect or dimension of world-creation.

This temporal aspect of narrative worldmaking can be analyzed into a number of sub-aspects, each of which can be captured as a question for which interpreters seek to frame answers as part of the larger process of co-creating storyworlds—based on inferences about the global as well as local designs subtending acts of narration. Relevant questions include the following:

1. How does the time-frame of events in the storyworld relate to that of the narrational or world-creating act (in Reichenbach's terms, what is the relation between *event time* and *speech time*?).
2. What is the relation between the temporal structure of events in the storyworld (insofar as that can be reconstructed) and the profile they assume in the process of narration? (As discussed below, this question encompasses issues of *emplotment*, that is, the way events are, in being narrated, set out in a particular order that in turn implies a particular way of understanding causal-chronological relationships among them.)
3. How does the chosen narrational mode and/or method of temporal profiling affect the process (or experience) of co-constructing the narrative world?

Taken together, these questions encompass the issues on which the present chapter focuses—time, plot, and progression—but allow those issues to be recast in the terms afforded by an approach centering on narrative worldmaking. Thus, when Genette (*Narrative Discourse* 215–27) distinguishes among simultaneous, retrospective, prospective, and "intercalated" modes of narration (as in the epistolary novel, where the act of narration postdates some events but precedes others), these narrative modes can be interpreted in light of the different kinds of structure that they afford for world construction—in ways that bear especially saliently on question 1 above. Likewise, connecting up with questions 2 and 3, Genette's ideas about duration, order, and frequency highlight key aspects of the way narratives prompt interpreters to configure events temporally, as part of the process of mapping textual cues onto the WHEN dimension of a narrative world.

In the case of simultaneous narration, like that used in sports broadcasts or on-site news reporting about occurrences still underway, events are presented in concert with tellers' and interpreters' attempts to comprehend the contours and boundaries of the narrated domain; inferences about the impact of characters' doings on the larger history of the storyworld remain tentative, probabilistic, open-ended. By contrast, retrospective narration such as McEwan's accommodates the full scope of a storyworld's history, allowing connections to be made among earlier and later actions and events (Margolin, "Past"). Narration of this sort allows for flashbacks to formative occasions as well as proleptic foreshadowings (anticipations-in-hindsight) of the eventual impact of a character's behavior on his or her cohorts—and also of future events over which the characters have no control. Thus, by alternating among narration of what transpires on Florence and Edward's wedding night, allusions to how their words and deeds will shape the future, and analeptic references to earlier actions and events that led them to this moment, McEwan draws a time-line that zigzags between present and past while also shadowing forth a future time-frame when the present, too, will have become past. In doing so, he manipulates narrative *order* in a way that frames the present moment within a longer life-course that stretches back into characters' past and extends forward into their future, grounding what they do or fail to do in larger patterns of motivation—sets of interconnected reasons for acting—that would otherwise remain inaccessible.

McEwan situates actions and events within a longer time-span, so that they can be evaluated more holistically, at a key point late in the novel. Just after Florence turns away from Edward on the beach and walks back to the hotel, having said, "I am sorry, Edward. I am most terribly sorry," the narrative continues:

> Her words, their particular archaic construction would haunt him for a long time to come. He would wake in the night and hear them, or something like their echo, and their yearning, regretful tone, and he would groan at the memory of that moment, of his silence and of the way he

angrily turned from her, of how he then stayed out on the beach another hour, savoring the full deliciousness of the injury and wrong and insult she had inflicted on him, elevated by a mawkish sense of himself as being wholesomely and tragically in the right. (192)

Here McEwan uses the subjunctive verbal mood (*he would wake, he would groan*) to provide a kind of thumbnail sketch of actions that, stemming from the episode on the beach, take place repeatedly in the future.[6] Telescoping forward in time, the passage also compresses into a reportable sequence a wide array of occurrences—thereby bringing into relation Edward's angry spurning of Florence's final gesture of conciliation and the years and indeed decades over the course of which that action bears the fruit of regret, self-analysis, and ultimately self-contempt. In this way, the passage just quoted, like the novel as a whole, demonstrates how narrative provides equipment for modeling networks of temporal relationships in a world, whereby actions and events at one temporal location carry effects that are distributed across time.

Then, in the final ten pages, after the couple's angry exchange on the beach, McEwan shifts to a strictly chronological mode of narration but now resets the parameter of *duration*. Covering a relatively long period of time in a relatively short span of text, McEwan provides the narrative equivalent of time-lapse photography, enabling readers to witness the unfolding of the consequences of characters' actions over the longer term—especially for Edward. And the parameter of *frequency* also comes into play. The text repeatedly alludes to the sailing trips that Florence took with her father and also to actions associated with Florence's pursuit of a musical career, thereby highlighting the salience of these elements of the storyworld and prompting construction of a story line in which past sexual abuse by her father constitutes a reason for Florence's compensatory immersion in the world of music (see 152, 182)—and also for her actions on her wedding night. More generally, by starting with world-creation as a basic cognitive and communicative function served by storytelling, and then working backward to the formal structures that support this root function of narrative, it becomes easier to motivate—to provide warrant for—Genette's foundational account of time in narrative. Fluctuations in the speed of narration along with manipulations of frequency can be viewed as metrics of value or at least attentional prominence—that is, as means for distinguishing between focal and back-grounded elements in a storyworld. For their part, flashbacks and flash-forwards can be studied as means for "thickening" the history of a narrative world and for underscoring how no action can be understood in isolation from the history of conduct from which it emerges and on which it impinges in turn.

As already indicated in my previous comments about order, storytelling constitutes a basic technology for modeling events in ways that facilitate their arrangement, or *emplotment, into larger patterns*.[7] These strategies for event-sequencing produce text-specific plot structures that correspond to the entwined destinies of the characters as they pursue, with more or less success, sometimes conflicting goals in a narrative world. At another level, distinct modes of emplotment are also associated with generic or canonical plot types such as the marriage plot, of which McEwan's novel can be viewed as a postmodern debunking. At a still more general level, emplotment yields the patterns of causal-chronological connection that make a story a story, as opposed to a mere assemblage of events (as in a list).[8]

Furthermore, even as methods of emplotment and other discourse features cue readers to map textual designs onto the WHEN dimension of a storyworld, that mapping process itself has a temporal structure—which is partly controlled by textual means (e.g., gapped-out information that is then returned to via analepses) and partly under interpreters' own control (as when I flip back through McEwan's novel to connect up into a sequence the passages that can be read as figuring forth the story line of sexual abuse [8, 20, 61–62, 123, 131, 140–41]). In the same vein, research by Sternberg (*Expositional*) and Perry highlighted processing strategies, such as the "primacy" and "recency" effects, that arise from the situation of a given event vis-à-vis the two temporal continua of story and discourse, or *fabula* and *sjuzhet*. Events that happen early in story-time can be encountered late in discourse-time, or vice versa, producing reading experiences different from those set into play when there is greater isomorphism between the time of the told and the time of the telling. Consider the different methods of world-construction that would have been set into play if *On Chesil Beach* had begun with an older Edward looking back on lost opportunities, or alternatively with his first glimpse of Florence at the Campaign for Nuclear Disarmament meeting in Oxford, many months prior to their wedding night (58–59). For that matter, rereading a narrative entails different modes of worldmaking than does reading it for the first time. Thus, with repeated readings of McEwan's novel, my own initial focus on reconstructing a time line for events has given way to an appreciation of the emplotment strategies that invite me to shuttle back and forth among present, past, and future and to explore how events have the significance that they do because of their relation to a larger world emergent in time.

My contribution to the next chapter discusses other aspects of the WHEN dimension of narrative worlds. I have distributed this time-related material across the two chapters because, as Mink (146) argued, the hallmark of narrative as a mode of representation is that it makes constant and necessary reference to the location of entities, situations, and events in a larger process of development (cf. Ricoeur). Hence, in narrative contexts, time must be factored into accounts of space; narrative representations of space in actuality consist of spatiotemporally configured scenes within storyworlds.

Brian Richardson

BEGINNINGS

Narrative beginnings are usually thought to be unproblematic. And to be sure, in most natural narratives and short stories, the beginning introduces a problem that needs to be solved. But as soon as we enter the larger canvas of a complex social world (or as soon as we are in the hands of an experimental writer), beginnings start to become more elusive. In life, things don't simply start up from nothing. If one wishes to describe the life of an individual, it is not enough to start with his or her birth: the personal, social, and economic conditions of the child's parents are relevant, as is the social milieu the child is born into. Biographers know this, and most provide the earlier history of their subject's family and a general account of their social condition. Richard Ellmann's biography of James Joyce, for example, begins with a chapter titled "The Family before Joyce." Novelists know this as well: Fielding gives us a detailed account of Squire Allworthy's family history reaching back several decades before the birth of Tom Jones. As Henry James has observed: "Really, universally, relations stop nowhere, and the exquisite problem of the artist is eternally to draw, by a geometry of his own, the circle within which they will happily appear to do so" (171). It is for this reason that authors such as Balzac or Faulkner can keep returning to the same fictional world and provide accounts of the antecedents of events already narrated and published. This is the same principle behind the Hollywood "prequel" that provides backstory to films that have already been produced.

Many modernist authors push this practice still further by providing what Melba Cuddy-Keane has called "beginning's ragged edge": that is, numerous references to earlier events that are never fully related or explained. Modernists also frequently delay the beginning of the central action, using the first part of the text to establish the work's mood, set up symbolic correspondences, and narrate parallel events that have little or no relation to the action of the main story line. Postmodern authors often mock or deconstruct the idea of a fixed beginning. The first words of Raymond Federman's *Double or Nothing* (1971) state "This is Not the Beginning." Italo Calvino's *If on a winter's night a traveler* is a novel that is largely made up of beginning chapters of different novels. Rushdie plays with beginnings by having his narrator first hide and then reveal that he was born exactly at the moment that India achieved independence on August 15, 1947. At the beginning of the eleventh chapter, he refers to the beginning of the *Ramayana*, one the great epics of Sanskrit literature—and gets it wrong. Throughout, he suggests that the beginning of a nation can also be an arbitrary, dubious, or fabricated event. He goes back in time thirty-two years to start the account of his life with an important incident from his grandfather's life and, just like Tristram Shandy, takes so long to move forward in the narrative that Padma, the woman he is reading the manuscript aloud to, admonishes him: "At this rate you'll be two hundred years old before you manage to tell about your birth" (37). Throughout, the narrator points to the interpenetration of beginnings, middles, and ends: "Even ends have beginnings" (404), he notes, as a new stage of his life is about to emerge; at the beginning of the chapter titled, "Alpha and Omega," he admits that this is "a curious heading for what will be my story's half-way point, one that reeks of beginnings and ends, when you could say it should be more concerned with middles; but, unrepentantly, I have no intention of changing it" (255). There are in fact "beginnings here, and all manner of ends" (255).[9]

FABULA AND SJUZHET

A fundamental distinction in narrative theory and analysis is that between (1) the story or *fabula* that one derives from the text and (2) the *sjuzhet*, the presentation of that story in the order that it appears in the text. Modernist authors such as Conrad, Proust, and Faulkner frequently produced work that was presented in an extremely nonlinear sequence but from which a consistent, linear story could be readily extracted. In the work of many contemporary authors, the text from which the story is extracted has become increasingly unusual or unlikely. Such narratives may take the form of a dictionary (Milorad Pavić, *A Dictionary of the Khazars: A Lexicon Novel,* 1988), a critical commentary on a poem (Nabokov's *Pale Fire,* 1962), the index to a biography (J. G. Ballard, "The Index," 1990), or a standard test question in arithmetic (John Updike, "Problems," 1979). They may even consist of piles of unbound or unnumbered pages, which the reader must arrange into an order for it to be apprehended (B. S. Johnson's *The Unfortunates,* 1969) or take the form of thirteen large playing cards that can be arranged in multiple possible orders (Robert Coover's "Heart Suite," 2005). The books that contain them may have two front covers and no back cover—and no instructions for reading such a Janus-faced text, as in Carol Shields's *Happenstance* (1991).

Contemporary antimimetic novelists transgress the principle that a coherent and chronological *fabula* should underlie the *sjuzhet*. Some of these narratives circle back on themselves, as the last sentence becomes the first sentence, and thus continue for eternity (Joyce's *Finnegans Wake,* 1939).

In other works, time passes at different speeds for different groups of people (Woolf's *Orlando,* 1928). Some invert temporality so that the characters move forward into the past (*Time's Arrow,* 1991). Others have multiple, contradictory chronologies that are impossible in the real world (Robert Coover's "The Babysitter," 1969). Ana Castillo's *The Mixquiahuala Letters* (1986) consists of a series of letters sent by one of the characters, but not all are intended to be apprehended by any reader. Instead, the author offers three different reading sequences depending on the reader's sensibility. Thus, the conformist is told to begin with letters 2 and 3 and then to go to number 6, while the cynic is to start with letters 3 and 4 before going on to number 6. The quixotic reader is offered yet another different sequence: 2, 3, 4, 5, 6. Significantly, each sequence produces a different story.

In none of the examples just noted can one easily extract a single, consistent story from a fixed *sjuzhet* the way one might remove the plum from a pudding. Alain Robbe-Grillet, referring to the contradictory *fabula* in his antinovel *Jealousy,* stated: "It was absurd to propose that in the novel . . . there existed a clear and unambiguous order of events, one which was not that of the sentences of the book, as if I had diverted myself by mixing up a pre-established calendar the way one shuffles a deck of cards" (*New* 154); he went on to state that for him there existed no possible order outside of that found within the pages themselves. An antimimetic narrative theory would incorporate these practices and stress that a text's *sjuzhet* may be fixed, variable, or multiple, while its *fabula* may be fixed, multiple, indeterminate, unknowable, or denarrated.

Rushdie also plays with these issues. In *Midnight's Children*'s twenty-fifth chapter, "In the Sundurbans," time follows unknown laws. In this jungle, an impossible temporality emerges: a literal 635-day-long midnight. The reader is treated to the kind of creative transformations of quotidian experience that are possible only in fiction. At the same time, the fictional experiences produce both a dramatization of the effects of trauma (unmoored temporality) and an allegorical vision of human evil (the endless night).[10]

PROGRESSION

Phelan and Rabinowitz use the term "progression" in their section; I wish to clarify that I am primarily interested here in what they call "textual dynamics," that is, the principles of movement underlying the *sjuzhet* (and distinct from what they call "readerly dynamics"). Postmodern authors occasionally employ traditional narrative patterns in order to parody them; at other times they create alternative ways of ordering their texts. The narrator of *Midnight's Children* claims that Padma is attempting to bully him "back into the world of linear narrative, the universe of what-happened-next" (37). In fact, however, apart from a number of digressions and flashbacks, the book's narrative is generally linear, moving forward chronologically from the story of his grandfather's doubts right up to the moment of the book's composition. What is unusual is that so much of the book is devoted to events before the birth of the narrator and that the duration or time it takes to read the book is frequently referred to.

Other authors employ different ways to establish the progression of their narratives. Some model the events of their texts on a sequence of events in an earlier text, as Joyce patterns *Ulysses* on Homer's *Odyssey;* others may draw on musical forms the way Thomas Mann uses the sonata form to structure "Death in Venice." Still others use geometrical or architectural patterns. Rushdie parodies this practice by insisting that he has exactly thirty-one chutney jars to fill with the story of his life, which contains thirty-one years, in a book that has thirty-one chapters and whose narrative goes back thirty-one years before Saleem was conceived.

Many experimental authors use still more unusual methods of establishing a narrative progression. James Joyce   as well as authors associated with the *nouveau roman* use pictures, key words, or ideas to generate their texts. In the "Circe" episode of Joyce's *Ulysses* there is a good example of a verbal generator producing a substantial stretch of text. As Bloom denounces tobacco, the prostitute Zoe retorts: "Go on. Make a stump speech of it." What follows next in the novel is the figure of Bloom in workingman's overalls, giving an oration on the evils of tobacco before an adoring populace (390–93); the phrase "stump speech" thus produces the event it names.

Still other kinds of textual progression (and even regression) are possible. At the end of *Midnight's Children,* shortly after the narrator announces the death of Shiva, a character who is closely linked to Saleem's life and fate, the narrator makes a very strange confession: "I lied about Shiva's death. My first out and out lie" (510). This practice, in which an author affirms certain aspects of a fictional world and then denies them, is one I have called "denarration." It is not uncommon in postmodern works, especially those written by or in the spirit of Samuel Beckett or Alain Robbe-Grillet. It points to the performative nature of fictional narration, that is, that people and events exist by the very act of a narrator's affirming that they exist—unless or until the narrator goes on to deny their existence. This unnatural kind of narrative construction and deconstruction is especially prominent in postmodern narratives, points again to the constructedness of every work of fiction, and also gestures toward the self-interested and personally motivated aspect of all narrative composition.[11]

ENDINGS

In a natural or conventional narrative the role of the ending is to wrap up the plot, reveal all the mysteries to all the relevant characters, provide some sort of poetic justice, and resolve the major problems that generated the story in the first place. While Victorian authors regularly attempted to satisfy these requirements, the more thoroughgoing realists and many modernists resisted such satisfying closure by pointing out its unreality: life simply does not usually resolve itself into happy units where all the threads are nicely knotted at one point in time; things always just keep on happening, and today's resolution prefigures tomorrow's crisis. Poetic justice is a rare commodity in life: when asked how her novel ended, Oscar Wilde's Miss Prism responded: "The good ended happily, and the bad unhappily. That is the meaning of fiction" (26). Something had to change.

Modernists developed a kind of conclusion that provided a sense of an ending without resolving all the major issues of the narrative. The final description of events in *Ulysses* or *To the Lighthouse* offers at most a fleeting moment of minimal resolution; we have no clear idea what will happen to Stephen or Bloom on June 17 or what will happen to the Ramsays after they return from the lighthouse. Joyce and Woolf do, however, provide a vivid sense of an ending through the works' construction: we know that the book is completed even though the characters' fates are up in the air. Conventional storytelling demands a conclusive ending, and these works refuse to provide one even as they signal their closure in other ways. In the final pages of *To the Lighthouse,* Lily finishes her painting and has her vision, Mr Ramsay finishes reading his book, the children become reconciled to their father, and the long-promised trip to the lighthouse is completed—ten years after it had been planned and long after the voyagers had forgotten its original purpose. Woolf provides a powerful sense of closure here even as she indicates that, in the real world, life goes on without any permanent resolutions or fixed boundaries.

There are many antimimetic forms of ending. These include the ending that occurs but is not told to the audience (Thomas Pynchon's *The Crying of Lot 49*); the ending that returns, Ouroboros-like, to the beginning of the story (*Finnegans Wake*); the ending that negates itself and presents a second, revised ending (John Fowles's *The French Lieutenant's Woman*); and a multiple ending that offers different possibilities for a reader to choose from (Malcolm Bradbury's "Composition"). An especially interesting kind of ending is present in *Midnight's Children*. "One empty jar . . . how to end?" Saleem wonders self-consciously and then goes on to consider comic, melancholic, and tragic possibilities (531). The narrative is ceasing, the time of the narrative has merged with the time of the writing, and the thirty chutney jars, each of which represents a year of his life, have been filled as the narrator contemplates the final one. The narrative thus symmetrically begins thirty-two years before his birth and extends to the start of his thirty-second year; it begins with the story of Aadam Aziz and ends with the birth of a son, Aadam, named after his great-grandfather. Saleem himself feels that he is exploding, and he is about to stop writing, but the events around him refuse to settle into place. His personal fate is unknowable, and so is the fate of the Indian subcontinent. A historical narrative that ends in the present is not normally supposed to have any closure, and this narrative of (among other things) India's history is similarly without any closure or tying up of narrative strands. The future remains open.[12]

NOTES

1. In Part Two of *Experiencing Fiction,* Jim discusses the relation of progression in narrative to progression in lyric and in portraiture, whose progressions are not governed primarily by change over time, and especially in hybrid forms of lyric narrative and portrait narrative. [JP/PJR]

2. It is far easier to sketch a viable plan for resolution than to execute it, but here is ours: Twain should have shown Huck helping Jim escape from the Phelps farm and then shown the two of them coming up with a clever scheme to get Jim to the free states. [JP/PJR]

3. One bibliography on the World Wide Web lists at least forty-one continuations of, sequels to, or alternate points of view upon Austen's completed and fragmentary novels, not including adaptations along the lines of Helen Fielding's *Bridget Jones's Diary* (1996) or the widely circulated *Pride and Prejudice and Zombies,* a 2009 spoof by Seth Grahame-Smith. See http://www.pemberley.com/janeinfo/austseql.html. [RW]

4. "She would, if asked, tell us many little particulars about the subsequent career of some of her people. In this traditionary way we learned that Miss Steele never succeeded in catching the Doctor; that Kitty Bennet was satisfactorily married to a clergyman near Pemberley, while Mary obtained nothing higher than one of her Uncle Philips's clerks, and was content to be considered a star in the society of Meriton; that the 'considerable sum' given by Mrs. Norris to William Price was one pound; that Mr. Woodhouse survived his daughter's marriage, and kept her and Mr. Knightley from settling at Donwell, for about two years; and that the letters placed by Frank Churchill before Jane Fairfax, which she swept away unread, contained the word 'pardon.' Of the good people in *Northanger Abbey* and *Persuasion* we know nothing more than what is written: for before those works were published their author had been taken away from us, and all such amusing communications had ceased for ever" (Austen-Leigh, Chapter X). [RW]

5. Anthony Trollope's novels, similar to Austen's in their focus on the marriage plot, have inspired few sequels, though Father Ronald Knox wrote a seventh Barsetshire novel in 1935 and in the late twentieth century the novelist's descendant, Joanna Trollope, published a few continuations under the name of Caroline Harvey. Apparently, a six-volume series like Trollope's Palliser novels offers a sufficiency of the kind of chronicling that Austen's fans seem to crave. [RW]

6. In the Genettean terms that I go on to discuss, this technique can be characterized as iterative narration, a mode of frequency in which what happens more than once is narrated only once (*Narrative Discourse* 113–60). [DH]

7. Thus, as with the concept of narrative referentiality, which I discussed in the introduction to this volume, I use the term "emplotment" in a broader sense than it has in the account that Dorrit Cohn develops in *The Distinction of Fiction.* In my approach, emplotment is a way of talking about the event-ordering potential of narrative—a potential also suggested by distinctions between story and discourse, or the chronological sequence of events told about (*fabula*) and the sequence in which those events are told (*sjuzhet*). By contrast, Cohn suggests that the idea of emplotment is pertinent only for nonfictional narratives: "A novel can be said to be plotted, but not emplotted: its serial moments do not refer to, and can therefore not be selected from, an ontologically independent and temporally prior data base of disordered, meaningless happenings that it restructures into order and meaning" (114). [DH]

8. The three effects of emplotment described here correspond to the three under-

standings of the concept of "plot" identified by Abbott ("Story"). Meanwhile, my next paragraph is indebted to Dannenberg's discussion of approaches to plot that foreground narrative dynamics ("Plot"). [DH]

9. For further reading on Beginnings, see Cuddy-Keane and Richardson, *Theory*. [BR]

10. For further reading on time, *fabula,* and *sjuzhet,* see Heise; Kafalenos; and Richardson, "Beyond Story" and "Denarration." [BR]

11. For further reading on progression, see Nelson; Richardson, "Beyond the Poetics"; and Tyrkkö. [BR]

12. For further reading on endings, see Miller (52–77) and Richardson, "Endings." [BR]

4

Narrative Worlds
Space, Setting, Perspective

James Phelan and Peter J. Rabinowitz

Run a Google search for study questions on *Huckleberry Finn*, and, whether you click on reputable sites like the Duluth Library or the discount stores of academic wisdom like CliffsNotes, the role of the Mississippi River is liable to pop up.[1] SparkNotes raises the issue in what might be its *ur*-form, at least for high-school education: "Discuss the use of the river as a symbol in the novel." We shudder at that prompt for several reasons. Peter has hated "symbols" since high school. Although he couldn't articulate why at the time, in retrospect he believes that he was already wary of the dangers of abstraction. As he has argued elsewhere, such interpretive practices can result in the erasure of concrete particulars, often muting the politics of the text at the same time. For his part, Jim believes that symbol-hunting is a surefire method for transforming the complex experience of reading narrative into the deadening exercise of searching for neatly packaged Hidden Meaning.

But at the same time, we acknowledge that questions about setting are both important and theoretically uncomfortable. It's easy for us to criticize the impulse to interpret setting symbolically, but, despite some earlier notable efforts by A. J. Greimas and Gabriel Zoran, it is only recently, as a result of work by David Herman, Susan Stanford Friedman, and others, that narrative theory has begun to take up more sophisticated questions about space and setting and to give them the attention they deserve. We believe that two interrelated difficulties have obstructed progress in this territory.

The first difficulty concerns how we determine the range of setting and the nature of its borders. Setting has a tendency to spread out from geographical space to the objects within it until it becomes synonymous with background in the broadest sense, even including the sociological or theological characteristics of the world of the work. In this broader sense, setting begins to merge with character—among other things—because "environment" and psychology begin to intertwine, both causally and symbolically. No surprise, really: interpretive analyses of setting tend to spill over into commentary on character precisely because so many narratives, including *Huckleberry Finn,* establish links between these elements. Still, we believe that it is heuristically useful to maintain the distinction, blurry as it sometimes is.

The second problem is that setting is often conflated with "description"— and hence serves as the portal through which a number of vexed issues enter the field. Among other things, blurring setting with description can turn setting (one element *within* narrative) into a discursive mode that is, from certain philosophical perspectives, *in opposition to* narrative.

Given our pragmatic orientation, our aim is not to draw artificially sharp lines around "setting" or to resolve the philosophical debates about description and narrative, but rather to determine the rhetorical function of setting within narrative. Or, more accurately, the variety of functions possible for setting within narrative. Fundamentally, setting, like character, has three components, the synthetic, the mimetic, and the thematic, any or all of which can take on important functions in a given narrative—depending on the nature of the narrative's progression and purpose.

First, we have the synthetic or the formal. As Evelyn May Albright puts it in a guide for writers, the first "function of the setting is to furnish, in the best possible way for any given story, the conditions of time and place and characters which shall make that story possible and actual" (149). This framing dimension of setting is so fundamental to narrative that it largely goes undiscussed. What are the characteristics of that frame? At its simplest, we have what we might call the "contrastive" or the diacritic. Most narratives take advantage of the way representation of distinct spaces (from a minimal "here" and "there" to the complex topography of Proust's *In Search of Lost Time*) can signify, support, or heighten differences of various kinds. At their most schematic, these distinctions are only loosely connected to the *content* of the setting: that is, it may be the contrast itself, rather than the inherent qualities of the settings, that's crucial—as we can see if we think of an urban variation of "Little Red Riding Hood" in which the walk through the woods is replaced by a ride on the New York subway, and grandmother's cottage by a Hundredth Street apartment. The River in *Huckleberry Finn* surely serves this kind of diacritic function.

But it is not only through contrast that setting can serve synthetic functions. A plot may also demand a certain *kind* of location—or at least put some limits on location. Little Red Riding Hood could meet the wolf on a subway or in an elevator; but she couldn't meet him in her prison cell and still have the plot work. Similarly, the plot dynamics of *Huckleberry Finn* depend on the River's providing Huck and Jim with a means of transportation—and, as we'll discuss later, Twain links this synthetic function with the River's mimetic and thematic functions. Furthermore, this particular form of transportation—one way, in a preordained direction, with certain constraints on variations in speed—evokes rules of configuration, that is, standard procedures by which readers infer the shape and direction of the narrative and set up our expectations as the plot dynamics develop (for more, see our discussion in chapter 3).

Setting may also perform many other synthetic functions. Sometimes, for instance, the setting itself can instigate or alter the direction of the narrative—as Raskolnikov's living conditions influence his action.[2] Settings familiar to the authorial audience can serve as a backdrop to generate not only particular rules of configuration but also particular rules of notice, that is, standard procedures by which readers give greater emphasis to some textual signals than others. Then, too, the level and accuracy of a narrator's account of setting can influence readers' decisions about the reliability of the narration and, more generally, about the web of relationships between narrative, authorial, and actual audiences. The magnificence of Huck's descriptions of the River, combined with our knowledge that Samuel Clemens had experience as a steamboat pilot, does a great deal to align Huck with Twain—and the authorial audience with both of them. That is, to the extent that we sense the authorial voice behind Huck's descriptions, our sense of Huck's reliability about the River, about nature, and about other things relatively untainted by civilization is increased. Furthermore, to the extent that we are encouraged to see Huck's descriptions as ones that apply to the world in which the authorial audience lives, we are encouraged to take seriously the ethical and political arguments in the novel.

More generally, focusing on the synthetic functions of setting (like attention to the synthetic functions of character) highlights the complex relation between the mimetic and the synthetic components of realistic fiction. This relation is itself the consequence of the double logic of realism, both in terms of its construction and in terms of its reception. From the author's perspective, as Ralph Rader has argued, realistic fiction entails creating the illusion that the characters are acting autonomously in a world like our own even as those characters are fulfilling an underlying constructive purpose. From the reader's perspective, realistic fiction entails responding to the characters and setting as if they were independent of any authorial construction (that's in part what it means to read as the narrative audience) even as one retains the tacit awareness that the characters are doing the bidding of their authorial designer and that the setting is represented in the service of that authorial design (that's in part what it means to read as the authorial audience). We shall return to this point when we discuss the River's role in Huck and Jim's sailing past Cairo and into the slave states.

WHEN THE *mimetic* dimension of setting is discussed by theorists, it's often treated as a weakness to be avoided. Brooks and Warren are typical. "Description of setting is not to be judged simply in terms of realistic accuracy; it is to be judged in terms of what it accomplishes for a story" (647–48). The second clause makes it clear that "realistic accuracy" has no value on its own, that it is useful *only* insofar as it serves the "higher"—and typically thematic—needs of the story. This is merely one variant of a repeated refrain that relegates the mimetic to a confined cubicle in order to create more office space for the synthetic and thematic.

Of course, such dogmas are apt to engender radical counterpositions, and under the influence of poststructuralist theory, some critics, for example, Keith Cohen, have argued for the value of setting (or description) precisely to the degree that it *does* distract us from matters such as plot and character.[3] But between these two extremes lies a vast area of readerly pleasure in the purely mimetic aspects of setting and description: pleasure in its function as a window on what the reader views as the "real world."

Finally, setting can also have a thematic function, one evoked clearly by that dreaded and dreadful prompt with which we began: "Discuss the use of the river as a symbol in the novel." It's often the thematic function that rescues setting from disdain, since this function, to borrow a phrase from D. S. Bland, "lifts . . . description beyond utility" (316). Some obvious cases? The House of Usher, the courtrooms of Kafka's *The Trial,* and the Arctic in *Frankenstein* all have clearly symbolic roles. And even without resorting to symbol-hunting, you can learn a lot about a culture by exploring the thematic function of the settings that take on a conventional status in a particular set of texts (say, the middle-class home of so many domestic sit-coms).

But thematic functions can be far subtler as well, as we can see by considering the role of the Mississippi River in the progression of *Huckleberry Finn.*

An important first step in appreciating the Mississippi's functions is to remind ourselves that although the River is always part of the novel's landscape, it is not always in the foreground. Instead, it is one of several important settings in the novel, and, thus, we should consider its mimetic, thematic, and synthetic functions in relation to the functions of these other settings. We don't have space (!) to give a full-scale analysis, but here's a brief sketch of the initial settings. As we noted in chapter 3, before Huck and Jim take to the River, Twain places Huck in two main settings in the environs of St. Petersburg: the Widow Douglas's house and Pap's cabin. In both, Twain emphasizes the lack of fit between Huck and the place, though the lack of fit, stemming from a combination of elements of the setting itself and the people within it, is different in each case. The Widow's house is a model of Christian, middle-class respectability, a milieu that Huck can neither adequately comprehend nor comfortably conform to. Physically, we see the lack of fit in Huck's exiting and entering the house via his bedroom window rather than using the stairs and the door. As for the people, the Widow is kind and generous, and Miss Watson is strict and severe, but neither has the slightest idea of who Huck is or what he needs. At Pap's cabin, Huck is in one sense more comfortable as he lives in nature away from "sivilization," and, in this way, Twain begins to establish a thematic hierarchy of settings. But, in another sense, Huck's life at the cabin is much worse because Pap, having kidnapped Huck, treats him as both prisoner and punching bag. Consequently, the first two settings, in addition to establishing the thematic hierarchy, also contribute to the synthetic function of establishing the mimetic and thematic dimensions of one of the narrative's global instabilities: Huck is a young adolescent without any adequate home or any adult who can properly guide him as he tries to find his way in the world. Twain reinforces the depth of this instability by having Huck fake his murder and by shifting the setting from Pap's cabin to Jackson's Island where Huck is initially alone. As we noted in chapter 3, this shift in setting coincides with the launch.

Twain skillfully uses Jackson's Island to begin complicating this global instability. Not only does he bring Jim as a fugitive to the Island, but he also gives it an important role in the intertwining of Huck's story with Jim's. Once Huck discovers Jim on the island, they join forces, first, to keep their presence hidden from everyone in St. Petersburg, and, second, to make a comfortable life for themselves. The setting reinforces the thematic hierarchy Twain has already established because Huck and Jim have a satisfactory life lived close to nature on the island, content in their makeshift home in the cavern on the island's ridge and their ability to provide their own food. In addition, Huck and Jim's shared outsider status enables them to connect in a way that Huck never connects with the Widow, Miss Watson, or Pap. Because Jackson's Island is otherwise uninhabited, Huck and Jim have some freedom to define their relationship, even as they carry with them their assumptions about how adult slaves and free white adolescents should behave toward each other. In this setting, they begin to establish some of the paradoxical qualities of their relationship: Huck does not immediately grant authority to Jim, yet with respect to some important decisions—such as choosing the cavern as their home base—Jim takes the lead. In this way, the interlude on Jackson's Island offers a glimpse of a positive direction for the trajectory of the instabilities surrounding Huck. But the instabilities surrounding Jim bring this interlude to a close in a way that emphasizes Huck's intuitive sense that he and Jim are now a unit: as we noted in chapter 3, after Huck learns from Judith Loftus that her husband plans to search for the runaway Jim on the Island, Huck races back and awakens the sleeping Jim by shouting "They're after *us!*" (81, our emphasis).

Once they begin their journey on the raft, Twain uses the contrast between life on the River and life along the shore to underline his thematic point about the superiority of a life lived close to nature to one lived in allegedly respectable civilization. But some of the functions of the River are more subtle than that, as we can see by examining the way that Twain handles its role in Huck and Jim's missing Cairo and, thus, their opportunity to head for the free states. Twain gives the River a major synthetic function here, since this event allows him to contrast Huck's adventures along the shore and his experiences with Jim and, in so doing, to sketch Huck's informal ethical education. Nevertheless, because having Huck and Jim miss Cairo runs the risk of appearing just a cheap plot device, Twain faces a challenge: how can he make the development mimetically plausible? It's a sign of his artistry that as he does so, he complicates the River's thematic functions and, at the same time, also finds a way to use the River's mimetic function to deepen the ethical dimensions of Huck's relation to Jim.

Twain does two main things to make the passing of Cairo mimetically plausible. First, he has Huck and Jim miscalculate their progress on the River. At the beginning of Chapter XV, Huck notes that they "judged that three more nights would fetch us to Cairo" (95), but since they have no maps and no locals to consult, their judgment is plausibly fallible. Second, Twain rolls in the fog on the second night and at the same time increases the swiftness of the current in the River. Consequently, Huck and Jim's efforts to pull over onto a towhead ironically become the means by which they get separated, with Huck in the canoe and Jim on the raft. Enveloped in the fog and at the mercy of the current, they focus entirely on their exchange of whoops until they lose contact and both fall asleep. Sometime during this night they go past Cairo and are understandably unaware that they have done so. Since it is mimetically plausible for the fog to come in over the River and for the current to run swiftly at the same time, Twain is able to keep the synthetic function of the River backgrounded. But in drawing on this mimetic dimension of the setting, Twain complicates its thematic function. Whatever easy escape from civilization that the River seems to provide, the events of this night indicate that a life lived so close to nature is also subject to its dangers. The events also remind us that nature is both indifferent to and more powerful than human desire.

Even more impressively, Twain combines the mimetic functions of this night of fog and fast current with mimetic aspects of his characters to deepen the ethical stakes of Huck's cruel joke on Jim once they are reunited. When Huck gets back to the raft, he convinces Jim that Jim has dreamed everything he'd experienced that night. Jim then develops an elaborate interpretation of this alleged dream. Huck springs the joke by asking Jim to interpret the all-too-real detritus that has accumulated on the raft. Jim's response is one of the novel's most impressive passages, as it articulates the ethical difference between Jim's and Huck's responses to their ordeal and reunion:

> "What do dey stan' for? I'se gwyne to tell you. When I got all wore out wid work, en wid de callin' for you, en went to sleep, my heart wuz mos' broke bekase you wuz los', en I didn' k'yer no' mo' what become er me en de raf'. En when I wake up en fine you back agin, all safe en soun', de tears come, en I could a got down on my knees en kiss yo' foot, I's so thankful. En all you wuz thinkin' 'bout wuz how you could make a fool uv ole Jim wid a lie. Dat truck dah is *trash;* en trash is what people is dat puts dirt on de head er dey fren's en makes 'em ashamed." (99)

Jim's speech is powerful testimony about his own feelings during the night's ordeal and about the cruelty of Huck's joke. But Twain also invites the audience to recognize that Huck's effort to make a fool of Jim is also shamefully insensitive in light of Huck's own experience on the River that night. Twain's masterful handling of Huck's perspective is crucial to these affective and ethical effects. Consider Huck's description of how he felt to be alone in the fog:

> I kept quiet, with my ears cocked, about fifteen minutes, I reckon. I was floating along, of course, four or five miles an hour; but you don't ever think of that. No, you *feel* like you are laying dead still on the water. . . . If you think it ain't dismal and lonesome out in a fog that way by yourself in the night, you try it once—you'll see. (96)

It's striking that Twain has Huck render his account of his own feelings through a hypothetical focalization of the narrative audience. In having Huck say that "if you experienced what I experienced, you would feel as dismal and lonely as I felt," Twain gives him a Whitmanesque sense of connection with others. But when faced with the actual Jim who was out in the same fog, Huck's first move is not to empathize with but to find a way to belittle him. To his credit, Huck recognizes that he needs to apologize to Jim. But Twain invites us to find the reason for Huck's failure of empathy in Huck's confession that it took "fifteen minutes" before he could "work [him]self up to go and humble [him]self" to a slave. Despite their developing friendship and the role of their life on the River in that development, Huck still can easily revert to his assumptions about Jim's inferiority and thus treat him as someone whose feelings can be manipulated for his own amusement.

Robyn Warhol

In spite of the narrator's penchant for exposing her narrative as fictitious just as she and the reader are leaving it, Austen's storyworld is vividly created and quite consistent from novel to novel. Indeed readers—and I am no exception—become strongly attached to their own ideas of what that storyworld is like and what can or cannot happen there. For example, at the end of an otherwise-faithful 1995 BBC adaptation of *Persuasion,* Captain Wentworth and Anne Elliot, having just come to an understanding in a scene drawn from the original, "canceled" chapter of the novel, walk out a doorway into a busy street in Bath, throw their arms around each other, and share a big, romantic, Hollywood kiss. In the world created by Austen's novels, they might just as plausibly have sprouted wings and flown to Florida for a vacation. Austen is vigilant in her handling of public and private space, public and private actions. Kisses are too private—or too banal, depending on how one interprets Austen's consistent refusal to narrate them—to be rendered as part of the narrative world. If heterosexual kisses *were* present in Austen's world, though, they would never happen in a crowded street. In Austen's version of the scene immediately following Wentworth's communication of his continuing love, Anne and Wentworth meet by chance on bustling Union Street and then go by design to the "comparatively quiet and retired" Gravel Walk (193), a wide path behind the gardens of the houses on Gay Street, shielded by greenery from the surrounding roadways. A present-day visitor to Bath will find the Gravel Walk much as it was in 1817 and will understand that for Anne and Wentworth in this spot, "the power of conversation would make the present hour a blessing indeed" (193), because the two could find here the uninterrupted privacy they cannot, as an unmarried man and woman, share in any house or public building or on any street in Bath. Television adaptations are free to play fast and loose with setting for dramatic effect, but Austen's handling of the interplay between gender and space is both subtle and detailed; the settings of her fictions play as significant a role in the creation of her narrative worlds as do the thoughts and actions of the characters.

Feminist theorists working not just in literary studies but also in history, urban anthropology, and geography have established that nineteenth-century upper- and middle-class British spaces were strongly gendered: home, or the domestic realm, was the "private" world associated with femininity, while "public" life—including the worlds of commerce, religion, higher education, politics, and law—happened in spaces that were coded as masculine.[4] Living at home, men were supposed to be morally improved by the softening presence of the women who controlled the domestic domain, and women in turn were supposed to have a positive effect on the public realm indirectly, through the influence they had over their husbands and sons. Austen's fictions do not directly challenge these assumptions, in that the novelist never created a female character who ventured into the public realm by trying her hand at any profession (not even authorship). Indeed, the masculine realm is literally invisible in Austen's fictional world. In all six of her completed novels, Austen never once wrote a scene dramatizing action between men with no woman present. Sometimes in Austen's world, conversations or actions happen among men that get reported secondhand. This is particularly true of *Persuasion*, where the backstory of Captain Wentworth's adventures at sea—including his acquaintance with the unfortunate Dick Musgrove—is so important to his re-emergence as Anne's potential hero. But we learn about the details of Captain Wentworth's achievement, as it were, only secondhand. In this novel as in her others, every scene Austen ever dramatized happens in the presence of at least one female character.

This is not to say, however, that Austen restricts her represented world to the domestic realm. In a novel like *Persuasion*, Austen focuses not on the male/female, public/private binary, or on the differences between men's world and women's (in the way that Anthony Trollope, for instance, was to do in the next generation), but rather on the gradations of difference within the feminine realm of the "private." As the scene of Anne's and Frederick's retirement to the Gravel Walk reminds us, some public spaces are more private than others in Austen's world—in fact, some public spaces can offer more privacy than home can. Women in Austen's world operate within a wide range of private and public spaces. At home in Kellynch Hall, Anne has become used to the neglect and misprision she suffers from her father and sister—"She was only Anne" (11)—but prefers the privacy of country life to the prospect of moving to a crowded resort town. "She disliked Bath, and did not think it agreed with her—and Bath was to be her home" (17). Venturing outside her own house to her sister Mary's, and then to the comparatively public space of a walk in the countryside, Anne exposes herself to overhearing conversations she would rather not have known to have taken place, as when, shielded by a hedgerow, she becomes the reluctant auditor to Frederick Wentworth's flirting with Louisa Musgrove. The removal to Bath adds another degree of public exposure to Anne's experience, as she must appear at Bath's Assembly Rooms, Pump Room, and parties, the locations of her ever-increasing efforts to communicate her continuing interest in Wentworth.

Being on display in a vacation destination provides many opportunities for Anne to see and be seen by her hero, but tourism grants an even more important public occurrence, when Anne notices Wentworth notic-ing Mr. Elliot's look at her on the steps to the beach at Lyme Regis. "It was evident that the gentleman (completely a gentleman in manner) admired her exceedingly. Captain Wentworth looked round at her instantly in a way which shewed his noticing of it. He gave her a momentary glance,—a glance of brightness, which seemed to say, 'That man is struck with you,—and even I, at this moment, see something like Anne Elliot again'" (87). Wentworth's renewed appreciation of Anne's attractiveness and the triangulation of his interest in her with Mr. Elliot's are both important developments in the plot. In Austen's world, significant actions often happen in public places, and *where* something happens can carry as much meaning as the event itself. Lyme, home to the congenial family of Captain Harville, signifies what Anne comes to appreciate in her own ultimate union with a naval officer, a man from "that profession which is, if possible, more distinguished in its domestic virtues than in its national importance" (203). The domestic realm, for Aus-ten's happily married couple, is both a feminine *and* a masculine space.

The beach at Lyme, or rather the Cobb, the harbor wall adjacent to it, also serves as the setting for the critical moment when Louisa childishly insists that she must be "jumped down" the steps one more time by Cap-tain Wentworth and ends up falling on her head. The aftermath of Louisa's accident puts Anne once again in Wentworth's sights, as he relies on her levelheaded competence for help: "If Anne will stay, no one so proper, so capable as Anne!" (95). The public location of the incident allows a momen-tary glimpse from a perspective rarely rendered in Austen's fiction, the point of view of working-class folk.

> By this time the report of the accident had spread among the workmen and boatmen about the Cobb, and many were collected near them, to be useful if wanted, at any rate, to enjoy the sight of a dead young lady, nay, two dead young ladies, for it proved twice as fine as the first report. To some of the best-looking of these good people Henrietta [who fainted on seeing her sister's fall] was consigned. (93)

Finding working people even mentioned in Austen's fiction is unusual, but finding a passage of free indirect discourse—even one so brief as "to enjoy the sight of a dead young lady, nay, two dead young ladies, for it proved twice as fine as the first report"—is remarkable.

In *Persuasion* this passage signifies the novelist's partial turn from the exclusively upper-middle-class view that dominates her previous fictions, a turn that is highlighted by Anne's relationship with her old school friend,

Mrs. Smith. The very location of Mrs. Smith's rooms ("Westgate-buildings must have been rather surprised by the appearance of a carriage drawn up near its pavement!" [128]) is as objectionable to Sir Walter as her common name ("an every day Mrs. Smith, of all people and all names in the world" [128]). Close to the highly populous baths and the mercantile center of the city, Westgate Buildings is an address without prestige, and Mrs. Smith ("A poor widow, barely able to live," as Sir Walter has it [128]) subsists at a social level of dependency and near-destitution equaled in Austen's fiction only by *Emma's* Miss and Mrs. Bates. In terms of narrative perspective on the fictional world, what makes Mrs. Smith's condition particularly interesting is her access to people of even lower status than she, particularly Nurse Rooke, who circulates as a servant through the households of the rich and casually carries important intelligence back to Mrs. Smith. It is from Nurse Rooke that Mrs. Smith gathers she should warn Anne against her would-be suitor. What Anne can't seem to find out about Mr. William Walter Elliot's disreputable past from the social circles in which she usually travels, she can learn from Mrs. Smith because the lower-class perspective in this novel carries insights to which the heroine's own point of view is blind.

Anne benefits in this instance from opening herself to a network that is as strongly marked by gender as by class. Nurse Rooke gets her information by overhearing the conversations of the ladies she attends, and she repeats them to Mrs. Smith, whose connection to Anne originated in the homosocial sphere of a girls' school. Women's way of knowing in this world comes through narratives, stories one woman tells another, intending for them to be passed on. To be uncharitable, one could call it gossip. Despite the negative connotations of this effeminate pastime, in Austen's world the network of storytelling women wields enough power to thwart William Walter Elliot's designs on Anne—enough power, that is, to ensure that the novel reaches its happy ending. The power of Mrs. Smith's knowledge is limited, though, because as a woman she cannot act on her own behalf to have her fortune reinstated. In the end, it is Anne's husband, Captain Wentworth, who must exercise masculine prerogative by taking the necessary actions to restore Mrs. Smith's financial security.

After the first three chapters, perspective in *Persuasion* is almost exclusively focalized through Anne. This makes Austen's last published novel similar to all the rest except for the first, because only *Sense and Sensibility* extensively dramatizes episodes which neither Elinor nor Marianne Dashwood witnesses. In *Persuasion,* as in *Pride and Prejudice, Emma, Mansfield Park,* and even *Northanger Abbey,* what the implied reader knows is, for the most part, limited to what the heroine knows. Like all of Austen's novels

Persuasion begins with a perspective providing an "establishing shot" of each main character's personality and circumstances, but after that, the perspective follows Anne but for a few telling exceptions. One is the brief insertion of the workingmen's perspective on the Cobb. Another, more instrumental in developing the plot, is a glimpse into Frederick Wentworth's perspective, shortly following his seeing Anne after their long estrangement.

> He had not forgiven Anne Elliot. She had used him ill; deserted and disap-
> pointed him; and worse, she had shewn a feebleness of character in doing
> so, which his own decided, confident temper could not endure. She had
> given him up to oblige others. It had been the effect of over-persuasion.
> It had been weakness and timidity. . . . Her power with him was gone for
> ever. (54)

This passage gives the implied reader knowledge about Wentworth's state of mind that Anne can only surmise. Even this early in the novel, the implied reader takes Wentworth's assessment of Anne's past actions as mistaken, because the narrator has provided ample justifications for the heroine's decision to renounce her engagement under pressure. A rare view of an Austen heroine from the hero's perspective, Wentworth's reflections build suspense in *Persuasion*, because after this point the implied reader knows no more than Anne does about the gradual rekindling of Wentworth's love.

More than suspense, though, hangs on the focalized perspective of Austen's novels. Focalization is primarily responsible for the novel's effective representation of the heroine's interiority. Not until Henry James did anyone articulate the practice of organizing a fiction around a central consciousness, and James himself certainly gave his great female forbear no credit for having anticipated his own technique: "Jane Austen, with all her light felicity, leaves us hardly more curious about her process . . . than the brown thrush who tells his story from the garden bough" (229–30). What James dismissively understood as the fruits of Austen's "wool-gathering" over her needlework a feminist narratologist can recognize as a technical innovation representing a sophisticated development in the handling of perspective and characterization in the British novel. Before Austen, only epistolary fiction (whether in the tragic mode like Samuel Richardson's *Clarissa* or the comic like Fanny Burney's *Evelina*) could bring into being as elaborate an illusion of female subjectivity as Austen's narrative practice achieves, but the epistolary novels—unlike Austen's or for that matter James's—always hold the possibility of offering multiple perspectives on the action. In *Persuasion,* as in her novels generally, Austen recreates for the authorial audience the epistemological experience of living under the social and familial restraints placed on women during the first decades of the nineteenth century.

Feminist theorists have embraced "standpoint epistemology" as a way of framing what can be known.[5] While it is not a radical relativism—because it acknowledges that persons sharing certain identity categories are positioned to see the world similarly—feminist epistemology understands "objectivity" to be a politically and socially useful fiction. What one sees depends entirely on where one is standing while one looks. Austen's focalized perspective anticipates this feminist insight, framing a narrative world as only a female—or to be more precise, a feminine—consciousness could know it. To the extent that Austen's novels have engaged readers from across the gendered spectrum of identity positions, they have exercised readers' capacity for understanding Austen's world from a feminine perspective. For Austen, this in itself was a feminist achievement.

David Herman

My discussion of emplotment in chapter 3 raised issues that extend beyond the WHEN dimension to the WHAT and WHERE dimensions of narrative worlds. The emplotting of events entails creating not just a temporal sequence but a linked series of spatiotemporal contexts or environments (cf. Bridgeman; Dannenberg, *Coincidence*)—a series of situated actions and occurrences that, characterized from some vantage point on the storyworld, are connected with one another via the process of narration. At issue is what I termed in an earlier study the "spatialization" of storyworlds, the process of building mental representations of narrated domains as evolving configurations of participants, objects, and places (Herman, *Story Logic* 263–99).

Again, the spatial aspect of narrative worldmaking—more precisely, the spatiotemporal configuration of narrative worlds—can be analyzed into a number of sub-aspects, each of which can be captured as a question for which interpreters seek to frame answers as part of the larger process of co-creating storyworlds. Relevant questions include the following:

1. Where did/will/might narrated events happen relative to the place of narration—and for that matter relative to the interpreter's current situation?
2. How exactly is the domain of narrated events spatially configured, and what sorts of changes take place in the configuration of that domain over time?
3. During a given moment of the unfolding action, what are the focal (foregrounded) constituents or inhabitants of the narrated domain—as opposed to the peripheral (backgrounded) constituents?
4. Whose vantage point on situations, objects, and events in the narrated world shapes the presentation of that world at a given moment?

Approaches such as deictic shift theory (Duchan, Bruder, and Hewitt) and contextual frame theory (Emmott) can illuminate the cognitive relocation that enables interpreters to take up residence in a narrative world like McEwan's (question 1); such approaches can also elucidate how interpreters are able to remain oriented within that world by monitoring changes in the space-time configuration of characters, objects, and places (questions 2, 3, and 4). Also relevant for question 4 is work that rethinks narratological approaches to focalization or perspective via ideas from cognitive linguistics, which studies how the structure and use of language reflects the capacities and dispositions of embodied human minds (Herman, "Beyond").

Consider the opening sentences of *On Chesil Beach:*

[1] They were young, educated, and both virgins on this, their wedding night, and they lived in a time when a conversation about sexual difficulties was plainly impossible. [2] But it is never easy. [3] They had just sat down to supper in a tiny sitting room on the first floor of a Georgian inn. [4] In the next room, visible through the open door, was a four-poster bed, rather narrow, whose bedcover was pure white and stretched startlingly smooth, as though by no human hand. [5] Edward did not mention that he had never stayed in a hotel before, whereas Florence, after many trips as a child with her father, was an old hand. [6] Superficially, they were in fine spirits. [7] Their wedding, at St. Mary's, Oxford, had gone well; the service was decorous, the reception jolly, the send-off from school and college friends raucous and uplifting. (3–4)

These seven sentences evoke a fictional scenario to which the world-building logic of the referring expressions ("They," "a Georgian inn," "the send-off") and deictic terms ("this," "before") invite me to relocate.[6] Reading the passage in accordance with protocols for fictional world construction, I map these expressions and terms onto the space-time coordinates organizing the account being presented—rather than those associated with the worlds that McEwan occupied as text producer or that I currently inhabit as text interpreter. In other words, while interpreting the narrative, I make a *deictic shift* to a particular night in 1962 (as stipulated by subsequent textual cues), which is in turn part of an autonomous, stand-alone world that contrasts with storyworlds evoked by accounts of the past that make a claim to fact. Granted, toponymns included in the title of the novel and in the text's opening pages (Chesil Beach; St. Mary's, Oxford; the Dorset coast) provide general geographic coordinates in which to situate the world of the novel. These toponymns function as what Even-Zohar would term "realemes," or units within a larger repertory of real-world elements deemed to be insertable within a given narrative. Generic conventions, authorial preferences, and text-specific patterns constitute criteria for realeme insertability in a given narrative; such criteria afford scaffolding for particular kinds of world-construction and, while obviating the need to build the storyworld from scratch, also determine the degree to which (and ways in which) narrative worlds can be cross-referenced with the world(s) in which they are interpreted.

The relative abundance of place names distinguishes McEwan's novel from the storyworlds of some science fiction narratives, for example, where tighter constraints on realeme insertability translate into different methods of world-building. Yet a note included at the end of the novel signals the divergence between, on the one hand, the fictional situations and events recounted in the novel and, on the other hand, circumstances and occurrences about which falsifiable claims can be made: "Edward and Florence's hotel—just over a mile south of Abbotsbury, Dorset, occupying an elevated position in a field behind the beach parking lot—does not exist" (205). This note underscores how interpreting McEwan's text requires making a deictic shift away from the world of the here-and-now, and also the world of a (dis)confirmable historical past, to the world of the story. But understanding McEwan's text also requires shifting among different sets of space-time coordinates *within* this narrative world. Here Emmott's idea of contextual frames can supplement deictic shift theory, indicating how narrative worlds are in fact composite constructs, built from a constellation of mentally projected scenes or contexts linking characters, locales, and events. Indeed, the dynamics of frame shifting suggests that the traditional concept of "setting" operates at too gross a scale to capture the fluctuating relations between focal and peripheral elements as one navigates space-time regions of the storyworld.

To parse the first sentences of the novel, readers who use the world-building methods I am outlining have to move from the spatiotemporal configuration, or contextual frame, that corresponds to the present moment in the narrated domain, or what can be called the story-NOW (sentence 1), to a frame associated with a gnomic statement anchored in the present moment of narration, or the discourse-NOW (sentence 2). There is then a shift to a different configuration immediately preceding that of the story-NOW (sentence 3), followed by a further elaboration of the current frame (sentence 4). Tracking such frame-shifts, and in longer episodes monitoring when circumstances and participants are bound into or out of a given frame, allows readers to navigate (by bringing into relation with one another) the WHAT, WHERE, and WHEN dimensions of the storyworld under construction. Thus, recognizing the frame shift between sentences 5 and 6 allows readers to anchor referring expressions to appropriate subdomains of the storyworld. It is because of this frame shift that "they" in sentence 6 can pick out Edward and Florence in the space-time coordinates corresponding to the story-NOW rather than during the separate lives they led in the past.

Modes of perspective taking likewise bear crucially on narrative world-making, suggesting the need to reorient accounts of focalization around the key question of how storyworlds are spatialized. Up to now scholars of narrative have for the most part concentrated on developing taxonomies of modes of focalization, distinguishing, for example, between fixed modes of focalization, where the vantage point on the events being narrated does not change (as with Jack's perspective in *The Cement Garden*), and variable modes like that used in *On Chesil Beach*, which switches back and forth between Florence's and Edward's vantage points. Theorists have also contrasted internal or character-specific modes, where the action is filtered through the perspective of one or more characters, with external modes, where, as in the opening pages of McEwan's novel, the vantage point is wider in scope than any character's and is thus "ambient" rather than "strict," to use Manfred Jahn's terms. But an emphasis on worldmaking necessitates a less taxonomic and more functional approach to narrative perspective. Tracking frame-shifts of the sort just discussed requires monitoring what vantage point orients the configuration of circumstances, participants, and events in a given frame and across frames. In turn, in ways that can be illuminated by recent work in cognitive linguistics, perspective-marking features are part of the blueprint for world-building included in a narrative's verbal texture.

Cognitive-linguistic research (Langacker; Talmy) suggests how perspective-marking features of stories can be situated within a wider array of *construal operations*—ways of organizing and making sense of domains of experience—that are anchored in humans' embodied existence and that may be exploited in different ways in different narratives (for fuller discussion, see Herman, "Beyond"). The opening of chapter 5 of McEwan's novel suggests the advantages of assimilating issues of perspective to a broader concern with the construal of situations and events in narrative worlds. Here, having hurried away from the honeymoon suite after her and Edward's unsuccessful attempt at sexual intercourse, Florence watches Edward approach her on Chesil Beach as the last of the daylight fades:

[1] She watched him coming along the strand, his form at first no more than an indigo stain against the darkening shingle, sometimes appearing motionless, flickering and dissolving at its outlines, and at others suddenly closer, as though moved like a chess piece a few squares toward her. [2] The last glow of daylight lay along the shore, and behind her, away to the east, there were points of light on Portland, and the cloud base reflected dully a yellowish glow of streetlamps from a distant town. [3] She watched him, willing him to go slower, for she was guiltily afraid of him, and was desperate for more time to herself. . . . [4] Briefly, she saw the outline of his shoulders against a silver streak of water, a current that plumed far out to sea behind him. [5] Now she could hear the sound of his footfalls on the pebbles, which meant that he would hear hers. (169; 172–73)

In this passage, the retrospective narration is oriented around Florence's sighting of a scene that, featuring Edward as the focal participant, unfolds in the real time of the story-NOW. Yet the scope of the construal fluctuates from sentence to sentence—indicating that, as with the concept of "setting," distinctions like internal vs. external focalization operate at too gross a scale to capture moment-by-moment processes of worldmaking. Thus, within sentence 1, the scope of the construal widens as one moves from the first to the second clause—a widening that continues in sentence 2, which presents elements of the scene that are situated behind Florence and thus outside her visual field. The scope then narrows again in subsequent sentences, with Florence's standpoint orienting the narration of events, although in sentence 5 Florence does imaginatively project herself into what Edward must be able to hear as he approaches her on the beach. As Edward nears the proximal end of the line of sight from which Florence watches his approach, the degree of detail of her visual and auditory perceptions increases, prompting continued spatialization of the scene from Florence's standpoint.

This passage thus underscores how what can be seen or perceived alters with the spatial coordinates of the embodied self who is doing the looking or perceiving. But more than this, it suggests that a self is in part constituted by what it perceives, and when and where such acts of perception take place— with narrative being one of the principal means for situating selves, or persons, in evolving sets of space-time coordinates. In the next chapter I build on these last remarks concerning the interconnections between perspective and character or identity. There I explore in more detail how stories portray *model persons* in narrative worlds, and in doing so at once draw on and contribute to the *models of persons* circulating in a given culture or subculture.

Brian Richardson

Narrative space can be approached from a number of vantage points: we may investigate geographical, psychological, social, metaphorical, allegorical, ideological, and self-reflexive sites and spaces. For an antimimetic approach, it is the ontological nature of the fictional storyworld—that is, what exactly exists in there—that most insistently demands our attention. The space of the fiction is also the site where mimetic and antimimetic impulses are often engaged in a dialectical interaction. We can see this particularly sharply in *Ulysses*. Unlike Victorian realists, who might set a work in a partially invented (Hardy's "Wessex") or incompletely unidentified location ("In the town of _____"), Joyce uses the exact topography of 1904 Dublin. It is so accurate that reenactors can follow in the exact steps of the fictional characters. At the same time, many of the spatial depictions are deceptive. Eric Bulson observes that even with such precise coordinates, readers typically "get a fragmented image of Dublin, one responsible for a lot of wrong turns, dead ends, and retracing of their steps" (73), particularly in the labyrinthine "Wandering Rocks" episode. The routes traveled by the characters regularly trace out revealing geometrical designs, such as the "X" marked over the city of Dublin made by the intersecting paths of the representatives of the church and the state in this chapter.

The mimetic/antimimetic dialectic affords us a clearer sense of the fabrication of space in fiction; Nabokov's *Pale Fire* is a particularly instructive example. This work refers to a number of actual spaces in the real world, such as Paris and New York. Other areas are fictionalized versions of actual places ("New Wye" stands for a town in upstate "N.Y."). The ontological status of the country of Zembla, "a distant northern land" (315), however, is much more indeterminate; it seems to be a Baltic state on the border of the Soviet Union. It may not exist at all; it may only be an elaborate figment of the imagination of Charles Kinbote, the book's deranged narrator. John Shade, the poet in the text, does, however, refer to it as a country, suggesting it may be "real" within the storyworld of the novel. On the other hand, its very name suggests an illusory existence; many of the descriptions of it, including those of its history and inhabitants, seem to come from a parodic version of a popular romance such as *The Prisoner of Zenda*. At the furthest reach from the mimetic, we see a reference to Illyria, the fictional land invented by Shakespeare as the setting of *Twelfth Night*.

Many other writers construct space in original ways; there are the dreamlike worlds of Kafka or the magical realists; the unreal psychotropic world of Anna Kavan's *Ice* (1962), the postmodern fantastic realms of Angela Carter's

The Infernal Desire Machines of Doctor Hoffman (1972) and Italo Calvino's *Invisible Cities* (1972), and the impossible space of Mark Danielewski's *House of Leaves* (2000).

Samuel Beckett extends and distills many of these strategies. We observe him constructing indeterminate, contradictory, and what I call "denarrated" spaces. Some of Beckett's spaces, like the world of *Endgame,* are inherently ambiguous zones. It refers to actual and fictional places, it has a dubious historical setting, it makes several metadramatic allusions, and the very shape of the stage space it is enacted within has two windows that suggest two eyes. These multiple, mutually contradictory references simultaneously suggest historical, invented, postapocalyptic, purgatorial, psychological, allegorical, and metadramatic domains. The work partakes of each of these spaces without being reducible to any one.

An especially illustrative example of Beckett's practice is found in the troubled narrative of Woburn in "Cascando." In this piece, Woburn keeps trying and failing to establish the spatial setting of his story: "down . . . gentle slopes . . . boreen . . . giant aspens [. . . .] face in the mud [. . . .] soon the dunes . . . no more cover [. . . .] face in the sand . . . arms spread . . . bare dunes [. . . .] face . . . in the stones . . . no more sand . . . all stones . . . that's the idea . . . we're there . . . no, not yet [. . . .] no tiller . . . no thwarts . . . no oars . . . afloat [. . . .] face in the bilge" (138–41).

Beckett clearly enjoys erasing or "denarrating" the spaces he has created; he affirms and then negates several descriptions in many of his works. In *Worstward Ho* we see him constructing, altering, and deconstructing the narrative space of his story. We may also note that here Beckett has come about as close as possible to creating a setting that has almost no space. The depictions begin with: "A place. Where none. A time when try see. Try say. How small. How vast. How if not boundless bounded. Whence the dim" (11). This attempt at invention leads at first only to: "Beyondless. Thenceless there. Thitherless there" (12) and then to a "dim bit of void" (13). Two figures start to plod though the void, the dim, "far and wide unchanging" (17). They come to what is called "a grot in the void. A gulf. Then in that dimmest grot or gulf such dimmest light as never" (17). From now on the void only grows more encompassing: "Shades dimmed. Void dimmed. Dim dimmed" (40). The characters start to vanish, the events are denarrated, the images fade. The drama of space in this text ends with the words, "At bounds of boundless void. Whence no farther" (47), as the void consumes all that it had held. While the discourse of *Endgame* suggests numerous possible, contradictory spaces without any one established as definitive, "Worstward Ho" never provides enough description for any coherent spatial setting to emerge. We remain, as it were, at the edge of space looking in on opacity.

Perhaps the most fantastic impossible space is that contained within Borges' Aleph:

> The Aleph was probably two or three centimeters in diameter, but universal space was contained within it, with no diminution in size. Each thing (the glass surface of a mirror, let us say) was infinite things, because I could clearly see it from every point in the cosmos. I saw the populous sea, saw dawn and dusk, saw the multitudes of the Americas, saw a silvery spiderweb at the center of a black pyramid, saw a broken labyrinth (it was London), saw endless eyes, all very close, studying themselves in me as though in a mirror [. . . .] saw my face and my viscera, saw your face, and I felt dizzy, and I wept, because my eyes had seen that secret, hypothetical object whose name has been usurped by men but which no man has ever truly looked upon: the inconceivable universe. (283–84)

Though not quite as radical as Borges or Beckett, Rushdie reconfigures space in a number of intriguing ways. He describes older spaces that are transformed by new names and identities, as during the creation of the state of Pakistan. Being "handcuffed to history," Saleem and his family always improbably and unwillingly find themselves in the place where major historical events are about to occur: in Amritsar just as the British assault is about to happen, in Gujerat during the language riots, in Pakistan as the new state emerges, in East Pakistan during its war of independence, and so forth (440). As the boatman Tai is about to enter the narrative, he is described as physically moving closer to it: "Tai is getting nearer. He, who revealed the power of the nose, and who is now bringing my grandfather the message which will catapult him into history, is stroking his shikara through the early morning lake" (9). Saleem comes to realize that he has experienced a number of unusual adventures in improbably confined spaces (439); this is especially true of the magical basket that transports him, invisible, back to India: "I was in the basket, but also not in the basket. . . . Present but insubstantial; actual, but without being or weight," he explains obscurely (438). Most unnatural is the labyrinthine geography of the Sundarbans where, as we have seen, time is dislocated, self-identity dissolves, teleology collapses, and pseudohistorical events transpire. Here, the "jungle closed behind them like a tomb, and after hours of increasingly weary but also frenzied rowing through incomprehensibly labyrinthine salt-water channels overtowered by the cathedral-arching trees, Ayooba Shaheed Farooq were hopelessly lost" (414). They quickly surrender themselves to "the terrible phantasms of the dream-forest" (417).

WHAT IS THE purpose of all these strange, unnatural, or impossible spaces? The answer is as multiform as the spaces themselves. One, it points to the fabricated nature of descriptions and places set forth as real and often gestures toward the ideological pressures that inform such constructions (think of "Greater Serbia" or "Manifest Destiny"). Postmodern metageographers like Rushdie show how new places come into being by verbal acts; this is no less true of Pakistan than it is of Utopia (etymologically, "No Place") or the state of Cooch Naheen (literally, "no thing") in *Midnight's Children*. Postmodern authors are especially deft in challenging existing allegorical constructions. The ancient association of the human body and the body politic is parodically set forth by Saleem's geography teacher, Mr Zagallo, who uses the boy's face as a map of India: the stains represent Pakistan: "Thees birthmark on the right ear is the East Wing; and thees horrible stained left cheek, the West! Remember, stupid boys: Pakistan is a stain on the face of India!" (265). Then, in a final illustration of India's sundering by the creation of Pakistan, Zagallo rips Saleem's hair out of his scalp. This kind of allegorical play with space is common among postmodernists.

Finally, antimimetic constructs of narrative space also demonstrate the imaginative as well as the documentary power of fictional narrative. Actual spaces may be accurately depicted, or hitherto unthinkable ones may be invented. This in turn draws attention to what analytical philosophers refer to as the ontological status of fictional entities. When a work is designated as fictional, the status of all its elements becomes different from similar elements in works of nonfiction. No matter how realistic it seems, no description or event in a fictional text can be falsified by reference to nonfictional evidence. One cannot say that Proust got his geography wrong in the *Recherche* because, at the time his narrative takes place, there was no such town as Combray—in the fictional world he created there is indeed such a place. Similarly, in *Ulysses,* it makes no sense to say that there was no Leopold Bloom living at 7 Eccles Street; in the fictional world of *Ulysses* Bloom does and will always inhabit this space, regardless of whoever actually lived there on June 16, 1904, the day the action of the book takes place (in fact, historically, the house was unoccupied that day; Joyce made sure that no "real" person was displaced by the Blooms). It is this very fictionality that is extended and underscored by the unnatural and impossible spaces of postmodernism.[7]

IN ADDITION TO a temporal and spatial setting, every narrative has a canon of probability that governs events in its world. Fictional worlds usually fall into one of four types: supernatural, naturalistic, chance, or metafictional. In a world with supernatural causal agency, some sort of superhuman force appears: gods, ghosts, angels, demons, or fairies are able to cause or influence events. In this realm, we usually observe an overarching order determined by the workings of providence, fate, or destiny. In a naturalistic world, which is the world of the nineteenth century realist novel, supernatural agents are banished and all events have strictly naturalistic causes. In many contemporary works and in the theater of the absurd, one finds a breakdown of conventional causal orders, as events seem to unfold randomly or with no discernible order. There is an unnatural proliferation of chance events and coincidences; indeterminacy or contingency reigns. Finally, in a metafictional world, the narrator alters the causal laws of the world of the narrative, for example, by intervening to spare a protagonist who is otherwise doomed to a tragic end. Postmodern works that foreground the collapsing of their ontological frameworks are additional examples of this type.

Characters often struggle to determine the laws of their world: in *Oedipus Rex,* Jocasta believes that chance (*tyche*) rules all, and Oedipus and Laius both believe that human will can circumvent divine decree. All eventually learn that theirs is a thoroughly supernatural world where Fate cannot be eluded. Most realist and modernist authors establish naturalistic canons of probability as supernatural interpretations are shown to be illusory. A seemingly naturalistic causal setting can in its turn be disrupted by too frequent irruptions of chance events and uncanny coincidences, as happens in *Ulysses.* Authors may also keep readers guessing as to which laws a work adheres to.

Rushdie evokes all four types of governing causal systems in *Midnight's Children.* Supernatural figures and actions are regularly mentioned and at times insisted on: prophecies always prove correct and "yes, magic spells can occasionally succeed," we are informed concerning Saleem's invisibility (440). More often, however, other, more quotidian means are available to explain away such events. Thus, the djinns that torment Saleem's father turn out to represent a very ordinary kind of spirit: gin. The ability of his mother to perceive the dreams of her sleeping daughter is also suggested to be merely a case of a mother's intuition of her daughter's desires. Chance, determinism, and fate jostle together; Saleem himself can't decide which rules his world: the preternatural powers of the children born on the day of India's independence are due to "some freak of biology, or perhaps owing to some preternatural power of the moment, or just conceivably by sheer coincidence (though synchronicity on such a scale would stagger even C. G. Jung)" (224). In the end, we discover that fate is not preordained; human will can sometimes alter an apparent determinism. Saleem recognizes that the next generation will not be "looking for their fate in prophecy or the stars, but forging it in the implacable furnaces of their wills" (515). While supernatural explanations tend to get naturalized, these naturalistic parameters are themselves regularly exploded by the intrusion of antimimetic events, as supernatural marvels are replaced by playfully fictional ones. Chance remains unnaturally powerful as a series of wildly improbable coincidences land Saleem and his family in the most historically volatile areas year after year all over the Indian subcontinent. This in turn points to a metafictional intelligence that is arranging the events, even as it usually acknowledges the generally unalterable force of history. The book ends in a kind of stalemate between metafictional and historical/naturalistic ordering powers. Taken together, these examples disclose that the establishing of the canon of probability that governs a fictional world is of central importance and that characters and readers alike may be drawn into an interpretative drama concerning the precise nature of the storyworld.

FOCALIZATION is normally thought to be the perspective from which the narrated events are presented; this perspective is typically that of one or more individuals located at a particular point in space. In a mimetic first-person narrative told by a character, the only possible focalization would be the perceptions experienced by the narrator: after all, how can one individual know for certain exactly what any other is seeing, hearing, or feeling? Antimimetic fiction provides for many other options. An omniscient third-person narrator can abruptly lose his or her omniscience, as Gogol's famously does in "The Overcoat." First-person narrators in works of fiction can occasionally break into the minds of others, as when Marcel depicts the final thoughts of the solitary Bergotte in *In Search of Lost Time*. The focalization of collectives in "we" or "they" narratives is always intriguing, since all individuals in a group almost never have identical perceptions; there is always some variation among different observers. In extreme examples of this kind of narration, contradictory perceptions are set forth or shared thoughts stretching over centuries are delineated. The example of Borges' Aleph offers us one impossible space that provides the literal viewpoints of an infinite number of different spaces. In *Midnight's Children*, Saleem not only depicts his own perceptions but also offers the hypothetical focalization of his father ("maybe, yes, why not, my father sees a dark flurry of monkey out of the corner of an eye," 94); he also visualizes an illicit image privately seen by his mother (97).

He even learns how ghosts perceive the world (438). At other points he hears the private thoughts of other minds. The main source of these unnatural perceptions is what the narrator calls "All India Radio," or his ability to over-hear others' streams of thought. This too is spatially situated: "In the street, I learned how to identify the mind-stream of passing strangers [though] the law of Doppler shift continued to operate in these paranormal realms, and the voices grew and diminished as the strangers passed" (192–93). Antimi-metic texts thus locate impossible perceptions in natural spaces as well as fixing ordinary perceptions in impossible spaces.

NOTES

1. Thus, the Duluth Library website, asks us, "What is the role of the Mississippi River in this book?" Sometimes the question is disguised (CliffsNotes asks us to "Compare and contrast the environment on shore and the environment on the raft"), but you can count on its presence in one form or another. [JP/PJR]

2. Thanks to Michael Harwick. [JP/PJR]

3. Keith Cohen, taking a cue from Roland Barthes, argues that some kinds of description (in particular, *ekphrasis*) can be valuable artistically because they produce a kind of *jouissance,* a "textual thrill, when the ordinary limits of signification are exceeded . . . [and] the normal communication process is . . . short-circuited. . . . If ordinary pleasure confirms me and my cultural expectations, textual thrill unsettles me, decenters my worldview, challenges all symmetries" (Cohen, "Unweaving Puig's *Spider Woman,*" 18). [JP/PJR]

4. For examples of feminist geographical scholarship, see the journal *Gender, Place, and Culture,* published by Routledge; the founding editors were Liz Bondi and Mona Domosch. See also Joni Seager and Lise Nelson's *Companion to Feminist Geography* and the work of Linda McDowell. [RW]

5. Feminist standpoint theory was first outlined by Nancy Hartsock; Sandra Harding and Patricia Hill Collins extended standpoint epistemology to the disciplines of science and to include perspectives from all marginalized groups, including, but not exclusively, women. [RW]

6. Deictic terms like "I," "here," and "now" are expressions whose meaning changes depending on who is uttering them in what discourse context. [DH]

7. For further reading on narrative worlds, space, setting, and perspective from an unnatural narratology perspective, see Alber; Doležel, *Heterocosmica*; Grishakova; Richardson, "Poetics"; and Shen. [BR]

5

Character

James Phelan and Peter J. Rabinowitz

Two of the persistent questions about character in fiction are how seriously we should take its mimetic potential and whether character or plot is the more important element. One position on the first question is that only naïve readers take that mimetic potential seriously because characters are only words on paper, brushstrokes on canvas, images on celluloid, and so forth. Structuralist narratologists with their interest in laying out the grammar of narrative by identifying its fundamental units and the rules for combining them offer one version of this position. They define character as a set of predicates grouped under a proper name that performs one or more plot functions (e.g., sender, receiver, helper, opponent). A competing position, which can be traced back to Aristotle's *Poetics* and which has seen a contemporary flourishing in work on narrative's ability to exercise our Theory of Mind (Zunshine; Palmer), makes the mimetic potential of character its defining property. Our position is that we should eliminate the competition between these positions by recognizing that character has both mimetic and synthetic components—and thematic components as well. Characters do resemble possible people, they are artificial constructs that perform various functions in the progression, and they can function to convey the political, philosophical, or ethical issues being taken up by the narrative. For example, Miss Watson is a straitlaced, conventional, single, Christian woman who has no problem being a slave-owner, and we react to her as representing a kind of person we might actually meet if we time-traveled to pre–Civil War

Hannibal, Missouri. At the same time, Twain uses her to perform three main synthetic functions: to help demonstrate that Huck and "sivilization" are not a good match; to provide the spur for Jim's flight by entertaining the offer to sell him; and to resolve the global instability about Jim by granting him his freedom in her will. In addition, Miss Watson helps Twain make his thematic arguments about one brand of Christianity, about slave owning, and about the connection between those two things. While this view of character eliminates what we regard as an unnecessary theoretical competition, it also raises the question of how the three components of character interact in any given narrative. We can better answer that question after we take up the second persistent question, the one about the relative importance of character and plot.

This question also has its roots in the *Poetics,* where Aristotle identifies plot as the soul of tragedy and views character as subordinate to plot. Henry James famously tilts the balance back toward character by suggesting that events and characters are so interdependent that they blend into each other: "What is character but the determination of incident? What is incident but the illustration of character?" E. M. Forster goes further than James by arguing that character is ultimately more important than plot, and many subsequent critics and theorists, including Robert Scholes and Robert Kellogg in their influential *Nature of Narrative,* share Forster's view. Consistent with our pluralism, our first response to the question is that it depends on the nature and purpose of your inquiry. If you are interested in how the shapes of actions in literary texts reflect or influence social reality (e.g., how the nineteenth-century marriage plot ties in to cultural practice), then plot is clearly more important. If you are interested in literature as a window into psychology, then character is more important. Our second response is that even from the perspective of rhetorical narrative theory, once we locate character and plot as elements of the textual dynamics, their relative importance will depend on the particular progression of the narrative under consideration. In *Tom Jones,* for example, Henry Fielding subordinates character to plot as he directs our interest not to the psychological complexity of his characters but rather to the marvelous sequence of events that takes Tom first to the point of almost having a noose around his neck and then to his engagement with Sophia. In *Mrs. Dalloway,* on the other hand, Virginia Woolf subordinates plot to character as she directs our interest in the events of the novel not toward their contribution to any significant change in Clarissa's life but rather toward what they reveal about who she is and why she matters.

Similarly, the relationship among the components of character in any given narrative (or at any given point in a narrative) depends on the underlying purpose governing the progression. Some progressions will direct our interest primarily toward one component, some primarily toward two of the three (Italo Calvino's *If on a winter's night a traveler* plays down the mimetic in favor of the synthetic and thematic), and some toward all three—and no interest or set of interests is inherently superior to the others. Nevertheless, we can generalize about some tendencies in the relationships among the components and draw out some other important principles.

1. The mimetic and synthetic components are often (though not always) on a seesaw. When a progression increases our interest in one, it tends to decrease our interest in the other. Indeed, as we've already noted, the art of realistic fiction consists of conveying the illusion that the characters are acting autonomously even as their actions serve the implied author's overall purpose. From the perspective of this standard mimetic-synthetic seesaw, we can more clearly discern a problem with Tom Sawyer's delayed revelation that Miss Watson freed Jim in her will. Although Tom's delay is consistent with the mimetic component of his character—indeed, it explains both to Huck and to the authorial audience why Tom would side with the "lowdown Abolitionists" (for "the *adventure* of it")—Miss Watson's action all but punctures the novel's illusion that the characters are acting autonomously at this crucial point. Her decision comes across less as the logical consequence of her mimetic character than as the consequence of Twain's desperate need to resolve the global instability of Jim's story line.

2. The thematic component is a congenial partner of both the mimetic and the synthetic components. One typical underlying constructive purpose of mimetic characters is to link their mimetic traits with thematic functions. Furthermore, one typical consequence of an author's foregrounding the synthetic component of character is the heightening of our interest in the thematic. In *If on a winter's night a traveler,* Calvino flaunts the constructed quality of his protagonist, whom he calls simply Reader and addresses in the second-person, in order to direct our attention to his thematic exploration of readerly desire and its dependence on both the internal dynamics of narrative and the various institutions that support, profit from, or otherwise take advantage of that desire. Nevertheless, these frequent connections between the thematic and the other two components do not mean that the thematic component will necessarily be the dominant interest. Think again of Woolf's *Mrs. Dalloway,* which generates multiple thematic interests (about the effects of World War I, the chaos of life, the value of Clarissa's parties, etc.), but keeps our focus primarily on the mimetic component of Clarissa's character.

3. It is useful to distinguish between dimensions and functions of character—that is, to distinguish between the attributes that serve as the building blocks of character and the coalescence of those attributes into a larger entity. Thus, sometimes characters have a collection of mimetic traits but the progression does not convert those various traits into an overarching mimetic function. For example, over the course of Jonathan Swift's *Gulliver's Travels*, Gulliver is sometimes patient, sometimes impatient, sometimes perceptive and sometimes obtuse—and similarly inconsistent in relation to many other traits. In this sense, Gulliver has multiple mimetic dimensions, but these dimensions do not work together to produce a coherent mimetic character. In offering this analysis, we are not finding fault with Swift. Instead, the analysis helps support the points that different authorial purposes will lead to different relationships among the components of character and that judgments about the effectiveness of different relationships should be made in relation to those purposes. In our view, Swift's decision to give Gulliver multiple but inconsistent mimetic dimensions enables Swift to achieve his thematic—more precisely satiric—purposes far more effectively than if he had felt obligated to work with a mimetic character who was consistent across his different travels.

At other times a mimetic dimension of a character will contribute to her mimetic function but the progression will not thematize that dimension. In *Pride and Prejudice*, Elizabeth Bennet is given to spontaneous outbursts of feeling as when she expresses her shock at Charlotte's decision to accept Collins's proposal ("Engaged to Mr Collins! my dear Charlotte,—impossible!") and then later unguardedly expresses her grief in Darcy's presence about Lydia's flight with Wickham. This trait adds an important dimension to her mimetic character, and though Austen uses it to accomplish thematic or synthetic purposes (highlighting Charlotte's plight in the marriage market; disclosing to Darcy news that eventually allows him to demonstrate the best aspects of his character), she does not thematize the trait itself.

4. The particular balance of components of a character may or may not match the balance of components of the larger progression. In *1984*, for example, George Orwell directs our attention primarily to the mimetic and thematic components of Winston Smith's character, but he also foregrounds the synthetic component of his storyworld—one in which clocks strike thirteen and many other elements do not conform to Orwell's world in 1948. This foregrounding of the synthetic reinforces our central interest in the progression to the thematic component—Orwell's exposure of the evils of totalitarianism—even as we never lose our strong mimetic interest in Winston. That emphasis and the treatment of Winston also mean that *1984* is an exception to the usual rule about the seesaw relationship between the mimetic and the synthetic components of character. Because mimetic Winston exists as an integral part of this clearly synthetic storyworld, we also direct more attention to his synthetic component, particularly his function as the individual who initially rebels against but ultimately conforms to the totalitarian state.

5. The mimetic component of character may or may not alter over the course of a narrative, but, if it does, the change will typically be tied to the thematic functions of the character and hence to the thematic purposes of the narrative. The bildungsroman, for example, is a subgenre of the novel built on the principle that the protagonist will undergo some significant change not just in fate but also in character. In just about every case, the progression will tie the change in character to the thematic component of the narrative. For example, the change in Huck's character from someone with little conviction about the best way to act toward Jim to someone with firm conviction about how to act is clearly tied to the novel's thematics. Huck's change allows Twain to demonstrate the superiority of Huck the outsider's instinctive judgments, based on his direct experience of Jim, to the judgments that follow from shore society's links between Christianity and the legality of slavery. One of the problems with the Evasion is that it works against Twain's thematic points by undermining our sense that Huck has changed.

6. Our interest in the different components of character meshes with our theory of audience, which we discuss in more detail in the next chapter. Briefly, our interest in the mimetic component is a function of our participation in the narrative audience, which takes the events in a fiction as history and the characters as real people. Our interest in the synthetic component is a function of our participation in the authorial audience, which seeks to discern the underlying constructive purpose of the story as a whole. Our interest in the thematic component is always part of our participation in the authorial audience and sometimes part of our participation in the narrative audience (at minimum whenever the narrative engages in overt thematizing).

7. The synthetic component of character includes its contributions not only to plot dynamics but also to narratorial dynamics. As we noted in chapter 2, character–character dialogue, which typically heightens our interest in the mimetic component, can simultaneously be used—reliably or unreliably—to report, interpret, or evaluate. This aspect of the synthetic component deserves more attention than it has received so far.

8. As Alex Woloch has pointed out, the progression of some narratives can direct readerly attention to their "character systems," that is, the distribution of textual space allotted to each character and the larger network of relationships among those characters. In *Middlemarch*, for example, in

order to understand the fates of individual characters such as Dorothea and Lydgate, we need to recognize how they exist within the whole web of Middlemarch society. That recognition in turn highlights the tight link between the mimetic and the thematic, since one of Eliot's themes is the power of that web-like society.

CHARACTERIZATION AND CHARACTER FUNCTIONS IN *HUCKLEBERRY FINN*

To illustrate many of these points, we turn to the Boggs-Sherburn episode in Chapters XXI and XXII. This is one of the episodes in which the local purpose is to reveal the nature of shore society, but, since that purpose is shared by many other episodes, if Twain had not included it, we wouldn't notice a gap in the progression. More specifically, the episode has the thematic function of getting us to recognize the evils of the lynch mob—in particular, to convince us that mobs exist in part because ordinary people fail to resist their sway. This thematic point will be all the stronger if Twain can temporarily convince the narrative audience, if not to join the mob, then at least to watch with interest from the outskirts.

Twain achieves his purpose through his characterizations of Boggs, Sherburn, Boggs's sixteen-year-old daughter, the Bricksville bystanders who witness Sherburn's shooting of Boggs and then go after Sherburn with the intention of lynching him, and Huck. One of the synthetic functions of the Bricksville bystanders is to characterize Boggs through their interpretive and evaluative comments, which paint a thematic-mimetic portrait of a variation on the town drunk, an ultimately harmless man, who, fortified by drink, nevertheless periodically raises a ruckus. But even as the bystanders perform this synthetic function, Twain is also giving them mimetic and thematic functions. Huck refers to them as "loafers," a mimetic description that fits with their regarding Boggs only as a figure of fun whose monthly drunken rampage is a source of entertainment. That description in turn supports their thematic function of representing the deficient values of shore society. Twain then uses Sherburn, whom he mimetically presents as a proud, imperious, and cruel man, to represent another side of those deficient values. When the drunken Boggs does not obey Sherburn's command to cease harassing him by one o'clock, Sherburn guns him down in cold blood—and in front of his sixteen-year-old daughter. Why? Simply because he can. Twain uses Boggs's daughter to underline the self-indulgent viciousness of Sherburn's act: she has enough of a mimetic function to make her grief over her father plausible, even moving, but her main function is synthetic. Her presence adds to our repulsion at Sherburn—*something* ought to be done to punish this man.

Thus, as we watch the bystanders deciding that they should lynch Sherburn, Twain has set things up so that we have a least some sympathy with their goal—not enough, perhaps, to join the mob but enough to watch their actions with a certain detached curiosity (in radical contrast, say, to the absolute horror with which we watch the lynch mob in Richard Wright's *Uncle Tom's Children*). Thus, when Sherburn calls their bluff, we're caught as well—because to a certain extent, his criticism is directed to the narrative audience as well as to the "loafers" in the mob. In our momentary thematic shock, we do not notice a certain slippage from the mimetic toward the synthetic. The Sherburn who gives his speech is an authorial spokesman, a reliable interpreter who shows a wisdom and understanding of human nature and social debilitation (note his discussions of the legal system, the press, and the military) that seems inconsistent with the self-centered pride and cruel disregard for Boggs and his daughter he displays earlier. Even if we can imagine a plausible person who combines these traits, a little reflection reveals that the length and careful logic of Sherburn's speech is not mimetically motivated: rather than being what such a man would say in such a situation (he'd give another terse ultimatum), it is what Twain needs him to say in order to accomplish his thematic purposes. In a sense, Twain has made a sacrifice here, trading his usual concern for mimesis for greater thematic power—but the progression of the scene is so artful that we are likely not to register the sacrifice as we read.

And what about Huck here? Throughout this episode Huck's primary function is synthetic, as he reliably reports but only lightly interprets the events. But at the very end, after having Huck report that all the loafers fled from Sherburn's house, Twain moves his mimetic function back into the foreground of the narrative: "I could a staid, if I'd a wanted to, but I didn't want to" (148). This is a rare instance of estranging unreliability in the novel, as Huck misreports and misevaluates his motives for leaving in order to have his narrative audience think that he is not as scared of Sherburn as the Bricksville bystanders are. The estranging effects are not great, because we still sympathize with Huck in this situation—especially since we have nearly been there ourselves and, in fact, have watched the unfolding of the scene from Huck's perspective. Huck should have left much earlier—but we didn't notice it at the time any more than he did. In the end, then, the estranging effects contribute to the larger synthetic function of the whole episode in the progression. The episode gives Huck—and the authorial audience—experiences of shore society that provide a compelling contrast to Huck's experiences with Jim, a contrast that Huck registers at some level and that ultimately informs his decision (and our approval of that decision) to go to hell rather than act in a way that would return Jim to slavery.

Robyn Warhol

For many fans and students of Jane Austen, her characters are people. Such readers speak of Anne Elliot, Frederick Wentworth, Lady Russell, Sir Walter, and everybody around them as though they possessed agency and autonomy outside the confines of the text, speculating about whether Frederic "really" still loved Anne even though in his resentment he denied it at first, or whether Anne "was actually mature enough" to have handled getting married at nineteen. Indeed, given the vividness and the singularity with which Austen's characters are endowed, the temptation to think of them as if they were persons is very strong. The novelist herself was having fun with this conceit when she told her friends and family members what "happened" to some of her characters after their novels' plots had played out, as I mentioned in a footnote to the previous section. For both narrative theory and feminist criticism, however, remembering that characters are not people is crucially important. Characters are marks on the page, made up of the alphabetical characters that spell out "who" they are. They have no psychology, no interiority, no subjectivity. Characters are the representational effects the novelist creates in structuring the novel. The way characters like Austen's can leave the impression of being real people is one of the miracles of literary writing, and it produces one of novel-reading's greatest pleasures. But to achieve the ends of feminist narratology—that is, to understand how narrative participates in the construction, reinforcement, and subversion of gender—the critic who can feel the effects of Austen's characterizations needs to focus on how those effects are achieved.

In classical narratology (as inspired by linguistics and proposed by Vladimir Propp and A. J. Greimas), individual characters are superseded by "anthropomorphic actants" performing "functions" in the story; at the level of deep structure, they have attributes which, in combination with their fictitious actions, constitute their role in the narrative syntagm. Thinking about characters in this bare-bones way does not go very far toward understanding the subtleties of Austen's work, but it can be useful in describing the strongly gendered macro-structure her six completed novels have in common. As I have mentioned above in my discussion of the marriage plot, Austen's novels always center on an unmarried heroine between the ages of fifteen (Catherine Moreland) and twenty-six (Anne Elliot) and always present her with an apparent choice between the right suitor (e.g., Henry Tilney, Frederick Wentworth) and the wrong suitor (e.g., John Thorpe, William Walter Elliot). Following the long-established precedent of romance fiction, the heroine is invariably paired with at least one female foil or rival, who is in some ways like her but in important ways different (in *Sense and Sensibility* Elinor's foil is Lucy Steele, Marianne's is Elinor; *Pride and Prejudice* presents Charlotte Lucas, Miss Bingley, and Jane Bennet as foils to Elizabeth; Emma Woodhouse's foil is Jane Fairfax; Fanny Price's is Mary Crawford; Catherine Moreland's is Isabella Thorpe; and Anne Elliot's are her sisters and Louisa Musgrove). By her similarities to her foil (youth, eligibility for upper- or upper-middle-class marriage, attractiveness to men, quickness of mind and of perception) we know the heroine's character type; by her differences, we know what sets her apart as the character who gets to be the heroine. (Elinor is more well bred and less narcissistic than Lucy, while Marianne, a sort of junior heroine, is more expressive than her sister; Elizabeth is more romantic and less mercenary than Charlotte, less vain or snobbish than Miss Bingley, and more forthcoming than her sister Jane; Emma is more candid than Jane Fairfax; Fanny is more self-aware and far less sexually knowing than Mary; Catherine is much nicer and a little smarter than Isabella; and Anne is worlds above her sisters and Louisa in intelligence, manners, capability, education, sensitivity to others, and depth of feeling.)

Sometimes the heroine's evident superiority to her foil is vast, as with Elinor and Lucy or Anne and Louisa; sometimes it is not so obvious—or indeed, for some readers, it is debatable—as with Emma and Jane or Fanny and Mary. However, the familiar configuration of characters, the recognizable pattern of good suitor/bad suitor, heroine/foil, is not just a framework on which to build a plot but is also part of the substance of what the individual figures signify. Typical of generic patterning in general, the Austen novel rounds up the usual suspects in order to spotlight the variations on that pattern which the presence of secondary characters can introduce. To give just a few examples of deviations from the normal pattern: one challenge in interpreting *Sense and Sensibility* arises from the doubling of the heroine figure in Elinor and Marianne; the proliferation of foils for Elizabeth Bennet adds extra facets to those characteristics of the heroine that distinguish her from the women who are not-the-heroines; the introduction of a female peer and friend who is neither the heroine's rival nor her foil, such as *Northanger Abbey*'s Eleanor Tilney or *Persuasion*'s Mrs. Smith, increases the opportunities for registering the heroine's best qualities as they are reflected in her friend's affectionate regard. In short, we come to know a character by seeing examples of who and what she is *not* and by understanding how she is perceived by other characters, even as we attend to the attributes and functions assigned to her. This is especially true in nineteenth-century fictions about women, where the creation of characters is governed by the logic of what Helena Michie has called sororophobia—the cultural assumption that women exist in and through dyads of rivalry, love, and conflict with each other—as well as the paradigm of homosocial bonding that Eve Sedgwick has identified between pairs of men who compete over women in novels.

Another strong temptation for readers is to think of the attributes and situations of Austen's characters as an indication of what "life" was like in Austen's time and place. But the fictitious experiences of characters actually reveal nothing about the author's historical period except for the attitudes and assumptions that are reflected in and influenced by the text. To be sure, upper-class British women of the early nineteenth century were in an emotionally and financially unstable position if they were still unmarried at age twenty-six and therefore dependent, as is Anne Elliot, on patriarchs who might be no better at knowing the value of their money than the value of their daughters. But if we think about it candidly, practically everybody except upper-class men (those who could hang onto their resources more effectively than Sir Walter) was in a precarious condition in that economy, and women of all social classes beneath hers suffered more significant discomforts than Anne Elliot's disappointment in love. Longing, as many lovers of Jane Austen do, to have been alive during Austen's time reflects a naïve though understandable assumption that people in that world were like characters in Austen novels, with motives that were legible, actions that were consistent, and conversational diction and syntax that were superb. Like William Shakespeare's, Austen's characters are vehicles for conveying some of the most beautifully constructed sentences in the English language. One need only look at Austen's own letters or the draft of the canceled chapter of *Persuasion* to realize that not even the author herself "really talked like that." As part of my practice of feminist narratology, I try to encounter characters in all their facets as functions of discourse, not as mirrors of or windows on the extradiegetic world.

Characters, then, are creatures of the discourse of gender in *Persuasion*, the discourse most interesting to me as a feminist narratologist. An obvious way in which characters serve this function is by talking directly about gender, as Anne does in her important debate with Captain Harville about whether women or men love "longest, when existence or when hope is gone" (189). While dialogue about gender can mark a novel as explicitly feminist, as I believe that scene does for *Persuasion,* the construction of gender in the creation of the characters themselves is more subtle and probably more effective in both reflecting and influencing the culture's beliefs about masculinity and femininity. Austen presents secondary characters who embody gendered stereotypes, sometimes in the extreme, in order to challenge those stereotypes through other, more fully delineated characters with traits that complicate the expectations raised by the cultural norms. For instance, Anne's sisters exemplify different veins of the negative stereotypes of femininity which Austen's immediate predecessor, Mary Wollstonecraft, identified as the inevitable result of women's existence in a patriarchal system. If one binary assumption about gender was that because men are strong, women must be weak, Mary's ineffectual hypochondria and perpetual demands for attention seem to prove it; if another is that men are careless about their appearance and women are vain, then Elizabeth fills the negative feminine type perfectly. In a sense, these secondary characterizations suggest that Austen represents those stereotypes of femininity as in some way "true," or that she even endorses the binary reasoning behind them. To be sure, Austen is no gender radical. A character's complete reversal of gender norms is an index of that character's devaluation in the novel: Sir Walter combines Mary's selfish uselessness with Elizabeth's personal vanity to present the epitome of an objectionably effeminate man, strongly contrasting with the admirable and hypermasculine Admiral Croft, who, like Wentworth, is a self-made man ("having acquired a very handsome fortune" [23]) and unlike Sir Walter is not at all addicted to having multiple mirrors in his dressing-room ("Such a number of looking-glasses! oh, Lord!" exclaims the Admiral. "There was no getting away from oneself" [104]). Admiral Croft's character fits the norms of the new nineteenth-century masculinity almost as closely as Mary's and Elizabeth's conform to the negative types of femininity, but in the Admiral this conformity to the norms is presented as a good thing—particularly since he is willing to be led by his very savvy wife in matters of business and in driving, a flexibility that mitigates the consistency with which he fits the masculine type.[1]

To be an admirable character in Austen's world, then, a figure must be grounded in comprehensible gender norms but depart from them in selected and significant ways. Far from being a simple inversion of negative traits associated with femininity, Anne embodies many "feminine" norms: masculine men are supposed to be bold, but Anne is gentle; men are boisterous, while Anne is quiet; men project self-confidence, while Anne's reticence expresses a feminine self-effacement. As the heroine, Anne does represent the inversion of many negative traits culturally marked as feminine: she is wise, though it is feminine to be silly; she is efficacious, though women are supposed to be passive; she is unselfconscious about her own increasing physical attractiveness, though as a woman she ought to be vain. And, perhaps most importantly, though it was "feminine" to be not just sexually chaste but cold, Anne is represented as a fully sexual being whose ardent desire for Captain Wentworth expresses itself repeatedly in her trembling bodily reactions to moments of contact with the hero. Anne's conformities to and divergences from the gender norms of Austen's period are a key to the political positioning of the text.

Whereas secondary characters in Austen are mainly built out of narrator's generalizations, bits of dialogue, story-functions, and other characters' reactions to them, their social identities are partly constructed through Austen's characteristic use of free indirect discourse (FID).[2] Attitudes and expressions assigned to the secondary characters through free indirect discourse in *Persuasion* generally reflect what they say (or what they would say) out loud, as in the example of Sir Walter's free indirect discourse I have analyzed in the section on Narration. Lady Russell's character is formed chiefly by the opinions attributed to her in passages of free indirect discourse like this one, which summarizes the reasons she held for advising Anne against her initial engagement to Captain Wentworth:

> Anne Elliot, with all her claims of birth, beauty, and mind, to throw herself away at nineteen; involve herself at nineteen in an engagement with a young man, who had nothing but himself to recommend him, and no hopes of attaining affluence, but in the chances of a most uncertain profession, and no connexions to secure even his farther rise in that profession; would be, indeed, a throwing away, which she grieved to think of! Anne Elliot, so young; known to so few, to be snatched off by a stranger without alliance or fortune; or rather sunk by him into a state of most wearing, anxious, youth-killing dependence! It must not be . . . (27)

The exclamation points, the repetitions ("throw herself away at nineteen; involve herself at nineteen"), the hyperbole ("no hopes of attaining affluence," "to be snatched off by a stranger"), and the effect of "thinking aloud" that comes through in the building up and revising of Lady Russell's thoughts through the course of the passage ("to be snatched off . . . or rather to be sunk by him") all suggest what Lady Russell would sound like, if she were to express these thoughts. Indeed, the passage implies that Lady Russell did express them to Anne. Perhaps because the novelist needs to craft Lady Russell as a character with whom the implied reader can sympathize, she also uses free indirect discourse to render thoughts Lady Russell cannot be supposed to have said out loud, for example, her objections to Mrs. Clay's going in Anne's place to Bath with the Elliots: "Lady Russell was extremely sorry that such a measure should have been resorted to at all—wondered, grieved, and feared—and the affront it contained to Anne, in Mrs. Clay's being of so much use, while Anne could be of none, was a very sore aggravation" (32).

Here the narrator embeds a bit of free indirect discourse coming from Sir Walter or Elizabeth ("Mrs. Clay's being of so much use, while Anne could be of none") in Lady Russell's thoughts, which are in turn rendered in free indirect discourse that reflects her own diction ("extremely sorry," "wondered, grieved, and feared," "affront," "sore aggravation") but that would contradict her punctilious sense of propriety if spoken aloud. The effect of such a passage is that Lady Russell emerges as one of the few characters in the novel who seems to have an interiority. In the very brief glimpse into his feelings I discussed in the section on Perspective, Wentworth is another. But the novel's focalization through Anne means that she possesses by far the most detailed consciousness in the text. Every page of *Persuasion* contains passages of free indirect discourse reflecting Anne's thoughts, feelings, and bodily sensations, adding up to the powerful illusion of an independent psychology comparable to that of a "real person." Technically speaking, this is what makes Anne the heroine of the novel, more than any of her admirable characteristics or actions. For me as a feminist narratologist, the fullness with which the novel represents this strongly gendered interiority is what gives the character its interest.

David Herman

In the approach to be sketched here, characters in fictional narratives like McEwan's are textually grounded models of individuals-in-a-world (cf. Margolin, "Character" 70–76). More specifically, characters can viewed as a particular subsystem of the WHAT dimension of narrative worlds; they constitute a subset of the entities that, on the basis of textual cues, can be inferred to populate the storyworld. This subset, consisting of more or less prototypical members of the category of "persons," is a special class of entities. Capturing what distinguishes characters from other elements of the WHAT, and how those differences bear on the process of narrative worldmaking, requires taking into account the fundamental contrast between persons and things, or personal vs. nonpersonal entities.

This contrast is based on more or less widely circulating models of what a person is and of how persons relate to the world at large. Modes of characterization specific to particular narrative genres (e.g., picaresque tales, novels of manners, detective fiction), and for that matter modes specific to a given author's oeuvre, provide further scaffolding for the construction of individuals-in-a-world, who can conversely be used to throw light on—and potentially reshape—a culture's or subculture's understandings of persons. Hence my focus in this chapter is on interactions between, on the one hand, schemes for understanding persons (schemes that emerge from prior encounters with stories and other kinds of texts, as well as everyday social encounters) and, on the other hand, text-guided inferences about human individuals in narrative worlds.

CONTRASTING APPROACHES, FOUNDATIONAL ISSUES

Here again I should stress that although it explores issues that are broadly relevant for mind-oriented research on character, my account takes its place within a variety of approaches to this area of inquiry—a variety that in itself suggests the vitality of the scholarship in this domain. For example, Alan Palmer foregrounds intratextual over intertextual approaches to fictional minds; he focuses on how the cues included in a given text prompt readers to ascribe to characters reasons for acting, rather than on how that text draws on (or relates to) wider repertoires of mind-indicating cues (41–43). By contrast, to use terms that I discuss further below, my approach seeks to balance (1) an emphasis on how individual narratives trigger the construction of character profiles, or what I term *model persons*, with (2) an emphasis on how those profiles relate to broader *models of persons*—models deriving in part from the narratives circulating within a given culture or subculture (cf. Jannidis, "Character" and *Figur;* Schneider, "Toward"). Meanwhile, Lisa Zunshine uses ideas from evolutionary and cognitive psychology to argue that readers of fictional narratives recruit from an innate "Theory of Mind" to link what characters say and do to inferences about underlying mental states. The approach that I outline in the remainder of this chapter, however, grounds itself in different traditions of research in the philosophy of mind, social psychology, and other fields. This work, by scholars such as Lynne Rudder Baker, Jerome Bruner, Peter Hobson, Daniel Hutto, P. F. Strawson, and others, calls into question the assumption that there is a problem of other minds that must be solved by way of theory.[3] The resulting shift in perspective allows the grammar of questions featuring the theory-of-mind concept to be surveyed anew, in ways that are consequential for research on characters in storyworlds.

To elaborate further: in the research that informs my contribution to this chapter, the fundamental contrast is between not self and other but rather persons and things, or personal and nonpersonal entities. Thus for P. F. Strawson the concept of person is part of human beings' basic equipment for living, or the means by which they negotiate the world. Strawson argued further that the notion of "person" is a conceptual primitive; in other words, the idea of a person indissolubly combines mental or personal predicates ("intends to take a walk"; "doesn't feel well") with material predicates having to do with persons' bodies and those bodies' situation in space and time ("is currently seated on the couch"; "is lying down with a flushed appearance"). On this account, being able to ascribe mental as well as material predicates to one and the same entity—an ascriptional practice made possible by observed behaviors in the case of others but not in one's own case—is the criterion that establishes what counts as a member of the category "person." But what is more, this way of treating the idea of person reframes the entire question of other minds. Other minds are not a problem to be solved but instead built into the very concept of a person (see Hobson 243–52; Noë 29–35; Seemann). Hence the idea of person, from this perspective, *entails* that mental predicates will be self-ascribable in one's own case and other-ascribable in the case of others.[4]

On this view, narrators make sense of characters' minds, characters make sense of one another's minds, and readers make sense of both narrators' and characters' minds insofar as they situate those individuals in the domain of persons.[5] At issue is a process not of theoretical reconstruction or simulation of another's mind, but rather of *categorization*. When I categorize a being as a person, I ipso facto assume that he or she embodies a constellation of mental and material predicates—predicates that are linked together in patterns specified by *models of persons* circulating in my culture or subculture. In turn, characters in novels can be viewed as *model persons;* these fictional individuals are at once shaped by and have the power to reshape broader conceptions of what a person is and of how persons can be expected to respond in particular kinds of circumstances.

ENGAGING WITH CHARACTERS IN STORYWORLDS

An approach to character that connects these ideas with issues of worldmaking emphasizes not so much the assortment of psychological and physical predicates embodied in particular characters (or groups of characters) as the process that leads to the co-construction, or coordinated mental projection, of such individuals-in-a-world. At issue are the means by which, and the effects with which, texts evoke fictional individuals who can be inferred to possess more or less extensive constellations of personal traits, that is, fusions of mental and corporeal predicates that are a hallmark of persons. Once again, this aspect of narrative worldmaking can be analyzed into a number of sub-aspects, each of which can be captured as a question for which interpreters seek to frame answers as part of the business of world-building:

1. For which elements of the WHAT dimension of the narrative world are questions about WHO, HOW, and WHY pertinent? In other words, in what domains of the storyworld do *actions* supervene on *behaviors,* such that it becomes relevant to ask not just what cause produced what effect but also who did (or tried to do) what, through what means, and for what reason?
2. How does the text, in conjunction with broader understandings of persons, prompt interpreters to build a profile for the characters who inhabit these domains of action? Put otherwise, how do textual features along with models of personhood (deriving from various sources) cue interpreters to assign to characters person-like constellations of traits?
3. Reciprocally, how does the process of developing these profiles for individuals-in-a-world bear on broader understandings of persons?

In research in progress, I am drawing on work by Lynne Rudder Baker (*Persons; Metaphysics*) to argue that narrative is a mode of representation optimally suited for person-level phenomena. At issue are "medium-sized"

127

phenomena—objects, activities, situations, and events such as, respectively, tennis rackets, conducting a debate, living in a particular house, and witnessing a car accident—that are situated at the level of the everyday world of human experience. Thus, in connection with question 1 above, one can expect that when it comes to the WHAT dimension of a storyworld, actions will preponderantly supervene on behaviors—since stories are optimally calibrated for the representation of human actions (cf. Turner 26–37). Still, what might be termed the preponderance of the personal in narrative does not imply that storyworlds are wall-to-wall with characters. Rather, as in the world at large, in narrative worlds person-level phenomena unfold in a context consisting not only of other persons but also of nonpersons. Differences between kinds of narratives are based, in part, on different protocols for bringing into relation these personal and nonpersonal elements of the WHAT (see Herman, *Story Logic* 140–69). Such protocols fall under the scope of both questions 1 and 2.

McEwan's novel cues modes of worldmaking that range over the large middle zone that stretches between two poles. At one pole, the personal absorbs the nonpersonal, as with the use of anthropomorphic gods in ancient Greek myths; at the other, the nonpersonal absorbs the personal, as with the diminution of the personal in naturalism as well as the nouveau roman. For example, as the narrative unfolds, McEwan (23, 173) hints at parallels between the storms that have shaped Chesil Beach and the tempestuous interchange between Edward and Florence at that locale. The text thus raises questions about how to model the relation between, on the one hand, conduct explicable in terms of reasons and, on the other hand, behaviors driven by physical (including evolutionary) processes stretching back beyond the life span of any individual. But any suggestions of a parallel between the circumstances bearing on Florence's and Edward's choices and actions and the meteorological processes that have shaped the beach remain just that—suggestions. The narration places a question mark next to the scope of the personal, but without making fictional persons epiphenomenal (as in naturalism) or overtly marking them as heuristic constructs (as in the nouveau roman).

In any case, for sectors of the WHAT in which issues of WHO, HOW, and WHY are indeed pertinent, though not necessarily readily or straightforwardly resolved, the second question listed above comes into play. Here the concern is how interpreters of narratives map discourse cues onto individuals-in-a-world in a way that dovetails, in Strawson's sense, personal with material predicates. To address how interpreters construct profiles of fictional persons like McEwan's, I propose building on, and refining, Chatman's analysis of a character as a paradigm of traits. According to this analysis, a character is a "vertical assemblage of [a set of traits, or more or less enduring qualities or attributes] intersecting the syntagmatic chain of events that comprise the plot" (127). Although thirty years of research have provided new ways of understanding how textual cues prompt interpreters to map person-like traits onto individuals represented in narratives (see Schneider, "Toward," for an overview), I want to retain Chatman's insight about the importance of "trait-codes" for understanding characters—repertoires of trait-names that are culturally and historically variable (123–26; cf. Culler 236–37).[6]

I focus here on emotional traits in particular. My concern, more precisely, is how systems of emotion terms and concepts, which form one region or register of the trait-code(s) deriving from narrative genres as well as other kinds of discourses and also everyday encounters with persons, support the construction of character profiles. Recent work on such "emotionologies" suggests that to understand fictional characters, readers draw on models used to explain or predict how persons typically respond to particular kinds of situations. These models allow mental (here, affective) and material predicates to be grouped together in more or less person-typical ways. But beyond being anchored to such repertoires of affective traits, fictional characters can also, as models of possible individuals, reciprocally affect broader understandings of the minds of persons—to pick up with my third question about WHO, HOW, and WHY.

The concept of emotionology was proposed by Stearns and Stearns as a way of referring to the collective emotional standards of a culture as opposed to the experience of emotion itself (see also Harré and Gillett 144–61; Greimas and Fontanille). The term functions in parallel with recent usages of the term "ontology" to designate a model of the entities, together with their properties and relations, that exist within a particular domain. Possessed by every culture and subculture, emotionologies are systems of emotion terms and concepts deployed by participants in discourse to ascribe emotions to themselves as well as their cohorts. At issue is a framework for conceptualizing emotions, their causes, and the ways in which participants in discourse are likely to display them. Narratives at once ground themselves in and help build frameworks of this sort, as when ghost stories and romance novels link particular kinds of emotions to recurrent narrative scenarios. Indeed, in narrative contexts readers are able to understand characters' *behaviors* as *actions* in part because of the models of emotion on which they rely to interpret the text. McEwan's characters' activities can be construed as more than just a series of individual, unrelated doings because of the assumption, licensed by a model of emotions, that those behaviors constitute a coherent *class*. At stake is the class (or fuzzy set) of actions in which sexually inexperienced newlyweds, for example, are more or less likely to engage when motivated by anxiety about their wedding-night encounter, or alternatively the set of actions in which a person struggling with a (repressed) history of sexual abuse may engage at the prospect of that same encounter.

McEwan's novel reflexively calls attention to how systems of emotion terms and concepts make it possible to understand behaviors as actions—even as it prompts interpreters to use those systems to make sense of the characters' conduct. At a global level, the text models how emotionologies are shaped by sociocultural factors and are thus subject to change over time, leading to different methods for understanding one and the same form of conduct—for example, as idiosyncratic or not. For instance, when Edward learns of the accident on the railway platform that left his mother brain-damaged and then begins to keep to himself more, the text reads: "the term 'teenager' had not long been invented, and it never occurred to him that the separateness he felt, which was both painful and delicious, could be shared by anyone else" (93). But the narrative also underlines how emotion concepts organize thought and conduct at a more local level as well. As Florence and Edward dine in their honeymoon suite early in the novel, Edward self-consciously recruits from an emotionology in order to project a demeanor that is at odds with how he actually feels: "To show that he was not troubled by the presence of the waiters, though he longed for them to leave, Edward smiled as he sat back with his wine and called over his shoulder, 'Any more of those things [i.e., the glazed cherries served with their meal]?'" (14).

At the same time, the novel suggests the interpretive difficulties that can result from *not* having such emotionological facility; these difficulties translate into a disconnect between the mental and material predicates that must be linked together to construct profiles of persons, fictional and otherwise. A disconnect of this sort, arguably rooted in the repressed trauma that splits off Florence's experiences from any ability to take the true measure of their emotional impact, results in Florence's coming to the conclusion that she does not really know her own mind:

> Falling in love was revealing to her [Florence] just how odd she was, how habitually sealed off in her everyday thoughts. Whenever Edward asked, How do you feel? or, What are you thinking? she always made an awkward answer . . . she lacked some simple mental trick that everyone else had, a mechanism so ordinary that no one ever mentioned it, an immediate sensual connection to people and events, and to her own needs and desires. . . . (75–76)

Similarly, when family disputes break out at home, Florence finds that she has only a theoretical knowledge of how emotions inform conduct and make it recognizable as such. Unable to comport herself in ways specified by the emotionology that orients other members of her family, Florence resorts (or rather, regresses) to a simplified, literally cartoonish model of how emotions relate to action. This model reduces emotion to a physical process, shifting the locus of interest from the domain of action to the domain of behavior: "She knew very well that people fell out, even stormily, and then made up. But she did not know how to start—she simply did not have the trick of it. . . . She could only blame herself then, when she felt like a character in a newspaper cartoon, with steam hissing from her ears" (63).

In portraying how Edward and Florence attempt, with more or less success, to draw on emotionologies to make sense of their own and others' conduct, the novel uses fictional individuals to explore, reflexively, the scope and nature of models of what a person is. Such models, which include but are not limited to those associated with a culture's or a community's emotionology, in turn afford readers a basis for framing inferences about how a character's mental predicates are linked with her material predicates, in ways that make her behaviors legible as actions-in-a-world. In the next chapter I broaden my investigation of how readers' inferences bear on the worldmaking process. Indeed, as I hinted in the remarks that conclude chapter 2, the approach being developed here contests prior accounts of the role of the reader in narrative contexts.

Brian Richardson

Literary characters are agents within a work of fiction. They derive from a number of very different sources and fulfill several disparate functions in a narrative. We may begin with Phelan and Rabinowitz's model that argues for mimetic (realistic), thematic (ideological), and synthetic (formal) components, modify and extend their model, and add to it a fourth category, the intertextual.

MIMETIC

Many characters are thought to be modeled on human beings, but this is a considerably more difficult operation than is usually imagined. It is doubtless more accurate ·to say that realistic or mimetic characters are based on perceived, accepted, or imagined personalities of actual people. And these, of course, may be entirely fictional. Certain character types, for example, the miser or the braggart soldier, can be found in both literature and lived experience, but a large number of other such types are literary, cultural, or ideological fabrications.

Literature traditionally uses shortcuts: a characterization may be too simple (two-dimensional) or otherwise insufficiently complex to capture the behavior of actual people; thus, Proust's delineation of diffuse and partially self-negating characters is often praised for its verisimilitude in presenting human subjects in all their inconsistencies and contradictions. In other cases, pseudoscience precludes accurate depictions: Ben Jonson's characters are based on the false theory that four basic elements or "humors" govern human psychology; many dubious figures in nineteenth-century fiction embody personalities derived from the pseudoscience of phrenology; and characters studiously based on Freudian, Jungian, or Rankian psychoanalysis often prove to be equally false. Ideology is another powerful distorter of ideas regarding human behavior: for centuries, women and non-whites were depicted stereotypically and negatively in Western literary works. Each worldview should be expected to have a distorted presentation of human beings and to attempt to disguise those distortions. Even if one draws on the entire annals of narrative literature, it is very difficult to single out any individual character and say convincingly, "This one is entirely realistic: there are real people just like that." For the most part, "realistic" characters are merely characters whose essential fictionality is unacknowledged.

THEMATIC

Many other characters are not intended to be realistic portraits of humans. Some represent animals or extraterrestrial beings, though most of these usually wind up being thoroughly anthropomorphized. Many more or less realistic figures also represent themes or ideas in a text: in E. M. Forster's *Howards End* (1910), Mrs Wilcox stands for traditional England while her son represents the new, amoral capitalist order. Other characters are avowedly allegorical figures, from the personages in Bunyan's *Pilgrim's Progress* (1678) to Voltaire's *Candide* (1759) to Orwell's *Animal Farm* (1945). Here the ideological work is upfront and straightforward. The characters represent not types of people but rather particular ideas or, in the case of Orwell, groups at specific points before and after the Russian revolution. Writers often embody an idea without being fully aware of doing so; literary history is full of pseudo-realistic presentations of egregious cultural caricatures. This is especially true of the repetition of cultural stereotypes: women, aboriginal peoples, Muslim Arabs, and black Africans and their descendants have been the subject of centuries of insistent stereotyping. This is sadly and ironically the case in Eugene O'Neill's attempt in *The Emperor Jones* to provide a positive depiction of a black protagonist which nevertheless incorporated a number of negative perspectives from the white mythology of the time.

SYNTHETIC

Characters also have artificial or synthetic functions; that is, they act as part of a fabricated literary narrative. Characters in fiction are, after all, words on a page; they are both more and less substantial than human beings. On the one hand, we can know the thoughts of a character much better than we can ever know the mental processes of most people; on the other hand, any fact about them left unsaid by the narrator (did the protagonist have a large mole on her left shoulder?) can never be known. Characters may be elaborately developed or not developed at all; some are three-dimensional, some two-, and some one-dimensional, reduced to a mere function. If a tale requires that a door be opened or a hero stymied, a figure may emerge to open the door or block the protagonist. In a story, such figures may not be anything more than their function in the work.

 Authors frequently order the arrangement of characters so they form parallel or opposite patterns, and even create or re-form characters to produce this effect. The result of this kind of patterning is to illuminate the personalities of the individuals as well as to create formal, architectural symmetries. In Shakespeare's *1 Henry IV*, young Harry Percy ("Hotspur") is the exact opposite of young Prince Hal. Hotspur is proud, valiant, impetuous, and a good son; he lives for glory in battle. Hal is circumspect, cautious, a bit of a wastrel, and a disappointment to his father; he plans to exhibit his better self at a later, more appropriate time. The two have systematically opposed careers and, naturally, meet up for a decisive, man-to-man duel at the end of the play. To achieve this symmetrical effect, Shakespeare had to distort the historical record considerably. At the time of the actual battle of Shrewsbury, Prince Hal was only sixteen, while Hotspur was thirty-nine—older than Hal's father, King Henry IV. There is no historical record of the two meeting during the fight. In the real battle, Prince Hal was shot in the face by an arrow and nearly died. Shakespeare also invented the character of Falstaff to provide a number of other parallels and oppositions. When it came to creating good drama, Shakespeare never let mere history stand in his path.

In avant-garde and postmodern fiction, the idea of a self-consistent, single, unified, human-like character is regularly rejected. Postmodern characters transcend the limits of the merely human in a number of ways: they may be too flat or insubstantial, too fragmented or discontinuous; they may be self-contradictory, or multiple and fused with other selves. In short, they may far exceed or fail to embody the essential nature of a possible person. Ana Kavan's *Ice* (1967) consists of depictions of a hero's repeated attempts to save a weak young woman from the ravages of a cruel warden who holds her captive. At several points in the text, however, the hero notices a strange feeling of unity with the warden and suspects they are in fact the same person. The narrator of Beckett's *The Unnamable* consistently deconstructs its own identity as it claims both to have engendered characters in Beckett's other works and also to be the creation of someone else. Robbe-Grillet's Edouard Manneret in *La Maison de rendez-vous* (1965) is entirely and impossibly self-contradictory, as are many of the other personages in the book. Martin Crimp, in his play *Attempts on her Life* (1997), presents a series of scenes and discourses about a woman (or several women) named Anne, Anya, or Annie. They are presented as different people with different life stories in different situations: the girl next door, a performance artist, a rich woman, a terrorist, a scientist, a porno actress, a character in a script, even a new brand of car. Throughout the piece, Crimp refuses to provide either multiple discrete identities or a single, consistent identity for his protagonist(s); she/they remain insistently indeterminate, simultaneously one person and several people.

In addition, some characters acknowledge that they are fictional entities invented by someone else. In the case of Borges's "The Circular Ruins" (1941), this is a bitter discovery made by the protagonist; in Raymond Queneau's *The Fall of Icarus* (1968), the character escapes from the novelist and starts frequenting a café in Paris. Especially affecting is the fate of Harold Crick in Marc Forster's film, *Stranger than Fiction* (2006), who gradually discovers that he is a character in a novel, reads the entire draft of that novel, and nobly agrees that he needs to die in order to preserve the aesthetic integrity of the work. This kind of characterization is the least studied and is routinely neglected by narrative theorists. In summary, we can conclude that the synthetic category of characterization should be expanded to include three separate facets: (1) functional aspects that help keep the narrative moving along; (2) aesthetic aspects that produce, for example, an architectural symmetry; and (3) an antimimetic aspect that provides for the appearance of truly unnatural figures.

We see many antimimetic features in the characterizations in *Midnight's Children*. Saleem Sinai both represents all Indians of his era and is partially composed of other individuals. The evil Shiva is his double or "anti-self" and represents the part of modern India that Saleem would suppress. And Saleem contains still more individuals: "I have been a swallower of lives; and to know me, just the one of me, you'll have to swallow the lot as well. Consumed multitudes are jostling and shoving inside me" (4). This develops the idea of a multipersoned character even as it alludes to the god Krishna, whose special powers were discovered by Yasoda when she looked down his throat and saw the entire universe there. Krishna is also an avatar or incarnation of Vishnu, and Rushdie uses the trope of the avatar to refer to similar personalities in different people separated over time.

At other times, as we have seen, Saleem can lose his individual identity. As he is fighting in the atrocity-filled war with East Pakistan, his actions are so horrific and he is so ashamed of himself that he becomes unable to refer to himself in the first person: "I insist: not I. He. He the buddha. Who . . . would remain not-Saleem; who, in spite of running-from, was still separated from his past" (414–15). Rushdie is invoking the discourse of Buddhist strivings to free the soul from the ego and its desires in order to describe Saleem's very different slide into non-Being, one that bears more resemblance to what I have called the "pseudo–third-person" narration found in Borges and Beckett (*Unnatural* 10–13, 110–11). Still more radical character transformations occur in Rushdie's *The Satanic Verses* (1988); in the book's opening scene, the figures Saladin Chamcha and Gibreel Farishta exchange identities as they fall through the air, becoming "Gibreelsaladin

Farishtachamcha" (5) as they become "metamorphic, hybrid" (7) in the first of many such transformations throughout the novel.

INTERTEXTUAL

A last source of characterization is literary history itself. An author may stay with a source text and go on to narrate the central characters' further adventures, as in Ödön von Horváth's *Figaro Gets a Divorce* (1936), a continuation of the Beaumarchais' *The Marriage of Figaro* (1778). Alternatively, the author may wish to tell the other side of the story of the earlier text, fleshing out the lives of characters left undeveloped in the original version, as Jean Rhys does in her extension of *Jane Eyre* in *Wide Sargasso Sea* (1966) and Robin Lippincott attempts in his novel, *Mr. Dalloway* (1999).

Authors also create new versions of older fictional characters. To fully comprehend the behavior of Leopold Bloom or the anonymous Citizen in *Ulysses,* we need to know something about the characters they are modeled on: Homer's Odysseus and Polyphemous. Some characters will be closer to their literary models, while others will stray, but in each case it is essential to know the original story in order to follow the later incarnation. There are many motives for such rewritings; some authors may wish to place the same characters in a very different setting, as happens in *Throne of Blood,* Akira Kurosawa's cinematic remake of *Macbeth* set in feudal Japan. Others want to provide more realistic or current versions of distant figures and events (Turgenev's "A King Lear of the Steppe"). Authors can play with these expectations and make readers wonder how much of the original character will be retained and how much will be altered. At the beginning of Joyce Carol Oates's "The Dead," there are no obvious parallels for Gabriel, Gretta, and Michael Furey; as the story progresses, the reader naturally wonders who is going to emerge as whom.

Postmodern rewrites often exaggerate, distort, or parody the practice of literary reincarnation by refusing to maintain the identities of the originals; in Julian Rios's *Loves That Bind* (1998), the narrator recounts his love affairs with twenty-six literary characters, beginning with Proust's Albertine. In *Midnight's Children,* Saleem Sinai is a kind of version of Tristram Shandy, both as a frustrated narrator who has trouble telling his story economically and as one who experiences repeated difficulty with his nose and his penis. The point of the refiguring of this character would seem to be a demonstration of its portability across cultures and centuries and an affirmation of a cosmopolitan sensibility. At the same time, Rushdie's treatment provides more of a political bite than Sterne's does, as it shows how nations as well as literary characters are created by the stroke of a pen. There is also a touch of Scheherazade in Saleem: she narrated the tales of the *1001 Nights* in order to stay alive, while Saleem fears he will die once he reaches the end of his narrative. In these works, a major source of the characters' nature and behavior is an earlier literary text; this source is at least as important as the character's mimetic, thematic, or synthetic functions. These intertextual components need to be included in an expanded theory of literary character.

THE DIFFERENT ASPECTS of character that I have enumerated here may fuse together more or less seamlessly, as is often the case in Shakespeare. In Rushdie, we see recognizable portraits of fallible historical individuals, a playful allegory of the narrator's body as the body of the state of India, creative transformations of the idea of an individual character, and the refiguration of Tristram Shandy in the person of Saleem. At other times, these different aspects may be in a more disharmonious relationship. *Howards End* has often been critiqued because its allegory finally runs roughshod over its pretentions to verisimilitude: some of the key decisions made by the central characters breach psychological consistency so that Forster can sustain allegorical correspondences. In a similar vein, Marxist critic Georg Lukács once claimed that Dostoevsky slandered his more left-wing characters by causing them to act in psychologically inconsistent ways so that the author could more easily dismiss the characters' revolutionary politics. Other writers advocating a liberal, egalitarian agenda at times unwittingly deconstruct their own worldview by reinscribing social hierarchies into their texts, as unrealistic stereotypes take the place of more probabilistic portrayals. Overly schematized literary patternings can also be at war with psychological consistency, especially as the end of a work approaches and characters need to rapidly repent, forgive, or otherwise transform themselves in ways that will no longer obstruct the work's impending resolution. Antimimetic authors tend to be particularly alert to the different components of character outlined above as well as to the ways they often fail to fuse; their vigorous deconstruction of traditional characterization no doubt stems in part from this awareness.[7]

NOTES

1. For recent treatments of the developing notions of masculinity in Austen's period, see Garofalo; and Kramp. Wilt wrote a classic treatment of the topic, tracking the shift in ideal masculinity from Mr Woodhouse's old-style gentility to the more modern mode. [RW]

2. See Finch on how Austen uses FID to construct the voice of an entire community. [RW]

3. See also Noë, *Out of Our Heads;* Slors and Macdonald; and, for a fuller discussion of this tradition of research and some of its implications for narrative inquiry, Herman, "Storied Minds" and "Post-Cartesian Approaches." [DH]

4. As Strawson put it, "the concept of a person is to be understood as the concept of a type of entity such that both predicates ascribing states of consciousness and predicates ascribing corporeal characteristics [specific to human bodies], a physical situation etc. are equally applicable to an individual entity of that type" (104). For other accounts of the concept of person, see Goldie; Rorty; and Taylor. [DH]

5. The same goes for readers' attempts to make sense of authors' minds, as discussed in chapter 2. [DH]

6. See Goldie for a taxonomy of personality traits (which Goldie characterizes as *dispositions*), including ways of acting, habits, temperaments, emotional dispositions, enduring preferences and values, and skills, talents, and abilities (11–13). [BR]

7. For further reading on issues of character from an unnatural perspective, see Cixous; Docherty; Fokkema; and Richardson, "Beyond Poststructuralism." [BR]

6

Reception and the Reader

James Phelan and Peter J. Rabinowitz

Not all literary approaches need to consider the reader, at least in detail. It's possible, for instance, to explore the structures of particular genres or the ways in which texts reflect particular historical values or situations without paying close attention to the interpretive activities of readers or the differences among them. But once you accept rhetoric as your governing para-ⓧ digm, reception becomes key to analysis and evaluation. But exactly *who* is the reader of the text? The rise of reader-oriented theories starting in the 1960s brought with it a number of different concepts: ideal readers, implied readers, postulated readers, real readers. Each has its use for certain kinds of inquiry; but in this chapter, we'd like to set out in more detail the tripartite system—the *actual, authorial,* and *narrative* audiences—that we mentioned in our introduction and that stands at the center of much rhetorical narrative practice today. The nature of and the interrelations among these audiences vary from narrative to narrative, and attending to those interrelationships helps reveal any single narrative's distinctive qualities.

Every individual reader is different—and fabulously complex. As writers, we never fully know the audiences we address, which is why, for instance, it can be so difficult to calibrate a letter—say, a request for a favor or an expression of sympathy—even to someone we think we know well. How do authors of more widely read texts manage to write for the many people in their audience—an actual audience that they don't even know?

There's a mythology that serious artists don't pay attention to their audiences but instead focus only on expressing their visions. But it's impossible to make meaningful rhetorical choices without some sense of whom you are addressing—about their beliefs, background knowledge, values, taboos, sense of humor. For example, the implied Twain of *Huckleberry Finn*, in light of the occasion for his telling, had to decide whether or not to explain the system of slavery prevalent in the United States before the Civil War. In the absence of guaranteed knowledge about his actual audience, he had to make his best guess about what his imagined or "authorial" audience would know about that system. He decided to write for an audience that would be reasonably well-informed about the "peculiar institution"—a reasonable choice since the Civil War was still a fresh memory for so many Americans in the early 1880s. But that choice may unwittingly lead to a problem for at least some modern actual readers who do not know such things as the details of state law that made it necessary for a fugitive slave from Missouri like Jim to travel all the way to Ohio rather than simply to cross the River into Illinois. One major function of footnotes in editions aimed at students is precisely to give them the information necessary to join the authorial audience.

Works of fiction have another kind of audience as well. To the extent that a novel is an imitation of some nonfictional form (a biography, a memoir, a history), so the narrator (whether dramatized or not) is an imitation of an author; and just as an actual author always writes for a hypothetical authorial audience, so a narrator always writes for a "narrative audience" that treats the narrator as "real." Reading a work of fiction therefore always entails at least a double consciousness: we can treat the work neither purely as what it is, nor purely as what it pretends to be, but must hold these competing (and mutually incompatible) perspectives simultaneously in our consciousness. We are not reading *Huckleberry Finn* intelligently if we treat the story as "real" and criticize it because there are no public records confirming the murder of Boggs. At the same time, however, we would be negligent if we refused sympathy for Boggs's daughter on the grounds that she and Boggs are not "real" people. In other words, to read a text as fiction, an actual reader needs to recognize that it is an invented artifact (and hence that fictional characters are synthetic constructs) *and*, at the same time, to *pretend* to be a member of the narrative audience who takes what he or she reads as history and treats the characters as real. Having this double consciousness is another aspect of reading in the authorial audience of fiction.

The actual/authorial/narrative distinction helps us deal with numerous literary issues: it helps us to explain the relationship between truth and fiction, to reconceptualize the notion of authorial intention (with particular attention to the relationship between internal mental events and external conventions), to analyze the underpinnings of particular interpretive disputes. In what follows in this chapter, we'd like to focus on a different issue: the ways in which understanding of the three levels of audience can help us understand the tone or flavor of particular books. In choosing this topic, we are returning to two related issues we have emphasized in previous chapters: rhetorical theory's interest in the "purpose(s)" of narrative, and the way that this interest shifts analytical focus from the "meaning" (typically the thematic component) of narrative to the experience of narrative. We'd like to look briefly at two factors that can flavor this experience: the fuzziness of the authorial audience and the overlap between authorial and narrative audiences. Our overarching interest, we hasten to add, remains the ways in which (implied) authors communicate with actual audiences.

We said above that to experience a work as the author intended, we have to be members of the authorial audience "within some limits." That's because the authorial audience is fuzzy around the edges—although the nature and extent of that fuzziness varies from work to work and is, in fact, central to a work's rhetoric. Some books—say, Nabokov's *Pale Fire*—are sharply focused (in this case, written for a small group of extremely well-educated and careful readers); others—say, McEwan's *Amsterdam*—may also require advanced knowledge (in this case, of music) but are more forgiving of reader ignorance; others, such as Mickey Spillane's *I, the Jury,* have an authorial audience with very specific political beliefs—in Spillane's case, about the evils of liberal politics. What about *Huckleberry Finn*? It's fuzzier than any of these cases— but it's fuzzy in particular ways and in particular places.

Consider a few salient examples. As is obvious from the Duke's Shakespearean farrago, Twain was writing for readers with whom this kind of parody would resonate—but he wasn't too specific in his presuppositions of *exactly* what they would know. He probably expected that some of his readers would recognize all or most of the quotes—but he also calibrated the speech for less astute readers, peppering some of the less familiar lines with distortions of some of Shakespeare's most familiar ("To be or not to be; that is the bare bodkin"), setting up his readers to recognize the drift of the speech even if they can't catch all the references. He also made sure that understanding this speech was not *central* to the novel—that is, he wrote the book in such a way that readers with slightly different educational backgrounds (even people who had never read Shakespeare at all) would still be able to appreciate it, even if some understood it more fully than others. In this respect, *Huckleberry Finn* is a book that, among other things, encourages a broad feeling of community (something that supports its thematic development, too)—in contrast to *Pale Fire,* which fosters a sense of elitism in those who read it.

Yet the fuzziness around Shakespeare is not quite the same as the fuzziness around, say, religion: the book is written for an authorial audience prepared to question at least some of the givens of standard nineteenth-century Christianity, and here, failure to join the authorial audience is a more serious barrier to appreciation of the novel. Take, for instance, the passage where Huck describes dinner with the widow Douglas. "When you got to the table you couldn't go right to eating, but you had to wait for the widow to tuck down her head and grumble a little over the victuals, though there warn't really anything the matter with them" (33). There's a complex communication here, as Huck offers reliable reporting mixed with reliable and unreliable reading: he accurately recounts the dinner ritual and accurately (we assume) assesses the quality of the food, but he fails to recognize that what he calls grumbling the widow Douglas (along with Twain and the authorial audience) would call saying grace. The freshness of his "unsivilized" perspective allows him to raise the possibility that the saying of grace, even by someone as sincere as the widow Douglas, might be a rote and thoughtless activity. But the effect won't work on someone who is not at least *open* to entertaining the idea that the external trappings of religion are often a sham. And of course the book has an even more stringent set of expectations with regard to the ethics of race relations: the novel simply will *not* work for a reader who is ethically incapable of endorsing the friendship between a runaway slave and a young white boy. Put all these things together, and you are beginning to understand what it *feels like* to read *Huckleberry Finn* as a member of the authorial audience.

Much of the flavor of a work also stems from the relationship between the authorial and narrative audiences—in particular, on the extent, nature, and area of their overlap. Offenbach's *Les Brigands,* with a libretto by Henri Meilhac and Ludovic Halévy, takes place on the border of Italy and Spain. This setting not only opens a gap between the narrative and authorial audiences—it opens a slightly absurd gap, one that, when combined with the authorial audience's familiarity with Offenbach's previous works, gives us good reason to expect a certain degree of whimsicality, and one that discourages us from using too much real-world knowledge as we think about the plausibility of the operetta's romantic intrigue. Martin Amis's *Time's Arrow* works differently: its non-naturalistic scientific premise of reversing the direction of time's march might seem to make it a fantasy, but in many other ways, it conforms to the conventions of realism and it anchors itself in the central event of the Holocaust. Consequently, the narrative and authorial audiences share enough knowledge that our initial sense of fantasy morphs into a recognition that Amis is offering significant historical interpretations that are intended to be taken seriously by the authorial audience. Steinbeck's *Grapes of Wrath* aims for a kind of nearly complete overlap that moves the novel almost to the point of nonfictional chronicle.

As for *Huckleberry Finn*: We said above that we are not reading well if we try to determine the exact date of Boggs's death. But while the authorial and narrative audiences treat the "reality" of this event differently, they agree about the general geography of the Mississippi River—in particular, about the problems of traveling south in order to escape from slavery. They agree, too, about the inequity of slavery and about the admiration that should be accorded to acting according to your conscience. These overlaps contribute, among other things, to how "seriously" we take the text.

Attention to the rhetorical relationships among audiences can help us understand not only the particular tone of particular texts but also why certain texts—or portions thereof—simply don't work. We'll turn to this issue in our next chapter.

Robyn Warhol

For feminist narrative theory, "the reader" refers to two distinct entities, one of them made of text and one of them made of flesh and blood. Following the commonly accepted model of the narrative transaction proposed by Seymour Chatman and refined by James Phelan, a feminist narratologist would distinguish the implied reader or authorial audience on the one hand from the actual reader on the other, making a further distinction between these two figures and the narratee or the narrative audience.[1] Briefly, the narratee is constituted by the set of assumptions and attitudes the narrator invokes through word choices, explanations, direct address, and gaps in the storytelling. The narratee—whose characteristics emerge through close reading of what the narrator does and does not need to say—exists only in the text, to be uncovered by a method similar to Mikhail Bakhtin's strategy for finding dialogic voices in writing that only appears to be univocal. The actual reader, by contrast, is the embodied person who holds the book and reads. The implied reader is a figure hovering between these two entities, the virtual projection of a consciousness that can tune into the narrator's message—an imaginary reader who "gets it," even—or especially—when the narratee appears to be in the dark.

Jane Austen's most famous sentence, the opening of *Pride and Prejudice,* is a classic example of disjuncture between the narratee and the implied reader. When the narrator says, "It is a truth universally acknowledged, that a single man in possession of a good fortune must be in want of a wife," the narratee misreads the statement in an attempt to take it at face value. In fact, compendiums of literary quotations cite the sentence among other "Jane Austen quotes" as if it straightforwardly expressed an opinion Jane Austen held.[2] The narratee agrees with Mrs Bennet's view that an unmarried wealthy man is "in want of" a wife, which many casual readers of Austen—or of Austen quotes—take to mean he must desire to have a wife. The implied reader of *Pride and Prejudice* understands that Mrs Bennet's beliefs are strongly undermined by the dialogue with her husband that follows the narrator's assertion, while appreciating the joke: "in want of" doesn't mean "wants" in the sense of "wishes to have" but means "wants" in the sense of "lacks." To say as the narrator does that a single man lacks a wife is simply to couch a tautology in a shapely periodic sentence. The statement is therefore not only stylish but true on a literal level, since everyone will acknowledge that a tautology is not false. The implied reader grasps that this subtlety of diction is over the head of Mrs Bennet and that the joke is on her.

The implied reader of *Persuasion* (and of most of *Pride and Prejudice*) has less work to do in moving from what the narrator says to what the text is saying. The implied reader knows how to attribute free indirect discourse, whether it comes from Anne or from the other characters, and how to temper the narrator's penchant for hyperbole. This implied reader enters into the heroine's concerns about the ways people treat one another and about the appropriate attitudes to take toward such matters as class distinction. A single sentence (this one from the scene of Anne's arrival at the apartment her father and sister have rented in Bath after leaving Kellynch Hall) reveals the attitudes the implied reader would share with the heroine:

> She might not wonder, but she must sigh that her father should feel no degradation in his change; should see nothing to regret in the duties and dignity of the resident land-holder; should find so much to be vain of in the littlenesses of a town; and she must sigh, and smile, and wonder too, as Elizabeth threw open the folding-doors, and walked with exultation from one drawing-room to the other, boasting of their space, at the possibility of that woman, who had been mistress of Kellynch Hall, finding extent to be proud of between two walls, perhaps thirty feet asunder. (112)

The implied reader, as critical as the heroine of the elder Elliots' behavior, smiles and sighs with Anne at the stubborn vanity that cannot distinguish the decline in status and responsibility that has come with the move to Bath. At the same time, the implied reader is participating in a snobbishness the text does not treat as vanity, that is, Anne's assumption that this change in class status is "degradation," a word more associated with morals than with living quarters. For Anne, Elizabeth's pride in the size of the small apartment would more properly have been placed in an awareness that as mistress of Kellynch, she *really* had something to be proud of. The implied reader endorses this particular version of snobbery, as well as condemning the version embodied by Sir Walter and Elizabeth.

The degree to which the actual reader can identify with the implied reader establishes the actual reader's affective response to the text. If a twenty-first-century college student picks up *Persuasion* to find herself effectively interpellated by the narration—if some part of herself answers the call the narrator sends out to the implied reader—her reading experience will be absorbing; if she is offended by class snobbery or can't bring herself to care about the aggregation of tiny faux pas and minuscule interpersonal triumphs that add up to Austen's plot, this can be attributed to her own inability to identify with the implied reader. In approaching the topic of "the reader" in Jane Austen, a feminist narratologist could examine either the implied or the actual reader, or both. While their different positions in the narrative transaction are significant, the more important difference for feminism is the fact that the actual reader, unlike the implied reader, occupies a gendered and sexualized body in time and space. The implied reader is a virtual being. The actual reader lives in history, subject to the vicissitudes of cultural norms for gender and sexuality that sometimes seem dazzlingly mobile (it's hard to imagine what Jane Austen would make of a transgender romance) and at other times frustratingly fixed (it's even harder to understand why so many twenty-first-century women would be emotionally invested in Austen's matrimonial imperative, given the changes in women's options that have developed over the last 200 years). I often tell my students that as far as gender norms are concerned, the present historical period is more similar to Jane Austen's than different from it. Those among the students who can connect with Austen's implied reader are the ones who understand what I mean.

What a feminist narratologist would do with the figure of the implied reader might not vary much from what any narrative-centered critic would do. However, in attending to the actual reader, feminist narrative theory takes its biggest step away from its structuralist origins. I began my analysis of the narrator by speaking of how important the actual author is within Jane Austen studies. For Austen in particular, actual readers have also become the subject of much fascinating commentary, especially among feminist critics.[3] Unlike classical narratology, feminist narratology is free to draw on what can be known about actual readers to speculate about the impact of reading Austen novels upon individuals and, more importantly, upon the culture.

Sources of information about Austen readers are abundant. The Jane Austen Society of North America (JASNA) is rivaled in the community of nineteenth-century British novel readers only by the Dickens Universe in the longevity and vitality of its proceedings.[4] Since its creation in 1979 it has grown to include more than 4,000 members who attend annual conferences and local chapter meetings, receive copies of *Persuasions* (an annual journal designed to address both scholars and well-informed nonacademic readers), and reread Austen's six novels so frequently that some of them come to know the texts by heart. (Giving a paper at a chapter meeting of JASNA can be a daunting experience for visiting scholars, who often find that the audience will courteously and relentlessly quiz them on the finest-grained details of all the scenes their presentation has failed to mention.) Alongside the highly organized and structured JASNA there are countless spaces on the Internet where Austen readers congregate virtually. In the summer of 2009 I found on the World Wide Web more than a dozen blogs devoted to Jane Austen discussions, including "Jane Austen Today," "Jane Austen's World Blog," "Following Austen," "AustenBlog," "Austen-tatious," "Thoughts on Jane Austen and Other Cultural Icons," "Jane Austen Sequels," and "All Jane Austen, All the Time." Blogs on Charles Dickens—along with Austen the most popular of nineteenth-century British novelists—are few and far between, and blogs devoted to George Eliot or the Brontës are even scarcer. Large numbers of Jane Austen's twenty-first century readers are somehow more motivated to meet online to compare responses to novels, share historical anecdotes and information about Regency material culture, argue over how Austen's characters "really feel," talk about parallels between Austen's fiction and their own lives, and trash latter-day continuations of or sequels to Austen, which the bloggers always seem to read and seldom seem to like.

The Internet and JASNA make available to the feminist scholar a wealth of potential research material suitable for the kind of ethnography Janice Radway conducted in the 1980s on a community of actual readers of dime-store romance novels. In many ways anticipating feminist narratology, Radway considered not only the content of the readers' comments and reflections on their own reading but also the forms and conventions of the genre her subjects loved to read. Inspired by Radway's example, the feminist narratologist could draw on readers' self-reports to address questions about actual readers' expectations, interpretations, and evaluations of Austen's fiction and to link the ethnographic findings with analyses of narrative form. A feminist narratologist interested in discourse analysis, following the example of Ruth Page, might look at the construction of gender in the blogs themselves, scrutinizing not just what the fans say about gender but also how their own discourse performs gender. To do this kind of work responsibly, a researcher needs to keep in mind the demographic differences among readers. As I have said, actual readers have actual bodies, and those bodies are classed, raced, sexed, nationalized, and aged, as well as gendered. A drawback to using blogs as the subject or source of study is that one can make hypotheses or draw conclusions only about bloggers, who represent certain levels of economic and educational privilege, not to mention an enthusiasm for communications technology that could put them in the minority among Austen readers. How people represent their identity positions online is also a question to consider.[5] Virtual spaces for conversation enable participants to perform virtual identities that may or may not align with their own physical self-presentation. While the feminist narrative critic using such sources can speak with confidence about what some actual readers say, there is no way to delimit the identity positions from which those readers are speaking.

In my own work I have relied on more anecdotal evidence to speculate about what I call the "susceptible reader" or the "cooperative reader," any real-world person who is willing to engage in the set of emotional exercises set out in a narrative text. The susceptible reader shares much in common with the implied reader, one important difference being that the susceptible reader is an actual person. To be a susceptible reader, an actual reader needs to anticipate and enjoy the characteristic narrative moves of a given genre, to be awake to divergences from those typical moves, and to be able to take on—if only for the time of reading—the feelings and assumptions of the implied reader: in short, to be a fan. All the subjects of Radway's ethnographic study were susceptible readers of Harlequin romance, and practically all the bloggers on the Jane Austen sites (and presumably all the members of JASNA) are susceptible readers of their favorite novelist's texts. My project in *Having a Good Cry* was to analyze the affective experience exercised in susceptible readers of certain popular narrative genres and to consider how those repeated emotive experiences contribute to the constitution of actual readers' own gender performances. I have argued that susceptible readers do not necessarily imitate the gendered behavior of characters (indeed, as the sometimes-vehement debates on the blogs reveal, these readers are as likely to denounce their heroines' gendered behaviors as to emulate them). Nor do the moves of "feminine" narrative appeal to some essential gender trait supposed to be inherent in Austen's readers. Rather, the predictable trajectory of the marriage plot—which I have outlined above in the section on Time, Plot, and Progression—pulls the susceptible reader through a patterned sequence of affects: from excited interest, to uncertain anxiety, to heightened excitement, to gratification, to—in Austen's case—a bemused detachment born of the novelist's metaleptic refusal to come completely to closure. Repeatedly going through these affective motions, the bodies of actual readers are marked with the feelings the susceptible reader experiences. The susceptible readers' bodies thus bear the imprint of the continually reiterated affects inspired by the novels and by everything else in culture that interpellates those readers. This affective imprint constitutes, at least in part, the actual reader's gender identity and gender performance.

I have known actual readers who said that they loved *Persuasion* but reading it made them cry. I don't think this is solely the expression of self-pitying disappointment among readers who haven't found their own happy endings. A particular example I remember was a heterosexual professional woman *d'un certain âge*, unmarried and despairing of ever being able to find the life-partner she felt sure she wanted. She shed joyful tears for Anne Elliot's happy ending that were also bitter. For her, the metalepsis I have discussed in the section on Narration pointed up the fictitiousness of Anne's triumph, inspiring in my feminist friend a feeling of shame for investing so much emotion in an outcome for which she had a serious critique. Joy and pleasure, bitterness and shame are among the affects shaping the gendered experience of the susceptible reader of Jane Austen. The implied reader, then, is not the only creature of the text on this side of the narrative transaction: through its affective moves, the text comes to constitute the gender performance of the flesh-and-blood reader, too.

David Herman

As I have tried to emphasize throughout, narrative worldmaking is made possible by the active, ongoing participation of readers. (In using the term "readers," I mean to invoke the larger class of "story-interpreters," including viewers of films, interlocutors in face-to-face conversation, listeners to radio narratives, etc.) Figure 1 provides a flowchart (or decision tree) representing how readers cooperate in the worldmaking process by making interpretive choices at key stages—although arguably, as discussed in chapter 2, many readers coming to McEwan's text even for the first time already have enough contextual and paratextual information to move directly to the final stage of the process. That said, in other contexts, interpreters of someone's conduct or its results may have to make a first cut between caused behavior and reason-driven action; next decide whether a given action is communicative or non-communicative (compare writing down sentences vs. unselfconsciously rubbing one's arm because of a muscle cramp); and then, for communicative actions, decide whether the conduct at issue falls into the category of narrative or not (compare writing sentences listing off all the objects sitting on one's desk vs. sentences telling a story about how a thief stole those objects).[6] Finally, for the communicative actions that are in fact amenable to being interpreted as narratives, the two types of inferences mentioned in the opening chapter become relevant: (1) those concerning what sort of world is being evoked by the act of telling and (2) those concerning why or with what purposes that act is being performed at all.

Hence, if "narration" refers to the process by which story creators cue readers to construct, inhabit, and gauge the communicative purposes of narrative worlds, "reception" refers to the world-building practices of readers responding to those textual cues. Such practices can be studied diachronically or synchronically: contrast *Rezeptionsgeschichte* with attempts to model text–reader interactions at a given moment in the evolution of narrative forms—whether in a given culture or across different cultures (see Herman, "Introduction" to *The Emergence of Mind* 23–24). Reading practices can also be investigated via the observed conduct of others or else on the basis of the analyst's own intuitions, typically in dialogue with those of a larger community of experts. But however they are studied, readers' world-building methods involve inferential activities of a particular sort.

Readers use a textual blueprint, coupled with their prior familiarity with other texts and a repertoire of lived or imagined situations and events, to draw provisional inferences about the structure and inhabitants of a narrative world; to update or, if necessary, reorganize their mental representation

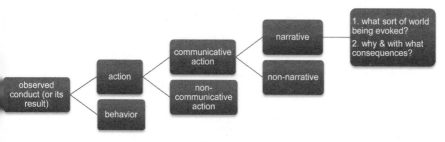

Figure 1
A Decision Tree for Narrative Worldmaking

of—and emotional responses to—that world, as they acquaint themselves with more details of the text while working their way through narrative; and to engage with the question of why the story creator has designed a narrative with these particular characteristics in this specific context or occasion for telling (Herman, *Basic Elements* 37–74). Crucially, inferences about both the internal structure and the communicative functions of storyworlds remain subject to revision, as when while rereading McEwan's novel a reader notices details skipped over on a first reading or (after visiting England) revises his or her mental estimate of the distance between Oxford and the Dorset Coast, or when it emerges that a text originally categorized as a memoir includes persons and occurrences that were invented whole-cloth. Likewise, if I have read a range of literary narratives and perhaps also some work in narrative theory and can situate McEwan's novel within this broader context, I will be likely to draw different conclusions about McEwan's textual designs than I would without such background knowledge.

The revisability of inferences about narrative worlds over time—and the variability of worldmaking methods used by different interpreters at the same time—has led theorists to develop a range of reader constructs (for helpful overviews, see Prince, "Reader"; Schneider, "Reader Constructs"). These constructs are premised on the assumption that "[r]eal, concrete readers . . . should be distinguished from more abstract readers" (Prince, "Reader" 398); they range from textually inscribed addressees, which Genette and Prince discussed under the heading of "the narratee," to the model reader, implied reader, or authorial audience (Eco; Iser; Rabinowitz), which are in effect names for the profile that an interpreter infers the reader targeted by a given author to possess.[7] Analysts have drawn on such constructs to suggest, for example, how characterized narratees can be used to model the (ideal or projected) responses of readers of the narrative as a whole (Williams) and to explore the complex, shifting functions of textual "you" in second-person narration (Fludernik, "Second-Person"). Yet there is in my view a danger associated with reader constructs and frameworks based on them, including the narrative communication diagram that assumes three levels or layers: in the outermost layer, the actual author and the actual reader; at the next level, the implied author and the implied reader; and finally the narrator and the narratee.[8] The danger is again that of losing sight of the heuristic status of these models and reifying or hypostatizing the entities they encompass—of forgetting that reader constructs are ways of describing phases or aspects of the inferential activities that support worldmaking, not preconditions for understanding stories.

Indeed, distinguishing between "real" and "abstract" readers seems to me to lead down a slippery slope toward hypostatization of this sort. Model readers, implied readers, and authorial audiences are less kinds or categories of readers than shorthand ways of referring to inferences about narrative texts—decisions about the structure of narrative worlds—arrived at by one or more actual readers and presented as having broad validity, that is, as interpretations on which other readers, given a particular text, should ideally converge. Like any other statement about McEwan's novel, a statement characterizing the assumptions and beliefs of the implied or model reader of *On Chesil Beach* derives from a particular reader's inferences about the nature and functions of the world McEwan has aimed to evoke via the textual cues he has here assembled. But expressions such as "the implied reader" can have the effect of occluding the way they, too, designate interpretations that stem from inferences made by actual readers. As I see it, furthermore, this occlusion serves a legitimating function: if a wedge can be driven between actual and implied readers, a specific interpretation of a narrative text or specific method of world-construction can be presented as the interpretation called for by the text itself—if it is to be read "authorially" or from a position aligned with an implied reader who is by definition tuned to receive the textual signals emanating from the implied author.

The approach that I am outlining in this volume makes no such claim for the storyworld that has emerged over the course of my discussion of McEwan's novel. Rather, I am making a claim for the general, trans-reader relevance of questions and subquestions of the sort discussed in my contributions to previous chapters—based on my assumption that the practice of framing tentative, defeasible answers to questions of this kind is what enables narrative worlds to be made and remade. Granted, when it comes to resolving such questions, there will be areas of convergence among readers who (1) make the initial determination that questions about time, space, and characters are pertinent, in ways I have outlined, for a given text (i.e., that the text possesses some degree of narrativity); (2) share broad familiarity with a larger tradition of narrative texts, competence in the language or other semiotic system(s) in which the story is told, and more or less comparable background knowledge; and (3) draw on the resources listed under item (2) to ascribe to story creators the aim of evoking a particular kind of world for particular reasons. Thus, my guess is that readers of the present volume would be likely to agree with me that *On Chesil Beach* does not evoke a world inhabited by green-blooded zombies who only act like normal people. They would also probably agree that McEwan is not seeking to convince readers to go back to older, pre-1960s social and sexual mores or to make a regular practice of handling arguments in the way that Edward Mayhew does. But I need not appeal to the concept of the implied reader to account for the disparity between these strategies for worldmaking and the strategies that I myself would be apt to use. Instead, factors (1)–(3) listed above constitute what can be described as constraints on the variable patterning of textual cues with inferences about storyworlds (Herman, *Story Logic* 12)—constraints that affect how much divergence or convergence there will tend to be among interpretations of a given narrative. Reader constructs do not explain these constraints on worldmaking; the constraints, rather, afford a way of explicating the constructs.

To be sure, there is no one-to-one relationship between textual blueprints and narrative worlds. Instead, a variety of discourse cues can prompt the same kinds of inferences about the world at issue, while the same cue can, if used in different contexts, prompt different sorts of inferences (Sternberg, "Proteus"). Thus a range of textual designs trigger the inference that Florence has been subjected to sexual abuse, whereas conversely McEwan's references to repressed memories serve different functions in connection with Edward than they do in connection with Florence. But the variability, in a given case, is not limitless. I do not assimilate Florence's mother's views about Stalinist Russia (65), for example, to the story line of sexual abuse; nor do I assign positive valences to any of the details that are in fact associated with that storyline. To extrapolate: the implied reader, model reader, and authorial audience are ways of referring to what constitutes, for a particular interpreter, the permissible range of inferences that can accrue to one or more textual features in a narrative—given the operation of factors (1)–(3) listed in my previous paragraph. Yet appeals to reader constructs can sometimes produce the impression that what is in reality the result of a chain of inferences is instead its cause or precondition. Narrative understanding—reconstructing a storyworld—is not contingent upon the actual reader's stepping into the role of the implied reader. To the contrary, the very division between an actual and an implied reader is contingent on using one's understanding of a narrative text to distinguish between inferences that can be felicitously associated with the text and those that cannot, and then (for heuristic or explanatory purposes) defining the implied reader as one who is immune to all the inferences that one has deemed infelicitous. But this explanatory move itself stands in need of further explanation; it presupposes, rather than provides, a criterion for what constitutes a permissible or appropriate range of inferences given a particular set of textual cues. Put another way, interpretive claims based on reader constructs like the implied reader beg fundamental questions about the felicity conditions for narrative worldmaking.[9]

As my appeal to felicity conditions here underscores, the practice of building narrative worlds, like other practices, is driven or organized by *norms*. My contribution to chapter 7 explores the nature and functions of these norms in the context of an approach that situates storyworlds at the meeting-point of narrative and mind.

Brian Richardson

We may begin with the model of reception offered by Phelan and Rabinowitz and affirm its usefulness for dealing with the majority of possible audiences. We may, however, need to mold these concepts somewhat if we are to include the central narratives of postmodernism and other antimimetic texts. We'll start with an admittedly extreme example from Samuel Beckett. His text "Ping" (1966) begins: "All known all white bare body fixed one yard legs joined like sewn. Light heat white floor one square yard never seen. White walls one yard by two white ceiling one square yard never seen. Bare white body fixed only the eyes only just. Traces blurs light grey almost white on white" (193). This writing is so unnatural that it is difficult to imagine a narrative audience for it: who could possibly be addressed by this strange text? We may postulate an authorial audience for it; we can imagine an ideal reader who would understand and enjoy the string of monosyllables, the odd syntax, the absence of verbs, the obscure setting, the vague figure, and the general suspension of narrative. Unless of course the authorial audience is any bright individual who refrains as far as possible from putting into place the normal rules of reading that Rabinowitz has outlined elsewhere (1997); such an audience would instead make only personal, provisional islands of meaning here and there and then move on to the next strange passage. And there is another possibility: as Rabinowitz shrewdly observes in the same work, sometimes a story "does not provide enough *internal* evidence for the actual reader to determine correctly the nature of the authorial audience" (42). Without the premise of a stable, retrievable meaning, the ideas of the narrative and the authorial audiences may become indistinct, irretrievable, or seemingly infinite. In this way, antimimetic texts play with and problematize our conventional reading practices.

More specifically, we may affirm that antimimetic texts generally tend to diffuse, or collapse, or multiply narrative and authorial audiences. Let's look at the interesting case of "autotelic" second-person narration at the beginning of Italo Calvino's *If on a winter's night a traveler* (1979): "You are about to begin reading Italo Calvino's new novel, *If on a winter's night a traveler.* Relax. Concentrate. Dispel every other thought. Let the world around you fade. Best to close the door; the TV is always on in the next room" (3). Who exactly is this "you"? Arguably, it is simultaneously the narrative, the authorial, and the actual audience. There are gaps between these conceptions; the actual reader starts to slip away almost immediately. It is not the case that he or she is "about to begin reading," but that he or she has just begun reading the book. As the scene is depicted with greater detail, the actual reader increasingly diverges from the authorial or narrative audience. If one is in fact reading the book in a library, one need not worry about television sets. This information is all noted and processed by the authorial audience, who presumably enjoys the way the distance shifts between the actual and the narrative audience. Moreover, the narrative audience becomes personified as a character in the text and enters the narrative's storyworld. This in turn produces a *new* narrative audience to which the adventures of this character, called "The Reader," are told. In this work we see the three audiences first fuse, then separate, then multiply, and later fuse and diverge again at different points: "One thing is immediately clear to you: namely, that this book has nothing in common with the one you had begun" (53). It would seem that every actual or theoretical audience could agree with this statement.

Postmodern texts regularly foreground the act of reading and often provide extravagant scenarios of processing words. The protagonist of Danilo Kiš's "Encyclopedia of the Dead" (1983) finds a library that contains an impossibly complete narrative of every aspect of his life; Orhan Pomuk's *The New Life* (1994) follows the adventures of characters whose lives have been disrupted and transformed after having read a particular, charismatic book; and in Julio Cortázar's "The Continuity of Parks" (1956), a reader is murdered by a character in the novel he is enjoying. Especially compelling is Borges's "The Book of Sand" (1975), in which an infinite book without beginning or ending is discovered and then deliberately lost.

The actual reading practices required of such works are, fortunately, rather less spectacular. Antimimetic works typically address an authorial audience that is well aware of the conventions of traditional fiction and is interested in their abrogation. In some texts, such as "The Continuity of Parks" or Fowles's *The French Lieutenant's Woman*, the antimimetic component appears with little foreshadowing and abruptly dissolves the mimetic framework that had been in place. In other cases, an antimimetic work addresses two or more authorial audiences, a "naïve" audience that keeps expecting some kind of mimetic narrative, and a more sophisticated audience that looks forward to antimimetic strategies. Umberto Eco has explained that what he designates a "metatext" must "be read twice: it asks for both a naïve and a critical reading, the latter being the interpretation of the former" (205). This idea of a double reading directed toward two different, incompatible authorial audiences will be of use in understanding many postmodern texts. Let us look at the beginning sentences of *Midnight's Children:*

I was born in the city of Bombay . . . once upon a time. No, that won't do, there's no getting away from the date: I was born in Doctor Narlikar's Nursing Home on August 15th, 1947. And the time? The time matters too. Well then: at night. No, it's important to be more . . . On the stroke of midnight, as a matter of fact. Clock-hands joined palms in respectful greeting as I came. (3)

The first clause, "I was born in the city of Bombay" reads like the beginning of a realist novel by someone like Dickens. But it is followed by "once upon a time," which is the traditional opening of fairy tales. This contrast within the first sentence suggests that the reader would do well to anticipate unexpected patterns and combinations throughout the book, including a juxtaposition of the realistic and the fantastic, of history and fable. The next sentences reproduce an oral discourse, as if the writer were pretending to be correcting himself as he speaks aloud. "And the time? The time matters too." These lines seem like half of a dialogue, as if the speaker is answering a real or likely objection to his account, by either an actual interlocutor or one internalized in his mind. This pseudodialogue in turn foreshadows the curious speech situation of the narrative, in which Saleem reads his written text aloud to the illiterate Padma and then transcribes their discussions about the narrative into his text, as the status and the time of the writing become somewhat unfixed. This practice inverts the classic situation of Vyasa, who dictated the Sanskrit epic, the *Mahabharata*, to the god Ganesh for transcription.

The reference to the clock hands making a greeting refers to the *Añjali Mudrā*, the Indian custom of pressing upright palms together in respectful greeting, typically accompanied by the word "Namaste"; this detail is something that a reader familiar with Indian culture would note, though a typical Western reader might miss. The date given in the text is also very important and is again primarily directed to those readers who appreciate its significance. Rushdie knows that many of his actual readers will, however, be ignorant of this fact, so he has his narrator address them, too: "Oh, spell it out, spell it out: at the precise moment of India's independence" (3). Rushdie employs this practice throughout the book, utilizing Indian expressions or practices and then contextualizing many of them so a non-Indian reader will be able to follow along. This addressing of a dual readership is particularly powerful in the second chapter as Aadam Aziz finds himself in the Jallianwala Bagh compound in Amritsar on April 6, 1919. Those with some knowledge of Indian history will realize well in advance that which will surprise the less well-versed: the British massacre of 400 unarmed Indians is about to take place.

Indian writers have a long tradition of writing for multiple audiences. To elude censorship, colonial authors often had to write in a kind of code, one that seemed innocuous to the imperial power but that could be quite subversive to indigenous audiences who were able to "read between the lines," as it were. Postcolonial authors often write to a slightly different pair of authorial audiences: one that is aware of indigenous culture, geography, and history, and a second, more traditional metropolitan audience that needs to be instructed in these areas.

The next few paragraphs of *Midnight's Children* allude to Scheherazade, the narrator of the *1001 Nights,* and the account in the Quran of the creation of man from drops of blood. These allusions are soon followed by references to popular culture in the form of Bombay musical films; Rushdie's range of reference is both Eastern and Western, high and low culture, local and cosmopolitan, classic and postmodern. The authorial reader is modeled in the following passage from the book's third chapter: "And there were so many stories to tell, too many, such an excess of intertwined lives events miracles places rumors, so dense a commingling of the improbable and the mundane" (4). This sentence might serve as a partial description of typical postmodern practice, and it further prepares the authorial reader for the book's extravagant content, unusual events, playful narration, and idiosyncratic style. The reader is told to expect the unexpected, to look forward to unnatural juxtapositions in the story and a frequently antimimetic style of narration.

The avant-garde has still more radical kinds of text. Some of these, for example, Gertrude Stein's or Samuel Beckett's more hermetic pieces, require the reader to act as a kind of collaborator, producing the interpretation of a multiform, protean work. Here, Eco's concept of the open work will prove very useful, as will Roland Barthes' concept of *text:* this kind of writing, he explains, "is plural. Which is not to say it has several meanings, but that it accomplishes the very plural of meaning: an *irreducible* (and not merely acceptable) plural" (159). The same may be said of many hypertext fictions.[10]

NOTES

1. I have commented at length on the gendered dimensions of the model of narrative transmission in "Teaching Gender and Narrative." Following the assigned topic, the present essay concentrates on the actual and implied readers but does not treat the narratee in detail. [RW]

2. See, for example, "Think/Exist" at http://thinkexist.com/quotes/jane_austen/ or the Jane Austen page at "Brainy Quote," http://www.brainyquote.com. [RW]

3. See especially Deidre Lynch's collection, *Janeites.* [RW]

4. The Dickens Project, hosted by the University of California Santa Cruz, has for more than twenty-five years held a weeklong "Dickens Universe" involving hundreds of faculty, graduate students, undergraduates, high-school teachers, elder-hostel participants, and Dickens fans in lectures and discussions of a single Dickens novel each year. [RW]

5. See Cherny and Weise, eds.; and O'Farrell and Vallone, eds. [RW]

6. Though figure 1 represents the narrative/non-narrative decision as binarized, see Herman, *Basic Elements,* and Ryan, "Toward," for arguments that narrativity should be viewed as a gradient, more-or-less feature of texts or representations rather than a binary, either-or feature. [DH]

7. As a textually inscribed reception position, the narratee has a different status than the model reader, implied reader, or authorial audience—these being labels for strategies of reception triggered by, rather than represented in, a given text. See, however, my next note. [DH]

8. For Chatman (*Story and Discourse* 151), the actual author and the actual reader remain outside narrative transaction as such; it is the implied author and the implied reader who, along with the narrator and narratee, are situated in the domain of the text. For Phelan (*Living to Tell about It* 38–49), by contrast, the implied author, being a label for the persona or "second self" adopted by the actual author while composing a given narrative, shifts to a position outside the text, while the implied reader remains internal to the text. I suggest, however, that debates about specific details of the narrative communication diagram should give way to a reassessment of its broader historical and conceptual foundations (see Shaw for a different take on this project of reassessment). Putting the same point in the Wittgensteinian terms I used in the introduction, my aim is to "survey," from the different vantage point afforded by a focus on worldmaking, the grammar of questions and claims based on the narrative communication diagram. Thus, in chapter 2, I discussed how my approach is informed by a thoroughgoing intentionalism that sees the idea of the implied author as an unwarranted concession to anti-intentionalist claims (see also my response in Part Two), and the narrator as a more or less salient concept depending on the structure of a given narrational act. In the present chapter, I extend my reassessment to the right-hand side of the diagram. Here I reconsider the descriptive status and explanatory force of heuristic constructs that should be viewed not as capturing conditions for successful interpretation but rather as shorthand ways of referring to (stages of) the inferential activity by means of which interpreters co-construct storyworlds. [DH]

9. For further discussion of the issues outlined in this paragraph, see my response in Part Two of this volume. [DH]

10. For further reading on these issues, see Barthes, "From Work to Text"; Eco; Rabinowitz, "Betraying the Sender"; and Richardson, "Singular Text." [BR]

7

Narrative Values, Aesthetic Values

James Phelan and Peter J. Rabinowitz

Rhetorical narrative theory provides tools not only for analytical descriptions of works of art but also for evaluations of them. We have touched on issues of evaluation before, especially in our discussions of Twain's deployment of bonding unreliable narration and of his management of Jim's role in the progression, but here we will address these issues directly. As noted in the introduction, the rhetorical approach considers three kinds of judgments involved in readerly dynamics: interpretive, ethical, and aesthetic. We make aesthetic judgments both as we read and again once we have finished the narrative and can look back on it as a whole. But these judgments follow from our interpretive and ethical judgments and, indeed, from our experience of the overall progression (as it is unfolding and as it gets completed). In this respect, aesthetic judgments are made by actual audiences about the quality of our participation in the authorial audience. We will illustrate these general points by focusing not on what we regard as an example of aesthetic success but rather one of aesthetic failure: the Evasion, and especially its narratorial dynamics. The success of Twain's ending has been debated by readers for years, and, though we do not claim that the tools of rhetorical theory can definitively resolve the debate, we do believe that they can allow us to contribute something substantially new to the conversation.

Simply put, we believe that in the first two-thirds of the novel Twain skillfully creates a relationship with his authorial audience based on shared ethical values, including a mutual respect and trust that underlies the communication of bonding unreliability, and that in the Evasion he betrays that relationship, both ethically and aesthetically. Before we demonstrate why we think that's so, however, we want to situate our analysis in relation to two defenses of the ending. These defenses are strong, in part because they begin by acknowledging some of the apparent problems with the Evasion section, especially Huck's going along with Tom Sawyer's demeaning treatment of Jim.[1]

Stacy Margolis contends that Twain uses the ending to stake out his position in contemporary legal debates about the relations among intentions and consequences in cases of liability. In Margolis's view, by showing that Huck maintains his good intentions toward Jim but fails to translate those intentions into action, Twain sides with those who believe that consequences matter more than intentions—a position that applies not just to Huck's relation to Jim but also to dominant white society's relation to slavery. Toni Morrison, in arguing that the ending is effective in spite of itself, finds a way to turn Huck's behavior toward Jim to the novel's advantage. Morrison deftly catalogues the problems with the ending, including its revelation that "freedom has no meaning to Huck or to the text without the specter of enslavement, the anodyne to individualism," but she concludes that the novel may still be "great" "because in its structure, in the hell it puts its reader through at the end, the frontal debate it forces, it simulates and describes the parasitical nature of white freedom" (309, 310). Although we find much to admire in each of these defenses, we find that they (and other defenses) are, as Huck might put it, too "intellectural": while they make sense on an abstract level, they strike no places to harden us against the sense of disappointment we feel when we read the last twelve chapters, a good quarter of the novel.

Margolis's thematic justification has a certain logical plausibility, but it requires her to downplay the reader's emotional and ethical experience of the progression through Chapter XXXI. As we have seen, Twain has signaled to his audience that Huck's decision to go to hell is the climax of his intuitive efforts to define his relation to "sivilization" and its dictates. In the final chapters, however, Twain undermines that climax by showing Huck aiding and abetting Tom's treatment of Jim. Whatever the thematic point here, it does not compensate for the experiential disappointment arising from the way the ending counteracts the progression of the first thirty-one chapters.

Morrison's emphasis on the "hell [the ending] puts its reader through" actually offers support for our case about the disappointment so many actual readers feel in the final chapters. Morrison doesn't deny the flaws but rather points out that they have unintended positive consequences. We would be more persuaded by her argument if the pain in the final chapters were of a different sort. It's not painful experiences in and of themselves that we are objecting to: the authorial audience has already dealt with considerable pain and anxiety in the text. But in such sections as the Grangerford–Shepherdson episode, our pain is rooted in sharing Twain's implicit ethical judgments, and it engages us fully as members of the narrative audience. Here, in contrast, the pain has both aesthetic and ethical sources, both of which serve to *distance* us from Twain as we read because of the tedium brought on by the seemingly interminable execution of Tom's plan, weakly justified as send-ups of chivalric romances—send-ups that are trivial in light of the serious social criticism that has marked the novel until then. Furthermore, the narratorial dynamics of the Evasion weaken our engagement with the narrative audience as our puzzlement about Twain's shift in tactics—including his sudden refusal to treat us as the sharp and sensitive readers he has addressed earlier in the book, and his apparent willingness to look down on us in the same way those "humbugs and frauds" (130), the King and Duke, look down on their audiences—greatly interferes with our concerns about the world of the novel and with our satisfaction in the ethical dimension of the implied author–narrator–audience relationships.

Consider one representative example of the change in Twain's technique. The passage is from Chapter XXXVI, just after Tom and Huck have dug the hole underneath Jim's cabin that would easily allow Jim to escape. Huck sees Jim for the first time since the King and the Duke sold him to Silas Phelps, but, while noting that Jim "was so glad to see us he most cried," Huck says nothing about his own emotions. The authorial audience that Twain has trained in the earlier chapters is sufficiently sensitive to notice this restriction—and sufficiently sensitive to see it as a mimetic implausibility and an ethical deficiency—a combination that makes it an aesthetic flaw: the Huck we've traveled with would, by this point in the novel, simply not treat Jim (or his narrative audience) in this way. Then after Tom explains all his elaborate plans to Jim, Huck reports Tom's reaction to their adventures.

> Tom . . . said it was the best fun he ever had in his life, and the most intellectural; and said if he only could see his way to it we would keep it up all the rest of our lives and leave Jim to our children to get out; for he believed Jim would come to like it better and better the more he got used to it. He said that in that way it could be strung out to as much as eighty year, and would be the best time on record. And he said it would make us all celebrated that had a hand in it. (228)

In this passage, Twain employs restricted narration as Huck reliably reports Tom's speech but refrains from offering any interpretation or evaluation of it. And, as he did in Huck's report about Tom's robber gang in the first chapter, Twain uses the technique to communicate far more than Huck realizes. But the effects here are significantly different: Twain asks his audience to see both the logical absurdity and the ethical deficiencies of Tom's hopes, but the humor here is so broad and—in this context where we've already seen similar absurdities from Tom—so repetitive that the restricted narration weakens rather than strengthens our bond with Huck and consequently with Twain.

We can understand why it might have been easy for Twain to fall into this way of writing. This is the same avuncular implied author we find in *Tom Sawyer,* and it's a voice that Twain could ventriloquize easily and well—and one that sold well in the public marketplace. But while that self-presentation may work toward the beginning of *Huckleberry Finn,* by this point in the novel, both the implied Twain and the authorial audience have changed too much for that self-presentation to seem anything but out of place. Furthermore, since the restricted narration requires Huck to shed much of the wisdom and understanding he had gained during the trip down the River, it comes at a very high price. The first thirty-one chapters build our appreciation of the relationship between Huck and Jim and nourish our understanding of how it is affected by Huck's efforts to find his place in the world and Jim's efforts to become a free man. Now those overarching purposes and their accompanying multilayered communications are replaced by Twain's ham-handed efforts to make us laugh at the excesses of a genre that the authorial audience of the first thirty-one chapters no longer takes seriously. This change is a serious come-down.

Furthermore, when the restricted narration in Chapter I allowed Twain and the authorial audience to share a joke that Huck was oblivious to about the contradiction of respectability as an eligibility criterion for Tom's band of robbers, there were no significant negative consequences of Huck's naïve obtuseness. Here, however, the restricted narration means that Huck remains silent not only about the absurdity of Tom's wishes but also about his demeaning assumptions about Jim, and that silence has estranging effects on our relation with Huck—and with Twain. Granted, Huck's experiences on the River make him more aware of the absurdity of Tom's games, but that only makes his silent acquiescence more troubling. How can the character narrator who reviewed the value of Jim's friendship so recently now report Tom's hopes for keeping Jim in captivity another eighty years and not register his dissent? How can the implied author who wrote Chapter XXXI also write this passage? Huck's silence weakens our previously strong affective and ethical bonds with both tellers, and it detracts from the overall quality of our reading experience.

The effects of this passage are, alas, repeated with small (depressingly small) variations at many other points in the concluding chapters. In episode after episode the pleasures and rewards of the first thirty-one chapters give way to the pains and disappointments of the last twelve. There are several ways we might describe this implied author–audience relationship: (1) Twain, expecting readers who would follow the ethical eddies of the first thirty-one chapters and also enjoy the humor of the Evasion, was writing for an in internally inconsistent authorial audience; (2) Twain, in the final chapters, is hypothesizing a *different* authorial audience from the one he'd been addressing until that point; or (3) Samuel Clemens, the actual author, constructs one implied version of himself in the first two-thirds of the book and a quite different and ultimately incompatible version of himself in the Evasion. In any case, as two *actual* readers, we find that our rhetorical analysis leads us to adapt Huck's vocabulary as our final assessment: *Huckleberry Finn*, stretchers and all, is a true book in the sense that it offers a richly satisfying affective, ethical, and aesthetic experience—until it gives way, during the Evasion, to humbug and fraud.

Robyn Warhol

The title of this chapter, "Narrative Values, Aesthetic Values," raises questions for the critic working from a politically committed perspective such as feminism. Does the comma between the two phrases suggest an opposition, as if narrative values were recognizable through their difference from aesthetic values? Or does the comma signify an appositive, asserting that narrative and aesthetic values are one and the same? The feminist narrative theorist cannot really separate narrative values—which I take to mean the ethical commitments reflected in the narrative structure of a text—from aesthetic values—which means judgments about the beauty of texts. To me, the pairing of the two terms seems to highlight the absence of a third term that is only implicit in this section's title: *political* values, the force behind the practice of any form of feminist criticism.

Often I tell my students that literary critics generally approach a text through one or more of three questions: (1) "How is it put together?" (the project of poetics); (2) "What is it saying?" (the work of interpretation); and (3) "Is it good?" (critical evaluation). Undergraduates usually come in assuming that "Is it good?"—the only question they have been taught in high school to associate with "criticism"—is a matter of aesthetics, a judgment of how effectively the text meets prescribed standards defined through poetics, or of how "universal" the text can be made to appear through interpretation. For the feminist critic, though, the question takes on a more practical valence. A better way for a politically committed critic to ask "Is it good?" is to rephrase the question as "Whom is it good *for*? That is, "Whose interests does it serve?" A feminist narrative critic will implicitly or explicitly evaluate a text according to its relation to patriarchy: the important question about a text's value is whether on the whole it operates to support patriarchal social and cultural arrangements or to subvert them.

Because of feminist criticism's focus on politics, aesthetics has dropped out of the feminist theoretical conversation, particularly in feminist narratological circles, where the question of textual beauty has never seriously been raised. Feminism's challenge to the canon in the late 1970s and the 1980s sought to undermine the whole idea of using preconceived aesthetic standards as a basis for determining which texts deserved critical attention. If the reason there were so few "great" women writers was that not enough women had written texts that matched the aesthetic standards of their male contemporaries and critics, then, according to feminism, there was something wrong with a set of standards that could so effectively exclude the creative efforts of half of humanity. Feminist critics followed Virginia Woolf's lead in

A Room of One's Own, looking at women's ways of writing and taking into consideration the conditions in which Jane Austen, for instance, educated at home because women were barred from universities, wrote domestic fiction and letters but not blank-verse epics. Austen had for most of the twentieth century hovered just inside the edge of the canon because her fiction meets so many of the aesthetic standards required of the "classics": she has always received credit for the beautiful symmetry of her periodic sentences and the post-neoclassical wit reflected in her dialogues and passages of narration, as well as for her vivid characterizations and her masterful management of free indirect discourse. By the end of the twentieth century, Austen had muscled her way onto the Columbia University reading list for the humanities survey course in literature. In 1937 there were no women on that two-semester syllabus, and in 1961 the list was still all male. Austen is on the 1991 list, however, along with Sappho and Woolf (but not George Eliot, who sometimes also appears on standard "great books" lists from the twentieth century).[2]

Since Austen had long been one of the few exceptions to the implicit rules of the Western canon, second-wave feminist critics did not need to "recover" her texts from obscurity. Rather, they worked to rehabilitate Austen for feminism, uncovering the subversive shadows behind her highly conventional marriage plots. When Sandra Gilbert and Susan Gubar introduced the first edition of the *Norton Anthology of Literature by Women* in the early 1980s, their selection from Jane Austen's writing caused a controversy in the popular press. Instead of choosing by an aesthetic standard, which might have meant including the whole of a novel like *Persuasion* to demonstrate the author's mastery of her craft, they excerpted a bit of *Love and Freindship,* the satire on eighteenth-century romance novels Austen wrote as a teenager. Gilbert and Gubar were looking for signs of feminism. Austen's spoof of the vapid and hypocritical heroines of the worst popular romances carries the same powerfully feminist significance as George Eliot's caricatures of "Silly Novels by Lady Novelists," published half a century later. The co-editors' choice raised skepticism and even hostility among commentators who believed an anthology's job was to represent the best of all the good literature that has been written. "Good for whom?" was Gilbert and Gubar's implicit question.

Still, it would be disingenuous for me to claim that no novel is better than another on aesthetic grounds. To remind myself that I do make distinctions despite my skepticism about the biases implicit in aesthetic standards, I need only pick up one of the many sequels to Austen novels published over the last ten years. Browsing through Barnes and Noble in January of 2010, I was frankly astonished at the number of novels I found that rewrite or continue *Pride and Prejudice* in particular. When I followed up my impression on Amazon.com, I was even more surprised at the quantity of these sequels and continuations: *Mr. Darcy's Daughters: A Novel* (2003); *Mr. Darcy Takes a Wife: Pride and Prejudice Continues* (2004); *An Assembly Such As This: A Novel of Fitzwilliam Darcy, Gentleman* (2006); *Darcy and Elizabeth: Nights and Days at Pemberley* (2006); *Mr. Darcy's Diary: A Novel* (2007); *Pemberley's Promise* (2007); *And This Our Life: Chronicles of the Darcy Family: Book I* (2008); *The Darcys and the Bingleys: A Tale of Two Gentlemen's Marriages to Two Most Devoted Sisters* (2008); *The Darcy Connection: A Novel* (2008); *The Darcys Give a Ball: A Gentle Joke, Jane Austen Style* (2008); *Loving Mr. Darcy: Journeys Beyond Pemberley* (2009); *Mr. Darcy's Dream: A Novel* (2009); *Mr. Darcy, Vampyre* (2009); *Pemberley Manor: Elizabeth and Darcy, for better or for worse* (2009); *Vampire Darcy's Desire: A Pride and Prejudice Adaptation* (2009); *Pride/Prejudice: A Novel of Mr. Darcy, Elizabeth Bennet, and their Forbidden Lovers* (2010). According to the Amazon website, this represents only a portion of the list (and of course I haven't even mentioned *Pride and Prejudice and Zombies* [2009]). Sometimes I open one of these volumes in hopes of finding some glimmer of the reading pleasure that surely inspired so many present-day novelists to undo the tentative closure of Austen's book and to keep the story going. What I invariably find are passages that strike me as wildly out of synch with Austen's texts. In one self-published sequel available on Amazon.com, Mr. Bennet assures Mr. Darcy that Elizabeth returns his affection, saying, "Lizzy has never acted as she did last night with anyone. I am quite sure that you were her first kiss. She would not have allowed it had she been disinterested" (*White Lies and Other Half-Truths* 14). If the author, Barbara Tiller Cole, does not know that "disinterested" does not mean the same thing as "not interested," someone like Mr. Bennet surely would have, just as surely as an upper-class Regency father would neither have had reliable access to information about whether his daughter had kissed any young man nor would ever have discussed such a matter with one of her suitors.[3] Indeed, in the entire text of *Pride and Prejudice*, Austen uses "disinterested" three times and "disinterestedness" once (something I can assert with confidence thanks to a Google Books search), in each case to mean someone is not motivated by expectations of personal advantage. Austen's word, in the extremely unlikely case of this episode's occurring in one of her novels, would have been "indifferent."

In another sequel, Darcy approaches his wife:

He embraces her lissome frame with stunned amazement. She is so small! Nearly from the moment his eyes touched hers at the Meryton Assembly, Elizabeth Bennet has loomed larger than life, to his reckoning. Her vibrancy, sharp intellect, and bold presence offset her svelte physique. As if designed specifically, her head rests perfectly on his breastbone and tucks exquisitely under his chin, while his arms easily surround her, broad hands flattening on her back. With a shock, he recognizes her fragility, coupled with an overwhelming strength. He could snap her bones facilely, yet she grips him with an unbelievably strong clench. (*Mr. and Mrs. Fitzwilliam Darcy: Two Shall Become One* 284)

I have to give Sharon Lathan points for gamely attempting a bit of free indirect discourse ("She is so small!"), but I can only laugh at her anachronistic diction ("svelte physique"? "unbelievably"? "clench"?), her resurrection of dead metaphors ("loomed larger than life"), her infelicitous adaptations of clichés ("his eyes touched hers"—really?) and the dopey absurdity of the interiority she assigns to Austen's inscrutable hero (he realizes with a shock that he could break his wife's bones "facilely"—is that a word?—in spite of the powerful grip with which she seizes him). The writing is just—well—bad. For a feminist critic to say so is to raise an irreconcilable paradox: who am I (a privileged, overeducated snob, strongly influenced by the old New Critics who taught me and the old copy of Fowler they said I ought to read) to say that novels are bad if some feminine readers are enjoying them?[4] Bad for what, besides the development of an ear for authentic Regency prose?

It would be equally disingenuous, though, for a feminist critic to say that this kind of writing provides harmless pleasure for the devotees of Austen fan fiction. Like most of the other sequels and adaptations, *Mr. and Mrs. Fitzwilliam Darcy* is not a satire but an evidently earnest attempt to give Darcy and Elizabeth's relationship a bodily dimension that is lacking in Austen's original. But what sort of eroticism suggests a woman might find it exciting to know that a man who says very little is actually fantasizing about snapping her bones? When I demonstrate an elitist dismissal of pop-culture aesthetics by laughing at the novel's prose style, I violate feminist principles of social egalitarianism and diversity. But when I consider the attitudes about gender that such novels are perpetuating, my feminist politics obligate me to call them bad books.

Feminist theory asserts that all literary critical approaches are political but that some are more honest about their politics than others. In my contributions to this book, I have tried to be consistently forthright about the ways that feminism guides and motivates my narrative–theoretically informed practice. Narrative values, aesthetic values, political values: from where I stand, they all come down to the same thing.

David Herman

In chapter 6 I discussed how questions about reception and the reader ulti-mately lead, in my account, to questions about the role of norms in narra-tive worldmaking. More generally, my focus on storyworlds raises questions about what sorts of narrative worlds (and worldmaking practices) are valued by readers, in what contexts, and why—and with what implications for the attempt to develop an approach that foregrounds the nexus of narrative and mind. In this chapter I suggest how norms orient worldmaking practices on multiple levels, while conversely narratives orient the construction and ongoing reassessment of normative frameworks. At the same time, as I dis-cuss in my concluding paragraphs, I view questions about how norms shape and are shaped by storytelling practices as separable from questions about the aesthetic value of particular (literary or other) narratives.

Like all practices, which are by definition rooted in the traditions and institutions of a culture or subculture, the practice of using textual blueprints to build storyworlds can be characterized in terms of norms viewed as codi-fied sets of expectations. These expectations have developed through a pro-cess of negotiating what should or should not be done in particular domains of conduct (cf. MacIntyre; Rouse). There are norms, specifying preferred and dispreferred modes of conduct, associated with practices ranging from table etiquette to academic writing; thus, in contemporary North America it would be frowned upon to spear one's food with a thumb tack or a pocket knife during a formal meal, just as claiming as one's own words written by another would violate the norms of academic conduct. More generally, a culture's moral and legal codes can be viewed as distinct but overlapping domains in which principles are developed to map norms for conduct onto the full range of recognized or attested practices. For its part, the domain of ethics concerns itself with how and why these mapping principles emerge—as well as their exact scope of applicability. Since narration constitutes a form of (communicative) practice among other culturally embedded practices, worldmaking through stories can be situated within this same broadly nor-mative context, as well as the meta-normative domain of ethics.

At least four (overlapping) kinds of interconnections between norms and narrative worldmaking can be identified, and McEwan's novel can be used to illustrate salient issues associated with each kind. Analysts can explore (1) how systems of norms shape what sorts of stories get told in what contexts. But they can also investigate, conversely, how (2) the telling of particular kinds of stories in particular contexts provides scaffolding for the construc-tion of normative frameworks. Further, (3) the degree to which what goes on in a storyworld disrupts normative or canonical situations is a factor contributing to the narrativity of a given text—that is, the degree to which it lends itself to being interpreted as a story in the first place. Finally, (4) narratives can reflexively model the nature and force of norms by representing how they operate within storyworlds, including how they affect characters' own (embedded or hypodiegetic) narrative practices.

In connection with (1)—the question of how norms shape the kinds of stories people tell—norms of several sorts are relevant, including norms pertaining to particular forms of communicative interaction, as well as the larger socio-ideological field in which such interaction takes place. Thus, as discussed in more detail in Herman (*Basic Elements* 37–74), narratives are told in the context of specific kinds of "occasions" with which various storytelling protocols are associated. People rely on different protocols to tell and assess stories told in a classroom, via an experimental literary fiction, or during an argument among family members. Narrators and their interpreters bring different protocols to bear on these storytelling situations because they frame them as different kinds of activities, to which different sorts of norms apply (cf. Levinson; Wittgenstein). The different norms guiding the reading of literary narratives as opposed to storytelling of the he-said, she-said variety in informal talk among peers lead to differences of story structure. Hence in McEwan's text, a compelling abstract or pre-announcement of the narrative's topic is not required to clear the floor for the story's telling; rather, contextual and paratextual features are sufficient to secure readers' engagement with the narrative. Different narrative occasions thus entail contrasting expectations about what sort of story warrants being attended to, and how to attend to its telling.

Meanwhile, both narratives told in everyday conversation and written, literary texts like McEwan's stand in a certain relation to more or less dominant storylines or master narratives about the way the world is (Bamberg and Andrews; compare Abbott, *Introduction* 46–49). Such master narratives likewise work to constrain what stories can or should be told in a given context. In a way that involves norm–narrative interconnections of both type (1) (norms shaping stories) and type (4) (stories modeling the force and effects of norms), *On Chesil Beach* positions itself in relation to global cultural narratives concerning sexuality and gender, the way family affects one's sense of self, the story-disrupting power of trauma, the institution of marriage, and so forth, with each such master narrative embedding a normative framework. As the novel suggests, there may be an emergent cultural script in conflict with a dominant-but-receding one, as was the case with global narratives about sexuality, and their associated systems of norms, in England in the early 1960s. But in any case, rather than simply shoring up a culture's major storylines, postmodern literary narratives like McEwan's engage with them (and the normative frameworks that they embed and work to reproduce) in a more or less critical or reflexive manner. That said, because of complex ways in which the institutions and practices of literary writing intersect with broader cultural institutions and practices, there is no a priori guarantee that a given literary text will align itself with the array of "counternarratives" circulating in a given setting, in opposition to more dominant storylines.

As these last remarks indicate, narratives do not merely convey or react to normative frameworks but also help constitute them—per norm–narrative interconnections of type (2), where stories provide scaffolding for systems of norms. Theorists such as Alasdair MacIntyre and Charles Taylor have explored this process at the level of actions performed by individuals. Arguing that "[n]arrative history of a certain kind [is] the basic and essential genre for the characterization of human actions" (208), MacIntyre suggests that narratives enable people's doings to be characterized as actions because they profile those behaviors as goal-directed and norm-driven forms of practice (215–16).[5] McEwan's text thematizes the way stories provide navigational resources of this sort. The novel suggests that Florence's and Edward's mutual misunderstandings result from their inability to construct larger storylines (e.g., about Florence's history of sexual abuse or Edward's proneness to violent outbursts [112–18]) that would allow them to make sense of their own and one another's conduct—in terms of reasons for acting whose intelligibility derives, in turn, from constellations of norms. But *On Chesil Beach* also reveals the dangers of overestimating the power of any single story to account for a person's goals and the norms shaping his or her pursuit of those goals. Thus Edward constructs an account of Florence as dishonest and deceptive only by "smoothing out the rough edges and the difficult transitions, the bridging passages that lifted free of his own uncertainties" (164–65).

Turning to interconnections of type (3), which concern the relationship between norms and narrativity, work by Bruner (*Acts;* "Narrative Construction") highlights how a basic orientation toward the normative helps define narrative worldmaking as a representational practice. Narratives do not merely evoke worlds more or less distant from or proximate to the world of the here and now; more than this, as early theorists such as Propp and Todorov emphasized, stories place an accent on unexpected or noncanonical events—events that disrupt the normal order of things for human or human-like agents engaged in goal-directed activities and projects, and that are experienced as such by those agents. Granted, what counts as normal or canonical will vary from world to world, narrative to narrative—as will, therefore, what counts as disruptive, disequilibrium-causing, noncanonical (Herman, *Basic Elements* 133–36). But the more general point is that "while a culture must contain a set of norms, it must also contain a set of interpretive procedures for rendering departures from those norms meaningful in terms of established patterns of belief. . . . Stories achieve their meanings by explicating deviations from the ordinary in a comprehensible form" (Bruner, *Acts* 47).

Thus, the interest-bearing events in McEwan's text are those that constitute a deviation from an expected or canonical sequence: the random accident that causes Edward's mother's brain injury, with consequences that affect the entire Mayhew family and that Edward's father conveys to his son by way of a narrative (85–94); the trauma of sexual abuse that, for Florence as well as Edward, remains at the edge of the comprehensible, precisely because of its resistance to narrativization; and the event-sequence of the wedding night itself, so much at odds with the canonical models of honeymoon encounters that Florence has picked up from "a handbook that was supposed to be helpful to young brides" (9) and that Edward has absorbed from more diffuse sources in the culture. Indeed, the shocking disparity between Edward's preconceptions about his wedding night and the actual unfolding of the encounter helps explain why it takes so long for Edward to be able to construct a narrative of the encounter that allows him to make sense of this noncanonical sequence of events: "Now [many years later], of course, he saw that her self-effacing proposal [that they remain married but that Edward have sex with other women, if necessary] was quite irrelevant. All she had needed was the certainty of his love, and his reassurance that there was no hurry when a lifetime lay ahead of them" (202). At another level, McEwan in the closing lines of the novel explicitly frames the narrative as one that uses a fictional storyworld to explore, counterfactually, possible responses to the non-fulfillment of normative expectations, and to suggest the damaging effects of an unyielding attachment (like the young Edward's) to contingent, context-bound systems of norms.

Finally, as I have already touched on in my discussion of the other types of norm–narrative linkage, McEwan's novel also demonstrates how stories can (4) reflexively model systems of norms by showing them in operation in a specific storyworld—and by using this counterfactual scenario to probe their scope, interrelations, and potential variability across different contexts. Thus, when toward the end of the 1960s Edward thinks back on the proposal that Florence made on their wedding night just a few years earlier, her suggestion has taken on an entirely different coloration, because of newly dominant master narratives about sexuality, marriage, and related institutions and practices: "her strange proposal . . . no longer seemed quite so ridiculous. . . . In the new circumstances of the day, it appeared liberated, and far ahead of its time. . . . Man, what an offer! his friends might have said" (196). *On Chesil Beach* reveals in this way what might be called the central paradox of narrative values. Using narrative to unmask narrative's own normative force, the novel stages in a fictional storyworld the ability of master narratives to occlude the contingency and variability of norms for conduct. The text thus dramatizes how pervasive, deeply rooted stories can suppress the capacity to imagine other possibilities for action—possibilities that, however, *other* narratives bring to light, through story-enabled forms of imagining.

I CONCLUDE with some brief remarks concerning aesthetic values. As mentioned at the beginning of my contribution to this chapter, I hold that questions about aesthetic value are separable from—orthogonal to—questions about the normative dimensions of storytelling practices. One reason why these two sorts of questions are distinct is that narrative, as a representational practice, exceeds the domain of literary art, providing resources for world-making in everyday interaction, courtroom trials, letters to the editor, and many other settings. In one sense, therefore, questions about norms and acts of narration are broader in scope than questions about the aesthetic value conferred on the result of any such act. What sort of story is it appropriate to tell when eulogizing a friend or a family member? How should I, as the witness of a crime, narrate what I saw—given that I must reconcile what I remember about what I saw with the constraints imposed by the legal system on persons giving testimony at trial? And, conversely, what criteria should I use, as an attendee at a funeral or a member of a jury, in order to evaluate the success or effectiveness of these narrative performances in their respective contexts? It seems safe to say that though producers and interpreters of stories do bring norms to bear on these storytelling practices, the norms are not aesthetic norms—or rather, the norms are not *only* aesthetic in nature.

The hedge used at the end of my previous sentence is telling, however, and points up a second reason why questions about narrative values should not be collapsed into questions about aesthetic values. The second reason is, in effect, the converse of the first: just as narrative practices extend beyond the domain of literary art, requiring the analyst to study how a broad range of norms impinge upon the diverse contexts in which stories are told, the domain of the aesthetic extends beyond any particular set of human practices, including those associated with artistic creation and interpretation. Here I take my cue from arguments outlined by John Dewey more than seventy-five years ago and recently re-framed and re-articulated by Richard Shusterman. In Dewey's account, the aesthetic is better thought of as a strand of or "strain in human experience rather than an entity in itself" (330). As Dewey puts it in *Art as Experience:* "When artistic objects are separated from both conditions of origin and operations in experience, a wall is built around them that renders almost opaque their general significance. . . . A primary task . . . is to restore continuity between the refined and intensified forms of experience that are works of art and the everyday events, doings, and sufferings that are universally recognized to constitute experience" (4). Thus, rather than being treated as part of an autonomous domain of practice that can be cordoned off and compartmentalized—for example, in museums or exhibits, or for that matter in literary narratives—aesthetic experiences need to be understood as part of the broader ecology or environment of human experiences from which they emerge and toward which they reflexively redirect our attention in new ways (cf. Shusterman 34–61). From this perspective the sharp division between the fine arts and the productive crafts, for example, can be questioned (Shusterman 49)—just as the pleasure and engagement afforded by literary narratives can re-integrated with a broader array of narrative pleasures and engagements, all stemming from the way storytelling practices are anchored in human experience.

For Dewey, one way to tear down the wall between art and experience is to consider how form itself relates to the structure of intelligent agents' interactions with their surrounding environments: "Interaction of environment with organism is the source, direct or indirect, of all experience and from the environment come those checks, resistances, furtherances, equilibria, which, when they meet with the energies of the organism in appropriate ways, constitute form" (147). Dewey's remarks here open out onto a whole program of research that lies beyond the scope of my contribution to this chapter. That larger research program concerns how aesthetic norms or values might relate to the specific sensorimotor capacities of humans and to the way humans use those capacities to negotiate social and material worlds. What range of world-types does humans' organismic structure enable them to "take in" experientially, and where does a storyworld like McEwan's fit within that range? Furthermore, how can the basic sensorimotor capacities shared by humans be reconciled with the different metrics of aesthetic value developed across different cultures, not to mention different communities within the same culture?

In keeping with the general tenor of a still-emergent framework for studying the art of narrative, as well as individual works of narrative art, I conclude with these far-reaching questions. They suggest breathtakingly vast areas of inquiry—areas that would not have come into view, arguably, in the absence of an approach (better, a family of approaches) dedicated to exploring the nexus of narrative and mind.

Brian Richardson

THE NATURE OF NARRATIVE

Victor Shklovsky once stated that the outrageous narrative *Tristram Shandy* is the most typical novel in world literature; its unexpected features lay bare and "denaturalize" the conventions of the novel. A primary value of antimimetic strategies of narration is to draw attention to the way narratives are constructed as well as to identify the desires that such constructions serve. There is perhaps no better way to point out the conventional nature of most kinds of ending than to refuse to provide them; this can be seen by the consternation and even outrage that John Fowles produced in some readers by the unexpected alternate endings to his novel, *The French Lieutenant's Woman.*

Antimimetic poetics has regularly provided a wonderful source of literary playfulness ever since Aristophanes' *The Frogs* was produced in 405 B.C.E. The work dramatized the contest in Hades that was to determine whether Aeschylus or Euripides was the greater tragic poet (to see whose words were "weightier," each author had a line of his verse placed on one side of a scale). Unnatural narrative practices readily align themselves with parody, above all the parody of predictable or outworn narrative formulas.

We might also note some paradoxical aspects of antimimetic fiction. Instead of constantly pretending to be nonfiction, antimimetic works are often nonillusionistic; that is, they openly acknowledge their own fictionality. As such, they are arguably more authentic in their self-presentation than are realistic pieces that try to disguise all signs of their fictionality. Repeated self-reference also introduces another layer of meaning: just as we follow the convolutions of the narrative within the storyworld, we can also trace out the developments of the narrator in his or her world, with its distinct temporal and spatial setting and its own dramas. We have, that is, the story that is told, and the story of its telling.

Antimimetic strategies also create a certain amount of distance between the reader and the text. They work against easy identification with characters and plot trajectories, they discourage conventional responses to stock devices, and they promote a critical stance that is at variance with illusionism or sentimentality. They are more Brechtian than Aristotelian; to extend Robyn Warhol's important concept of the "engaging" versus the "distancing" narrator, antimimetic narrators are typically emotionally disengaged with their protagonists but deeply engaged with their more understanding and ironic readers. The antimimetic distancing is not one that maps readily onto gender types, unlike the types of Victorian narrators Warhol discusses. A large number of feminist authors have used antimimetic techniques to foreground the gender bias of many traditional narratives; these techniques include second- and first-person plural narration (Mary McCarthy's "The Genial Host," Joan Chase's *During the Reign of the Queen of Persia* [1983]); multiperson and passive-voice narration (Fay Weldon, *The Cloning of Joanna May* [1989], Kathy Acker, "Humility" [1990]); denarration (Margaret Drabble, *The Waterfall* [1969]); antinomic temporality (Ilse Aichinger's "Spiegelgeschichte" [1952]); fragmented characterization (Djuna Barnes, *Nightwood* [1936]); unusual narrative progressions (Hélène Cixous, *Partie* [1976]); unconventional endings (Angela Carter, *The Passion of New Eve* [1977]); frame-breaking (Jeanette Winterson, "The Poetics of Sex" [1993]); and nearly all of these at once (Monique Wittig, *Les Guérillères* [1969]). In these works, antimimetic strategies are utilized both as alternatives to conventions associated with patriarchy and as devices to draw attention to insidious patriarchal cultural practices. In a somewhat similar manner, many gay authors have "queered" their texts by producing carnivalesque forms (G. Cabrera Infante's *Three Trapped Tigers* [1965]) or antimimetic narratives of illusion, masking, and unfixed identities (Severo Sarduy, *Cobra* [1972]).

POLITICS AND IDEOLOGY

Many antimimetic forms of narration have been effectively used as vehicles of social criticism and ideological critique. First-person plural or "we" narration typically comes highly charged politically, though it is used in opposed ways. It has been deployed to contest deindividualized social conformity as well as to articulate the shared social history and collective sensibility of marginalized or oppressed groups such as peasants, women, colonial subjects, and members of the African diaspora.

Authors can, with equal ease, defamiliarize a trope, a dogma, or a convention of representation. Thus, it should be no surprise that antimimetic practices readily lend themselves to a Rabelaisian mockery of the highly serious, the sacrosanct, the revered, and of all species of sacred cow, as is readily disclosed by a glance at Aristophanes' antiwar plays, Coover's depiction of Richard Nixon in *The Public Burning* (1977), and Rushdie's scathing portrait of Ayatollah Khomeni in *The Satanic Verses* (1988). This conjunction is particularly prominent in Joyce's joint attack on Christian dogma and on British imperialism (in the form of the Royal Navy) in his parody of the Apostles'

Creed in *Ulysses:* "They believe in rod, the scourger almighty, creator of hell upon earth, and in Jacky Tar, the son of a gun, who was conceived of unholy boast, born of the fighting navy, suffered under rump and dozen, was scarified, flayed, and curried, yelled like bloody hell, the third day he rose again from the bed, steered into haven, sitteth on his beamend till further orders whence he shall come to drudge for a living and be paid" (270). In *Midnight's Children* we see a sustained political satire on numerous historical figures whom Rushdie considers despotic, fanatic, or corrupt.

Antimimetic narratives, by contesting conventional or official accounts, invite us to imagine alternative narratives of the world we inhabit. Further, some authors have argued that antimimetic strategies help to expose the unreality of conventional ideas of order. Robbe-Grillet states that the unprecedented kind of textual order he constructs in a work like *Jealousy* "has the great advantage of calling attention to its own artificiality, of pointing to its mask with its own finger, instead of hiding behind the appearance of something natural, in essence, an ideological trap"; in this way it indicates the artifice of conventional mimetic orders. "One can only work against ideology," he continues, "on the one hand by pointing it out, and on the other hand by making it grind, so it can be heard, so that it will not be innocent, so that it will lose in fact that beautiful mask of innocence" ("Order" 5, 19).

Just as a number of feminist and gay authors have used antimimetic strategies to attempt to produce an original, egalitarian narrative form, so have other oppressed people, including U.S. ethnic and postcolonial authors. Though there is no necessary or logical connection between a particular ideology and any narrative form, there is often a perceived psychological connection; authors representing an oppressed group often reject the ruling class's preferred narrative styles and move instead to create alternate or original ones. My suspicion is that repressive governments tend to favor traditional, fixed, or neoclassical cultural forms and thus tend to view the innovative as oppositional. Looking at the poetics historically, one finds a proliferation of antimimetic texts during periods of major historical transformation: the Renaissance, romanticism, the years around the 1960s, and our own postmodern period.

REPRESENTING UNNATURAL EVENTS

Perhaps most compellingly, unnatural techniques are often used to depict traumatic or horrific actions that seem to defy the normal methods of ordinary narratives: the subjects of antinomic temporality, for example, include collective disasters and genocide. Martin Amis, author of the temporally regressive narrative *Time's Arrow* (1991), has stated that the Holocaust seemed to him "the only story that gains meaning backwards" (cited in Chatman 52). Trauma produces a skewering of normal perceptions of temporality as powerful past events come unmoored in time and haunt the present experience of the disoriented sufferer. Writers can and do reproduce these extreme situations for readers to experience in a way analogous to that of the protagonists. Toni Morrison has stated that she deliberately made the opening pages of *Beloved* to be confusing, so that the reader would be in a situation similar to that of a slave abruptly thrust into a new, unknown, dangerous situation.

As noted above, Rushdie's narrator experiences a particularly unnatural kind of temporality in the twenty-fifth chapter of *Midnight's Children,* "In the Sundurbans." Like other soldiers in the Pakistani army, Saleem Sinai has committed atrocities against the citizens of Bangladesh; feeling mortified, he cannot acknowledge his own identity or use the pronoun "I." He takes on a new name that suggests nothingness, and his body starts to become invisible. The betrayal of his personal values, that is, is represented by the transformation of conventional markers of the self: name, body, and the ability to say "I." Time is unnatural throughout the chapter as an allegorical long, dark night of the soul is given a literal embodiment; here, horrific events are given an appropriately unnatural presentation.

AESTHETIC VALUE

In my own work on antimimetic narratives, I continually find myself contextualizing a particular strategy within the framework of the text's central thematic concerns. These techniques, that is, are often selected to depict a specific textual situation rather than arbitrarily employed or chosen merely for the sake of novelty. A narratological analysis of such works typically leads us into a deeper understanding of the internal logic of the text and thereby helps us discern larger aesthetic designs. It is also the case that among the authors regularly considered the most prominent in Western literature, a large number often use antimimetic strategies; this suggests that there is some correlation between the kind of self-consciousness that produces literary value and that which exposes outmoded literary conventions. It seems plausible that a thorough account of aesthetic value in narrative will have to take antimimetic practices into account. It is certainly the case that the antimimetic elements of Joyce's *Ulysses* add to its undisputed stature as one of the two or three greatest novels of the twentieth century. A similar claim may be made of *Midnight's Children*—its antimimetic poetics was surely a factor in its winning the Best of the Booker prize in 2008 for the greatest Anglophone novel of the previous twenty-five years.

In the same general vein, it may well be that the more forced and formulaic the narrative is, the less aesthetic interest it provokes. This equation may lie behind one of the narrator's aesthetic warnings which is given as he is about to describe his period of forgetfulness: "With some embarrassment, I am forced to admit that amnesia is the kind of gimmick used regularly by our lurid film-makers. Bowing my head slightly, I accept that my life has taken on, yet again, the tone of a Bombay talkie" (402). Though Rushdie's works incorporate many aspects of Bollywood movies, his self-conscious and parodic emplotment of events differs radically from that of commercial cinema, especially when it comes to the use of formulaic patterns. This fact may in turn point toward the kind of aesthetic that postmodernism rewards. In general, few texts, by definition, are less formulaic than those experimental, antimimetic texts that defy all formulas. Readers who value creation, variation, and innovation will be drawn toward and rewarded by the more successful antimimetic narratives.

TO CONCLUDE, antimimetic texts thus provide an interrogation of the basic elements of narrative, a critique of overused narrative conventions, a challenge to official public narratives, an original vehicle for the self-representation of the oppressed, an exceptional way to express extraordinary events, and a different, challenging kind of aesthetic experience. The most innovative and exciting works of much of the twentieth century and the twenty-first century—late modernist, avant-garde, nouveau roman, *écriture féminine*, magical realism, postmodernism, and hypertext fiction—require an antimimetic theoretical framework in order to be fully comprehended. It is high time these works are fully included and centrally featured in the theory and analysis of narrative.[6]

NOTES

1. For a more extensive discussion of defenses, see Phelan and Rabinowitz, "'A True Book, with Some Stretchers'—and Some Humbug: Twain, Huck and the Reader's Experience of *Huckleberry Finn.*" [RW]

2. See Denby. [RW]

3. *White Lies and Other Half-Truths* turns out to be a self-published book produced by a service that Amazon.com offers for a fee. Perhaps it is unfair to criticize so severely a text that came out without the benefit of copyediting or peer review. Even so, it does present an excellent example of truly bad writing. [RW]

4. Henry W. Fowler's 1926 *A Dictionary of Modern English Usage.* [RW]

5. For criticisms of such narrative-based approaches to questions of identity as well as ethics, see Strawson. For a rejoinder to those criticisms, see Ritivoi. [DH]

6. For more on these issues, see Peel. [BR]

PART TWO

Responses

Headnote:

As noted in the Preface, this section contains responses in which we comment on one another's contributions to Part One. As also noted there, we view this section as only the first round in a discussion that we hope will continue on the companion blog for this book, generously created by The Ohio State University Press at https:// ohiostatepress.org/Narrative_Theory_Debates. We invite comments from readers who may wish to respond to our responses or to other aspects of the volume. We look forward, in short, to continuing the conversation with the help of other voices—and other stories.

RESPONSE
by James Phelan and Peter J. Rabinowitz

As rhetoricians, we value conversation. We especially value this conversation with Robyn Warhol, David Herman, and Brian Richardson because their work is so important to the larger project of narrative theory and because engaging with that work allows us to sharpen our sense (and, we hope, yours) of what the four perspectives have in common, what is distinctive about each, and what the stakes of the differences are. If you've gotten this far in the book, you won't be surprised by our two most general claims: (1) we find much in the work of our collaborators to be theoretically and interpretively persuasive; and (2) our dialogue with them strengthens, rather than diminishes, our commitment to rhetorical theory. As we seek to explain why we insist on both points—and how they relate to each other—we aim to go beyond what we said in Part One, deepening and extending our account of narrative as rhetoric.

Three interrelated principles guide our discussion. (1) *The a posteriori principle:* theory should not precede narrative, stipulating what it must be and do, but should rather follow from the myriad practices of actual storytellers; thus, we are inductive, rather than deductive, theorists. Since we are constantly encountering new narratives, and since storytelling practices constantly change, rhetorical narrative theory is a perpetual work-in-progress. Granted, our rhetorical orientation does influence our starting points and our general emphasis on progression and on author–narrator–audience relationships, but our goal is to develop theoretical concepts that are sufficiently flexible to be useful across as wide a range of narratives as possible. To put this point another way, the a posteriori principle does not mean that we approach our theoretical project without a general conception of what narrative is but rather that we approach any individual narrative without a priori assumptions about what that text must do or how it must do what it does. (2) *The pluralist principle:* rhetorical narrative theory is only one of many worthwhile approaches. Inquiries that originate in conceptions different from ours—in particular, inquiries that originate in questions different from those we are asking—often generate knowledge that is at least as valuable as the knowledge rhetorical theory can generate. Consequently, we actively seek out the insights of other approaches in order to identify and, in accord with the a posteriori principle, to remedy weaknesses in our formulations. More than that, our engagement with other approaches reminds us of the limitations built in to *any* theoretical commitments: pursuing certain kinds of knowledge inevitably means not pursuing other kinds. (3) *The some-answers-are-better-than-others principle:* still, we are pluralists not relativists, because we recognize that different theoretical positions and interpretive claims may share enough common ground that they represent genuine and substantial conflicts. In these cases, we seek to adjudicate the conflicts by testing the explanatory power of the different positions and claims against that common ground.

These three principles lead us to our two-part strategy for discussing the relationship between rhetorical theory and each of the other approaches. The first part follows from the a posteriori and pluralist principles as we focus on "differences, overlaps, and complementarities." The second part follows from the some-answers-are-better-than-others principle as we focus on "disagreements."

One further clarification: the four perspectives in this book are not perfectly parallel. Robyn Warhol, David Herman, and the two of us develop "Narrative as X" approaches based on differing conceptions of narrative *as a whole:* Narrative as a Site of Feminist Politics, Narrative as Worldmaking, and Narrative as Rhetoric, respectively. We build our theories and interpretive practices on the foundation of *our respective views of what narrative is and does.* Brian Richardson's, in contrast, offers a "Theory of X" (X in his case being antimimetic narrative) that focuses on *a particular type or aspect of narrative*—although that focus, too, ultimately has profound effects on how he approaches narrative more generally.

ROBYN WARHOL'S FEMINIST APPROACH

Differences, Overlaps, and Complementarities

For Warhol, gender, race, class, and sexuality are intrinsic aspects of narrative form, and form is always situated in history. In addition, her views of form and of feminism are capacious. She draws on work across the broad sweep of narrative theory, and her view of a feminist perspective has expanded over the years as feminist theory has itself evolved. What began as the study of "the impact of culturally constructed gender upon the form and reception of narrative texts" (p. 9) has now widened to include the study of the effects of such other culturally constructed identity markers as "race, sexuality, nationality, class, and ethnicity" (p. 9). Consequently, in her analysis of *Persuasion,* Warhol shows how the novel's formal components reveal Austen's attitudes toward these "politically significant and historically grounded differences" (p. 11), and she discusses the relation between Austen's attitudes and those of the dominant culture of early nineteenth-century England.

Warhol comments on the relation between her approach and ours: "For . . . James Phelan and Peter Rabinowitz . . . considerations of gender, sexuality, race, or class are only incidental to the fact that a genuine communication occurs when a person picks up a narrative text and reads it" (p. 10). We believe that her description, in particular the phrase "only incidental," understates the flexibility of our approach. Where Warhol always makes such considerations *central* to her analysis, we follow our a posteriori principle, taking our lead from the narrative we are considering. Thus, to us a more accurate description would be: "For Phelan and Rabinowitz the importance of gender, sexuality, race, or class in any narrative depends on the nature of its particular communication (including, crucially, the nature of the authorial audience)." To put it in different terms: we agree with Warhol about the centrality of gender and class to an understanding of *Persuasion*—but we locate this centrality in the specific rhetorical design of *Persuasion* not in the nature of narrative in general.

Consequently, the degree of our interpretive differences with Warhol will vary from text to text—although they will often show up as differences of emphasis rather than as fundamental disagreements. If a reader were to analyze *Huckleberry Finn* following Warhol's lead, we suspect that she would reinforce our attention to issues of race, but she might foreground issues of gender and class more than we have done. This reader might focus, for example, on Twain's use of gender and class stereotypes in his characterizations. Like Myra Jehlen, she might also play up the significance of Huck's cross-dressing. Furthermore, she might emphasize the roles of gender and class both in Twain's presentation of Huck's initial situation and in the ongoing complications of his story. Part of the gap between Huck on the one side and the Widow and Miss Watson on the other is attributable to the gender divide. Part of Pap's dysfunctional parenting is a consequence of his class- and gender-related assumptions about the relationship between masculinity and fathering. The raft is an exclusively male space, and such things as Huck's cruel practical joke on Jim, his apology afterwards, and the relations between the two of them and the King and Duke are all inflected by Huck's understanding of norms about gender as well as about race. In the end, such an analysis would complement, rather than conflict with, our analysis, adding to and refining, rather than overturning, our account of the novel's textual and readerly dynamics. For that reason, Warhol's approach and ours can be productive partners.

Disagreements

Still, we believe that our theoretical position allows us a flexibility that Warhol's does not allow her. This difference emerges when we ask how to determine the centrality of a particular issue to a given narrative. We suspect that Warhol would add nuance to her commitment to the centrality of gender, race, class, sexuality, nationality, and ethnicity by bringing in a question that she suggests in her discussion of aesthetic value—"more central for whom?"—arguing that in any given narrative, different readers would be likely to establish different hierarchies of centrality. For example, some readers might want to argue that *Huckleberry Finn*'s take on sexuality (recall Leslie Fiedler's famous "Come Back to the Raft, Huck Honey" with its attention to the erotic overtones of the Huck–Jim relationship) is more central than its take on race, claiming that the overt racial politics function as a screen behind which the novel plays out a more radical sexual politics. Similarly, some readers may find that *Persuasion*'s tacit assumptions about whiteness make issues of race more central to our understanding than issues of gender. For Warhol, we infer, these differences are all to the good.

Our a posteriori approach leads us to different claims about the relative centrality of gender, race, and sexuality in Twain's and Austen's novels. (1) Race is more central to the narrative communication of *Huckleberry Finn* than gender or sexuality, and gender is more central to the narrative communication of *Persuasion* than race or sexuality. (2) The narrative communication of both novels depends on other factors that are not adequately captured by the categories of gender, race, class, sexuality, nationality, and ethnicity. For example, the delicious ironies of each implied author, while often related to their gender, class, and sexuality, can't be fully explained in terms of those categories. (3) Our meta-claim: these positions do not come either from some general assumption about what's central in novels or from how it will manifest itself—indeed, Peter has argued elsewhere precisely that the overt racial politics in Nella Larsen's *Passing* provide a screen for covert lesbian politics. Rather, our positions come from observations about the *particulars* of the novels at hand. To put it in different terms: if we could not defend our judgments through an analysis of their role in the particular narratives' rhetorical designs, we would drop those claims.

When we move to the question of how to determine interpretive starting points, we have an even more profound disagreement with Warhol, one located in the contrast between our a posteriori approach and some a priori commitments in her critical practice. Warhol confesses that she is always looking for "signs of feminism in Jane Austen's texts," a search tied to her "sincere wish . . . for [her] favorite author not to have been an instrument of patriarchal oppression" (p. 11). Warhol consequently looks for "narrative practices that pull against received notions of what is suitable to a female character's life or a female novelist's text" (p. 12). While we share the politics underlying these starting points, we find her strategy methodologically problematic. As decades of reader criticism have made clear, texts do not enforce their meanings, and a sharp and committed reader can easily find whatever she sets out to find. The a priori commitment to discovering signs—especially covert signs—of forward-looking consciousness can thus easily override attention to the author's shaping of the narrative, and even reduce the text to a mirror of the reader's desire. For the most part, Warhol avoids this problem by attending carefully to Austen's communication, but she makes one significant claim that strikes us as a telling example of readerly desire trumping justice to the novel and its author:

> [T]he restlessness [in readers] inspired by Austen's endings has as much to
> do with the instability of her plots' closure as with the scarcity of Austen
> texts. Gestures like the unnarration at the end of *Persuasion* . . . suggest
> that the *texts themselves resist* the implication that the novel has really been
> "about" the marriage plot. . . . *Persuasion* is *less about* Anne Elliot's quest
> for marriage to Frederic Wentworth than it is about the subtle but crucial

ways in which the heroine achieves agency in circumstances calculated in every way to oppress her. The perfunctoriness of the way Austen ends her plots lets all the air out of the marriage plot. . . . (p. 70, emphasis added)

It's clearly possible to read the novel in this way—but how do we judge whether it is the "text itself" or the reader doing the resisting? What measure is being used to determine that *Persuasion* is "less about" a quest for marriage than about the achievement of agency? Obviously, we believe that the appropriate measure is the novel's overall design, and we believe that Anne's quest to marry Wentworth is fundamental to that design—as a brief look at its textual and readerly dynamics indicates. Anne's thought at the end of Chapter Three that "a few months more, and *he,* perhaps, may be walking here" not only generates the authorial audience's interest in this traitless "he" but also activates a desire that he can provide a means for her to escape from the Elliot household. The novel's middle represents Anne's unmerited suffering as she watches Wentworth get involved with Louisa Musgrove—even as it includes a few signs of Wentworth's solicitous attention to Anne. Both developments further nourish the authorial audience's desires for Anne and Wentworth to reunite. Given these dynamics, if the novel had actually "let the all air out of the marriage plot," Austen's ending would have introduced a disruption similar to (albeit on a smaller scale than) the one that Twain introduces in the Evasion section of *Huckleberry Finn.*

But does Austen's ending in fact puncture the tire? While Warhol astutely calls attention to the unnarration in the passage that begins "Who can be in doubt of what followed?" (p. 42), that passage significantly occurs *after* the arrival, that is, the resolution of the global instability: Anne's engagement to Wentworth. Furthermore, that resolution is far from perfunctory, involving as it does the following elements: (1) Anne's indirect but passionate appeal to Wentworth in the speech to Harville; (2) Wentworth's response in his direct and equally passionate proposal by letter; (3) her acceptance of the proposal with a look while in the company of Charles Musgrove; (4) their private colloquy shortly after in the gravel walk; and (5) their subsequent discussions of the past. Indeed, this more extended resolution is additional evidence for its superiority to the relatively perfunctory resolution in the canceled chapter. It gives greater play to the audience's own affective and ethical responses to Anne's long-deferred happiness, even as the narrator reminds us of what was lost in that deferral. Then, too, despite the unnarration, Austen's text in fact gives considerable detail about what happens after the engagement—particularly about how other characters are affected.

Furthermore, the novel's progression does not establish an opposition between Anne's quest for marriage and her achievement of agency but rather binds these two components together. Indeed, recognizing the crucial role of Anne's agency in bringing about the marriage does not make the marriage any less important but instead highlights Austen's skilled handling of the progression. She chooses a protagonist who, unlike her past heroines, does not need to change either in feeling or in ethical character and puts her in a situation where she must wait for her male counterpart to change. Nevertheless, Austen shows that Anne, by being true to herself in Wentworth's presence (e.g., in her level-headed response to Louisa's fall) and, as Warhol shows, by seizing the limited opportunities she has, is at least as responsible for that change—and thus for her own happiness—as Wentworth himself. Far from taking the air out of the marriage plot, Austen's connecting Anne's engagement to Anne's exercise of her agency is a key means by which Austen seeks to increase her audience's satisfaction in that resolution.

DAVID HERMAN'S APPROACH TO NARRATIVE AS WORLDMAKING

Differences, Overlaps, and Complementarities

David Herman's conception of "Narrative as Worldmaking" is an effort to do for our age what the structuralist narratologists of the 1960s and 1970s tried to do for theirs: develop a systematic account of narrative as part of a larger domain of inquiry. The structuralists located narrative under the domain of sign systems, and because they regarded language as the paradigmatic sign system, they turned to linguistics as their model. By contrast, Herman locates both language and narrative under cognitive studies, and he turns to "the sciences of mind"—including cognitive psychology, cognitive linguistics, and certain subfields of philosophy—for insights into how narrative works. Furthermore, where the structuralists typically established a one-way flow from linguistics to narratology, Herman establishes two-way traffic: just as the sciences of mind can illuminate narrative so too can narrative illuminate aspects of mind.

Herman's contribution here is grounded in a conception of both storytelling and "storyreceiving" as cognitive activities that converge in the process of worldmaking. Creators of stories produce "blueprints for world construction" and consumers of stories try to follow those blueprints as they build mental models of storyworlds. More specifically, from the perspective of the receiver, "engaging with stories entails mapping discourse cues onto the WHEN, WHAT, WHERE, WHO, HOW, and WHY dimensions of mentally configured worlds" (p. 17). The result is an elegant account of the interplay among these dimensions, which is to say an elegant mind-oriented account of narrative itself.

Herman's approach, like our rhetorical one, aims less at generating original interpretations than at identifying the underlying logic that grounds the interpretive process of worldmaking. For this reason, our approaches overlap with and complement each other on various points. Take our respective discussions of character: Herman's definition of characters as "textually grounded models of individuals-in-a-world" (p. 125) is consistent with our view of characters as having both mimetic ("individuals-in-a-world") and synthetic ("textually grounded") components. Granted, Herman puts primary emphasis on the mimetic both in this phrase and throughout the chapter, while we contend that different narratives balance the mimetic, the thematic, and the synthetic in different ways, depending on the author's purposes. Nonetheless, Herman's account of the interactions between "schemes for understanding persons" and "text-guided inferences" about character (p. 125) enriches our analysis of the mimetic component and particularly of how readers develop their conceptions of mimetic characters.

Despite our sympathy for Herman's aims, however, we ultimately conceive of the activity we're engaged in differently. There are two especially significant aspects to our response here, the first a matter of emphasis, and the second a matter of scope. Although Herman's other work provides ample evidence that he is adept at analyzing how the components of individual narratives do (or do not) work together, in his contribution here he is more concerned with descriptive poetics. His careful analysis illuminates the logic of *On Chesil Beach*'s worldmaking; but it does not then engage, as we would, with such key interpretive and evaluative challenges as those presented by the abandonment of Florence's perspective after the wedding night, the glossing over of Edward's marriage (what were his thoughts on *that* wedding night?), and the gender politics associated with the novel's handling of Florence's sexual abuse. As we've argued in *Understanding Narrative*, we emphasize and value the *interaction* of theory and analysis, and we hope our practice in Part I reaffirms that position. Were we writing about McEwan's novel, we'd seek to test our theory against its ability to meet those interpretive challenges.

As for scope: we value Herman's explanations of the cognitive logic underlying readers' acts of worldmaking but find that his account leaves out aspects of communication that are significant to our experience of countless narrative worlds—especially but not exclusively those found in literary narratives. Consider his "decision tree for narrative worldmaking" in the chapter on Reception and the Reader (p. 151). The tree captures one possible sequence leading from the initial observation of some kind of conduct to the conclusion that the kind is storytelling and that it therefore evokes a world for a certain purpose. But because the decision tree is restricted to what we would call interpretive judgments, Herman ends up with a far more limited notion of purpose than ours. In effect, he equates purpose with thematic points. In our view, he underplays too many of the other aspects of readerly dynamics—ethical judgments, their affective consequences, and aesthetic judgments—that are crucial to the multi-leveled experience of reading and to any account of narrative purpose.

Disagreements

Since Herman trumpets his disagreements with the concepts of the implied author and the authorial audience, we naturally want to respond to his objections. But first we want to underline the significant *overlap* between his stance and ours: we share Herman's interest in "reclaiming intentions," and we agree with his argument that "a form of narration is a form of communicative action whose interpretation . . . requires . . . ascriptions of reasons for acting" (p. 47). Herman's formulation endorses two key points of our model: authors design narrative communications for particular purposes; and one fundamental act of critical understanding involves reasoning back from the felt effects of those purposes to an identification of their sources in the authorial design of the text.

From this perspective, Herman shares some of our key goals but objects to some of our key means. His two main objections to the concept of the implied author are that it "arises from efforts to accommodate an anti-intentionalist position that . . . it is preferable to dispute from the start" and that it "entails a reification or hypostatization of what is better characterized as a stage in an inferential process" (p. 50). Herman extends this second objection to his argument against the authorial audience: "distinguishing between 'real' and 'abstract' readers [such as the authorial audience] seems to me to lead down a slippery slope toward hypostatization" (p. 152). He uses James Frey's purported memoir *A Million Little Pieces* to illustrate his preference for a model that characterizes inferences about intention as stages in an inferential process.

[Reading without knowledge of the controversy caused by Frey's fabrications,] I will assume that the storyworld evoked by the text is capable

193

of being disconfirmed through triangulation with other accounts of the events at issue. Once I know that James Frey concocted incidents in his putatively non-fictional account, however, I will use different strategies for world construction. . . . Specifically, I will interpret the text as one purposely—intentionally—designed by its author to prompt infelicitous modes of world building. (p. 49)

We agree that it is important to dispute anti-intentionalism from the start (see Chapter 2 of Jim's *Worlds from Words* for an early effort—or Peter's "Shakespeare's Dolphin" for a much more recent effort—to do just that). But Herman's focus on one of Booth's *motives*—specifically, his choice to avoid a direct dispute with the New Critics—leads Herman to neglect the significant *theoretical* component of Booth's scheme. Booth has many reasons for his formulation, whatever his relationship to the New Critics, and one of them is to emphasize the kind of intention rhetorical theory is *primarily* interested in: not conscious, unconscious, or other kinds of psychological, private intention but rather "textualized intention," inferable from the shape of the text (these signs in this order) and from its appearance in a particular public arena marked by a particular set of shared beliefs. At the same time (as the Frey case will make clear), initially private (even consciously hidden) intentions can be important to our understanding as well—and that is one reason why we still need the notion of actual author in our analytic arsenal.

This understanding of our interest in textualized intention helps meet Herman's second objection. If the implied author's intention were private, then positing such an intention *would* "entail reification or hypostatization," but since it is public and testable against the "completed artistic whole," any such positing is a defeasible hypothesis, and its power depends on how well it survives testing against alternatives. From this perspective, Herman's objections to the implied author and the authorial audience are objections less to the concepts themselves than to their misuse. In fact, the process of formulating, testing, and revising hypotheses about the implied author's intentions and of the characteristics of the authorial audience is wholly consistent with Herman's preference for a model that emphasizes phases in the inferential process of worldmaking.

With respect to the authorial audience (and similar hypothetical audience constructs) Herman claims that

the very division between an actual and an implied reader is contingent on using one's understanding of a narrative text to distinguish between inferences that can be felicitously associated with the text and those that cannot, and then (for heuristic or explanatory purposes) defining the implied reader as one who is immune to all the inferences that one has deemed infelicitous. But this explanatory move . . . presupposes, rather than provides, a criterion for what constitutes a permissible or appropriate range of inferences given a particular set of textual cues. (p. 154)

Herman here misses the heuristic purposes of the concept of the authorial audience. One purpose is to illuminate important dimensions of the reading experience that follow from the similarities and differences (of knowledge, beliefs, values, judgments, and so on) between actual audiences and the hypothetical audiences that writers address. For example, we do not share Jane Austen's views about the roles of chastity and of marriage in a woman's life, but we temporarily try on those views when we read her novels—and this aspect of our move into Austen's authorial audience highlights a significant component of the readerly dynamics of her narrative. A second purpose of the concept is to be a testable hypothesis that, if it survives comparison with alternative hypotheses, helps build a more general "understanding of a narrative text." To put it in different terms, to the extent that the characteristics and activities of the authorial audience are *presupposed* in the interpretive process, they are regarded as provisional and subject to revision in light of the next moves in the progression. Furthermore, the interpretive process is typically a complex one which, as we said in Part One, typically leaves us with a fuzzy conception. The process of discovery varies from work to work, and it may require scrutinizing textual features, exploring the cultural and historical context in which the work was produced and received, folding in what we know about the author's intentions from external evidence, and other activities. The process is rarely clean, but that's because narrative itself is often messy. Consider the first sentence of *On Chesil Beach,* which Herman also quotes: "They were young, educated, and both virgins on this, their wedding night, and they lived in a time when a conversation about sexual difficulties was plainly impossible." Does the phrase "plainly impossible" shift the narration from single-voiced, nonironic reporting into double-voiced indirect thought? Clearly, any actual reader who wants to answer this question has to stretch outside her own initial reaction—but there are no pre-existing hard and fast rules for how to make that stretch.

Frey's *A Million Little Pieces* offers a useful common ground for testing our claim that our explanation of the relations among authors, texts, and audiences is more capacious and flexible than Herman's. Herman promotes his account of stages in inferring Frey's intention on the grounds of efficiency: it avoids duplication of categories—we don't need *both* implied and actual author, and we don't need *both* actual and authorial audiences. We share Herman's interest in efficiency and, for that reason, in our engagements with certain specific texts, we wouldn't invoke these distinctions. There is not much to be gained by distinguishing Chekhov from "the implied Chekhov" when talking about "Lady with a Dog." But not all narratives conform to the model of "Lady with a Dog," and Frey's *Million Little Pieces* is one of the many cases where the distinctions *simplify and clarify* our understanding of the narrative communication, including its purposes and ethical dimensions.

With respect to authors: In telling his story of addiction and recovery, Frey has, among his purposes, the aim of making himself look admirable. In order to achieve that purpose he intentionally deceives his audience by constructing a version of himself—as both character *and* author—that is more deeply tested and resilient than he actually was. Thus, we have two distinct and incompatible authorial figures: the unadmirable figure who intends to deceive his audience and the admirable alter-ego whom we come to know through reading the memoir. Having the concepts of both actual and implied author at our disposal not only allows us to name and describe those two figures but also clarifies their relationship and the ethical breach involved in the actual Frey's construction of it.

With respect to readers: We again have two incompatible positions. (1) That of the reader who takes all the memoir's events as historically accurate: this reader is not simply making a temporary mistake that can be corrected through more careful examination of the textual information, but is rather *correctly* following the textual and paratextual signals that claim the narrative is a memoir. This position is that of the implied Frey's authorial audience. (2) That of the reader who learns that many of the events are simply not true. This position is of course available to actual audiences. The distinction between the authorial audience and the actual audience allows us not only to name and describe these positions but also to explore the ethical problems of Frey's storytelling. After all, the ethical problems do not lie within either of these audiences individually, but rather in the relationship between them.

With respect to both authors and readers: Frey as actual author *does not intend* for his actual audience to become aware of his fabrications, and our distinctions between kinds of authors and kinds of audience allow us to account efficiently for this undercover feature of the narrative communication. By contrast, Herman's account of a straightforward sequence of coming to understand Frey's intention glosses over the against-the-grain quality of any reading that takes into account knowledge of Frey's fabrications.

BRIAN RICHARDSON'S THEORY OF
ANTIMIMETIC NARRATIVE

Differences, Overlaps, and Complementarities

As noted above, Brian Richardson's approach is different from ours—and from Herman's and Warhol's—because it is motivated less by a different conception of what narrative is and does than by an effort to enrich our knowledge by accounting for a distinct and relatively neglected subset of narratives. That is, he seeks to fashion an account of narrative that is as adequate to the structures, techniques, elements, and effects of antimimetic narratives as it is to the characteristics of mimetic narratives. He remains in dialogue with what he might call the "Dominant Theory of Mimetic Narrative," often arguing that, in order to do justice to antimimetic narratives, theorists need both to alter concepts from dominant theory and to invent new ones.

Richardson's approach is also different in kind from ours—and from Herman's and Warhol's—because its underlying conception of narrative is looser. The contrast with Herman's approach is especially illuminating: where each of Herman's segments in Part One adds to his vision of the interconnections among the components of worldmaking, each of Richardson's segments adds to his expanding database of antimimetic phenomena that are not necessarily linked to one another. Nevertheless, by the end of Part One, Richardson's loose conception of narrative emerges: he adopts concepts from structuralist narratology, feminist narrative theory, and rhetorical narrative theory, among others, without fully claiming kin with any one of these approaches or proposing an integrated synthesis of them. We note, for example, that in discussing progression, he embraces our concept of textual dynamics but breezes past its rhetorical dance partner, readerly dynamics. In discussing character, he adopts the rhetorical approach's three components and adds a fourth called "intertextual" without asking, as we would, whether and how it intersects with the earlier three. Similarly, in his discussion of "narrative values" Richardson addresses the political and ideological implications of antimimetic narratives but he stops short of making feminist narrative theory's claims for politics an intrinsic part of narrative form.

As pluralists, we have no problem with such a loose conception. In fact, it's appropriate for *Richardson's* project, since it facilitates his efforts to account for the diversity of formal experiments carried out in antimimetic narratives. More than that, looking at our work from his perspective reveals a lot about our own position, in particular the degree to which we have sometimes failed to do justice to the range and importance of anti-mimetic techniques. Indeed, we value Richardson's work because it reminds us that rhetorical theory must be cautious about generalizing from examples in which the mimetic is dominant and because it highlights the way theories are influenced by their objects of study.

Disagreements

At the same time, looking at Richardson's work from our perspective suggests that he underestimates the ways in which our a posteriori approach to narrative as rhetoric cuts across his Theory of Antimimetic Narrative. Richardson implicitly—and in a few places explicitly—suggests that we are trapped by assumptions grounded in mimetic narrative. As should be clear by now, however, we seek to develop an approach that is sufficiently flexible to respond to narrative in all its variety, whether it be mimetic, nonmimetic, or antimimetic. This orientation means that we are less invested in drawing a thick line between mimetic and antimimetic narrative, and, thus, more inclined to see how these kinds are interrelated. Consequently, we would stress more than Richardson does that antimimetic narrative often depends on the foundation of mimetic fiction to do its work, a dependence that becomes evident through attention to the authorial audience of antimimetic fiction. Richardson distinguishes antimimetic narrative from "nonmimetic" narrative, and devotes his attention to the former because it is more challenging in the way it "contest[s] the conventions of nonfictional and realistic representation" (p. 28). We agree with Richardson's reasoning here; but, from our perspective, this contestation is possible because the authorial audience of antimimetic narrative has typically already incorporated the conventions of mimetic fiction—and because those conventions *continue to be activated* as the reader reads.

Richardson believes our view of narrative is skewed because we use mimetic narrative as our default; not surprisingly, we believe that Richardson's view of narrative is skewed because his focus on championing antimimetic narrative leads him occasionally to oversimplify how narrative works in general. For example, he claims that there is no falsifiability in fiction. "When a work is designated as fictional, . . . no matter how realistic it seems, no description or event . . . can be falsified by reference to nonfictional evidence" (p. 106). In a weak sense, this claim is correct: if it is posited as true for the narrative audience that the White Rabbit in *Alice in Wonder-*

land owns a watch, then you can't falsify this condition by pointing to the facts about rabbits in the real world. But Richardson's claim is stronger, as becomes evident when he argues that "*any* fact about [characters] left unsaid by the narrator (did the protagonist have a large mole on her left shoulder?) can *never* be known" (emphasis added). The claim is that gaps in the apparent knowledge of the narrative audience cannot be filled from the repertoire of "real world" knowledge of the authorial audience. But there are frequently matters left unsaid in fiction that *are* knowable. Nothing *in* the text of *Huckleberry Finn* provides a motive for Huck and Jim to travel to Ohio rather than simply to cross the river into Illinois. Even so, the authorial audience does "know" their motive because certain "facts" about slavery law are true in the novel, even though they are unstated—and because Twain designed his narrative with the expectation that his audience would use real-life legal knowledge to understand some of its action. The nature of the congruence of narrative and authorial audiences is text-dependent: they can overlap in radically different places and to radically different degrees. That often adds to interpretive difficulty—but it also adds immeasurably to the range of effects a narrative can have, including the effects that follow from the ways in which antimimetic narrative plays off mimetic narrative.

Sometimes Richardson's advocacy for the riches of antimimetic narrative and the need for narrative theory to account for it lead him to be too quick to categorize other approaches, including ours, as flawed because they take mimetic narrative as the norm. His comments about unreliable narration are a case in point: "The practice of unreliable narration, in which it is apparent that the narrator is deficient in factual knowledge, interpretation, or judgment, has been clearly set forth by Phelan and Rabinowitz. These categories, however, are all based on a mimetic model of narration, that is, of human-like narrators making typically human distortions as they narrate" (p. 53). Although the categories of unreliability may have originated in relation to mimetic narratives, they are not themselves "based on a mimetic model of narration." They are based instead on the assumptions that narrators, whether they are mimetic, nonmimetic, antimimetic, or anything else, typically will perform three main functions—reporting, interpreting, and evaluating—and that even in anti-mimetic narratives, we can gauge the distance between the narrator's reporting, interpreting, or evaluating and the implied author's own view of those actions. Thus, from our perspective a character narrator's reporting of antimimetic features of a storyworld will be reliable or unreliable not on the basis of comparing his reports against some standard of mimesis but rather against the implied author's stance toward those reports. More generally, Richardson's discussion of kinds of antimimetic narrators—the fraudulent, the contradictory, the permeable, and so on—is consistent with this view of a narrator's typical functions.

This response to Richardson's account of unreliable narration sheds some light on the ultimate challenge to the rhetorical model presented by Richardson's Theory of Antimimetic Narrative. How much does our model need to be revised? Our answer, despite Richardson's claim about the neglect of antimimetic narrative by "nearly all theories," is "some but not as much as he implies." Here's why: (1) the a posteriori principle means that we have always been open to whatever writers have chosen to do—and that includes composing antimimetic narratives; and (2) our interest in the synthetic component of characters and narrative progressions means that we have routinely incorporated attention to antimimetic narratives—and antimimetic components of otherwise mimetic narratives—into both our theorizing and our interpretive work. Jim's concepts of "paradoxical paralipsis" and "redundant telling" are two examples of the consequences of this attention. Similarly, Peter's theory of audiences grew out of attempts to explain Nabokov's *Bend Sinister* and, later on, *Pale Fire.*

Nevertheless, Richardson's work has convinced us that to this point rhetorical theory has not yet done adequate —much less full—justice to the synthetic component of narrative and its various consequences for textual and readerly dynamics. We look forward to continuing to learn from his detailed investigations—and from Warhol's and Herman's—as we seek to refine, expand, and otherwise improve our perpetual work-in-progress.

RESPONSE
by Robyn Warhol

A FEMINIST NARRATIVE THEORIST RESPONDS TO
PHELAN AND RABINOWITZ'S RHETORICAL NARRATIVE APPROACH

Rhetorical narrative theory, as defined by Jim Phelan and Peter Rabinowitz, and feminist narrative theory as I conceive it, are in substantial agreement on our fundamental assumptions. Both see narrative as an act of genuine communication that has consequences in the material world. Both take into account the motives of implied authors (though the rhetorical narrative theorists are more inclined to impute those motives to real-world authors), deducing those motives from textual evidence. And both are interested in the impact that reading narratives, whether visual or verbal, can have on flesh-and-blood readers—a term coined by rhetorical theorists that brings a welcome acknowledgment of embodiment to the narrative theoretical enterprise. Phelan and Rabinowitz's dedication to considering the ethics of narrative transactions is both congruent with and useful as a model for the practical application of feminist and queer narrative theories to texts. Indeed, there is significant theoretical overlap between our two approaches. For example, Phelan's distinction between "estranging unreliability" and "bonding unreliability" does for first-person narration what my own first project in feminist narratology attempted to do for extradiegetic narrators by distinguishing between "distancing" and "engaging" modes of narrative address; and I believe Phelan and Rabinowitz's reading of the way Huck's unreliability works toward a "bonding" effect goes a long way toward accounting for the complex responses *Huckleberry Finn* can inspire. Of the four approaches in the present volume, rhetorical and feminist are the two that go hand-in-hand most readily. But rhetorical and feminist narrative theory are not the same approach, for reasons I will outline here.

One of the features of rhetorical narrative theory I like best is its adherence to an inductive methodology. Looking at individual narratives and then abstracting what you see seems to me to be the only rational way to go about creating narrative theory. But results derived inductively depend altogether on the questions you ask before you start looking. I find myself emphatically shaking my head when Phelan and Rabinowitz say, as they are describing their a posteriori way of proceeding, "Of course we recognize that some narratives give special prominence to" issues or elements of gender (p. 5). To assume that gender is an element with more or less prominence in any given text is not to understand that gender is a part of everything people in this culture do, speak, write, or read. Gender actually has equal "prominence" in every cultural artifact under patriarchy. Recently I had an undergraduate challenge this assertion in class, thrusting her hand up and shouting at me after I called on her, "You don't know that!" All I can say is that I know it as well as so broad a statement can be known, and as I told that student, it's a good idea to read the accumulated research of forty years' work in feminist history, sociology, psychology, anthropology, political science, economics, philosophy, linguistics, art history, and literary and cultural criticism before drawing a conclusion about whether the assertion is true. Gender always signifies in this culture, as do race, age, sexuality, class, disability, and other categories of identity that structure social and cultural hierarchies and oppression. (Has anyone ever been in a class where a female student did anything as belligerent as yelling "You don't know that!" at a *male* full professor? I asked my friend Jim Phelan—who has taught for a long time in the department I recently joined—whether this had ever happened to him, and he laughed aloud before saying no. I laughed with him, because the very idea was so unthinkable.)

If you say that only certain texts give prominence to "issues" like gender, that means your default is male, masculine, and straight. But just as whiteness is structured as a race, masculinity is a gender, too, and—as a cultural construct—it can't help structuring the production and reception of texts. An act of communication can't exist outside the system of gender any more than it can exist without some form of language or sign system, verbal or nonverbal. If the deployments of gendered gestures in narrative are not readily visible to those of us who practice narrative theory, it is only because we haven't looked carefully enough, and we haven't adequately acknowledged that gender performance happens along a sliding scale, with macho-masculinity and ultra-femmy-ness at the two extreme ends. In the wake of poststructuralism, critics and theorists can't use the binarism of man/woman to analyze the gendering of texts, and even if we could, that would be boring. It would also leave out the perspective developed by the growing population of persons who identify as neither male nor female, but as transgender. To look at the gendering of acts of communication, narrative theorists need more information about which ways of speaking and writing are considered appropriate to men in dominant culture (i.e., "masculine"), which are considered appropriate to women (i.e., "feminine"), and how and when they combine and cross in acts of discourse, as well as—to invoke the rhetorical theorists' priorities—for what purposes.[1] We need more information about the circumstances in which men have used feminine gestures and women have used masculine ones, and about the purposes and material effects of such gender-crossing. A more comprehensive account of the gendered connotations of narrative gestures is what feminist narratology has been working on since the 1980s, when Susan Lanser and I made our tentative forays into the boys' club of narrative theory, where the few women who were working in the field followed centuries-old academic practice by ignoring gender or treating attention to it as a case of special pleading.[2]

Though many women are now using narrative theory to do important work in feminist criticism, they are still outnumbered dramatically by men: when I did everything I could to include women's contributions to narrative theory in an introductory graduate course I taught ten years into the twenty-first century, the syllabus ended up representing the work of forty men and twenty-seven women.[3] This might not sound so bad, given the gendered makeup of English faculty in the United States, where MLA statistics show that in 1995, "The largest group of white men were full professors [45.72 percent of all white men who are faculty members in English], the largest group of men of color were associate professors [35.66 percent], the largest group of women of color were assistant professors [33.62 percent], and the largest group of white women were instructors, adjuncts, or of similar rank [35.66 percent]" (201). However good the work of assistant professors, instructors, and adjuncts might be, it does not often find its way onto graduate syllabi, though there are a handful on mine. The disparity expresses itself another way when you consider the proportion of men to women who are senior scholars in English: of faculty who had completed their English PhDs before 1980, "White men had the highest percentage and white women the lowest percentage of full professors" (205). Indeed, at the rate we have been going, women won't be 50 percent of all full professors in the United States before the year 2149.[4] Imagine my dismay as I found—when my graduate students in the narrative theory survey asked me to distinguish between required and recommended readings—that unless the topic were feminist/queer narrative theory or narrative approaches to emotion and affect, I found myself giving priority to books and articles written by men because I had to acknowledge they were the most central to the field of narrative theory.

I freely admit that this digression from my direct response to the rhetorical approach is an example of what Virginia Woolf saw in Jane Eyre's solitary ruminations about the constraints on Victorian women's lives—Woolf called it the "swerve" that distorts a text when gender-based "indignation" makes its way into the writing.[5] Recognizing that it is awfully indignant, I considered putting the previous paragraph into a footnote, but I decided not to because the gendering of the professoriate is so telling an example of what gets put aside whenever gender is treated as a secondary category of analysis, as it is at present in rhetorical narrative theory. As I said at the outset, it seems to me today that the project of feminist and queer narrative theory could be completely compatible with the methodologies of rhetorical narrative theory. Of course I recognize that Phelan and Rabinowitz don't make this a priority (in the sense that they don't want to take gender on as a first principle, a priori, as they say), though both have been scrupulous about including the dynamics of gender, race, and sexuality in their analysis of texts where those categories stand out as "prominent."[6] In their social consciences and explicit politics, they are both feminists, without a doubt, but I would say their methodology and readings show that just as culture and academia are still segmented by gender, so are narrative theoretical methods. Much as I would love to have it happen, I don't expect to see what they call "that hybrid version of [their] actual selves . . . [the] version that readers come to know" come out as a feminist narrative theorist any time soon (p. 33).

Conversely, the reason I don't style myself a rhetorical narrative theorist is the same as the reason I doubt I can ever cross over into a cognitive or neuroscientific approach: that is, the presence of a normative or universalizing "we" in the critics' own writing.[7] Here I am not referring to the "we" in Phelan and Rabinowitz's text whose referent is the "hybrid self" whom the two theorists create in their combined writerly persona, as in "As our tone suggests, we greatly admire Twain's handling of the relationships" (p. 37) or "We will discuss what we regard as Twain's far less successful narration." I know from previous collaborations with Diane Price Herndl and with Helena Michie that there is pleasure in coming to the consensus represented by that particular usage of "we" and that the continual exchanging and revising of each other's drafted paragraphs yields a more rigorous and more readable product than I can produce by myself. When I am writing literary criticism alone, though, I use "we" very sparingly, and I try to be careful to specify the referent when I use the first-person plural: it might be "we feminist theorists," or "we narratologists," or "we susceptible readers," but I try to avoid saying "we readers" or using a universalizing "we" (or a universalizing "the reader") that implies what I am saying can speak for all persons who do not share my identity categories or political practices. Even the uses of the first-person plural pronoun I have just cited are problematic. If I speak for "feminist theorists," I can't be sure that what I am saying holds as true for feminists of color, queer feminists, feminists who write from positions of disability, and so forth, as it does for me and for those who have gendered experiences similar to my own. In their contribution to this volume, Phelan and Rabinowitz continually speak with well-warranted authority for "us rhetorical theorists." As their excellent, close-grained reading of *Huckleberry Finn* shows, however, they sometimes use a "we" whose referent is not "we rhetorical theorists," but rather "we, the members of the authorial audience." This presents a problem for feminist theory, because it suggests that the critic speaks from a position that is universally accessible to *any* careful reader of *Huckleberry Finn*. This "we" interpellates readers who can identify with Phelan and Rabinowitz's reading position, but it will marginalize actual readers whose identity categories incline them to come to *different* conclusions about the intentions of the text.

For example, consider the following passage from Phelan and Rabinowitz's section on Narrators:

> Thus, when Huck makes his decision to tear up that paper and—in a return to unreliability—evaluates his action most negatively, we feel our strongest sympathy and our greatest ethical approval of his actions. (p. 36)

Or this extract from their analysis of Progression and Plot:

> Among other things, this revelation means that we recognize the woeful inadequacy of Huck's judgment of his situation after the kidnapping when he says "it warn't long . . . till I was used to being where I was, and liked it, all but the cowhide part" (50). This recognition in turn influences our positive ethical judgment of Huck's later decision to fake his own murder. (p. 59)

These are strong statements. "We feel." "We recognize." "Our positive ethical judgment." Do all readers share those feelings? If they do not, are their feelings wrong? What if they are reading from subject positions that lead them to a different interpretation of the text's intentions?[8] The rhetorical narrative theorists would say that such readers have not made the imaginative leap necessary to becoming a part of the authorial audience. They also say they are pluralists, which is certainly true in that both Phelan and Rabinowitz are interested in and influenced by readings derived through other approaches to narrative. They might take a cue from Suzanne Keen, who suggests that "More self-consciousness about our own experiences of narrative empathy depends in part upon identifying where we stand as members of the diverse audiences reached by authors' empathetic representations" (223). Keen speaks here as a rhetorical narrative theorist influenced by neuroscientific approaches, not as an explicitly femininst narratologist; but her "we" is not normative because the pronoun here refers to a multiplicity of subject positions among the "diverse audiences." Ironically enough, Keen cites the earlier work of my friend Peter Rabinowitz as a model for how to take diverse audiences into account.[9] I would like to see the composite persona created by Phelan and Rabinowitz drop the "we" when speaking of the authorial audience that they have done so much to identify and define, and refer in the third person to "the authorial audience(s)" (what I in my own critical practice have called "the susceptible reader" or "the cooperative reader"), thus acknowledging through their own rhetoric that their take on the text's intentions, careful and logical as it is, is the product of an interpretive act inevitably colored by their own subject positions and cannot speak for the reading experience of everyone.

A FEMINIST NARRATIVE THEORIST RESPONDS TO DAVID HERMAN'S COGNITIVE APPROACH

Reading David Herman's account of cognitive narrative theory, I am lost in admiration. The theoretical sophistication and logical integrity of his approach are impeccable. The direct line of relevance between this work and the project of the original structuralist narratologists is both distinct and indisputable. His approach's integration of scientific and psychological research into the workings of cognition represents a profoundly interdisciplinary expertise, not to mention methodology. And the descriptive power of terms he elucidates here and elsewhere in his work—especially *storyworld,* which has permanently altered the way I teach the concept of diegesis—is invaluable. I understand why gender is not part of his analysis of the operations of the human brain—indeed, speaking as an anti-essentialist feminist, I am glad that cognitive narrative theory does not in any way emulate certain kinds of sociobiology by assigning gender to particular mental functions. However, cognitive theory is making a political decision when it avoids addressing gender difference, a decision that looks progressive when contrasted with essentialist models of gender but less so when the cultural history of gender oppression comes into the picture. David Herman's cognitive narrative theory eschews politics. The power dynamics among hierarchies of social categories such as race, class, gender, sexuality, or disability do not figure in his analysis. As a feminist, I must ask, "What is at stake in the cognitive approach to narrative? Whose interests does it serve?" Perhaps predictably, I find I can discern a politics in this rigorously apolitical method.

Read from a feminist perspective, *On Chesil Beach* is a novel about the persistent damage done to victims of sexual abuse and to those they love most intimately. Because it is a historical novel, *On Chesil Beach* underlines the pathos of people in Florence's generation who suffered from that damage in a moment of history just before a popular discourse of recovery from sexual abuse came into existence. Ian McEwan's text brilliantly manages the theme by keeping sexual abuse in the periphery of the actions that are narrated, thus mimicking the way memories of abuse hover at the edges of the survivor's consciousness, present to the mind only as a glimmer but powerful in their effect. As Herman usefully points out in his treatment of "frequency" in the section on Time, Plot, and Progression, the narrator of *On Chesil Beach* repeatedly brings up sailing trips that Florence took with her father during her childhood, "prompting construction of a storyline in which past sexual abuse by her father constitutes the reason for Florence's compensatory immersion in the world of music . . . and also for her actions on her wedding night (p. 73)." The abusive actions themselves are never named in McEwan's text, but the narrator alludes to them through descriptions of Florence's post-traumatic feelings in her father's presence on those and other occasions. Indeed, it would be possible for a careless reader to finish the novel without gathering that Florence has this history with her father. Writing in the twenty-first century and having access to the range of literary conventions available today within the genre of realist fiction, McEwan might have chosen to foreground the abuse, even to dramatize it as a series of directly rendered flashbacks in the novel. His choice to keep the clues of abuse out of the center of the novel's action has the powerful effect of keeping Florence's feelings and motives partially obscure, not just from Edward and herself but also from the interpreter of the text. The actual reader who picks up the clues of Florence's past comes to understand her better than Florence can understand herself and to comprehend the young couple's situation within a framework that is not accessible to either of them but fully present in the text, that is, the twenty-first century belief that the process of remembering and telling about trauma is the key to recovering from its effects.

Admitting that my previous paragraph proceeds from an explicitly feminist-narratological analysis of the novel's narrative structure, I was nevertheless surprised that Herman did not mention sexual abuse in his introduction's summary of the salient features of the novel's plot. I was even more surprised (though relieved at last), to find that he did not mention Florence's trauma until chapter 3 (p. 73) of his essay. While the novel's treatment of the abuse is indeed a perfect illustration of the point Herman is making on that page about narrative frequency, Herman's approach has the consequence of subordinating the fictional actions that a feminist narrative theorist would see as central to the novel's organizing principle. The way Herman finishes his introductory summary of the novel, too, seems to me to miss the point of the novel's ending, for the same reason. Herman says of the last few pages of the novel, "Most of this final section is refracted through the vantage point of Edward, who eventually comes to the realization that . . . 'all [Florence] had needed was the certainty of his love, and his reassurance that there was no hurry when a lifetime lay ahead of them' [202]" (p. 19). Herman's placing this quotation at the end of his summary (and returning to it in the final pages of his own contribution to this volume) gives it a degree of authority I do not believe is warranted by the text. Particularly interesting to me is Herman's characterization of Edward's thought as a "realization," implying that the conclusion Edward has come to is correct. I would argue that the novel knows Edward is wrong about this: the narrator's handling of the incidents of abuse suggests an awareness that childhood sexual trauma is not so easily overcome. Sweet though it may be, Edward's belief that all Florence needed was time and a good man's love to get over her revulsion is simply mistaken. The aftereffects of trauma are more insidious than that, the process of recovery much less dependent on the power of romantic or conjugal "love." In my reading, the novel does not condemn Edward for this still-naïve view of the mysteries of his bride's sexuality any more than it condemns either Edward or Florence for the badly misguided ideas about sex they play out on their wedding night. McEwan makes an interestingly gendered move by giving the final section wholly to Edward's point of view, but I don't think the absence of Florence's perspective here undoes the detailed construction of her subject position the novel has achieved up to this point. For a reader who focuses on the ways gendered subjectivity takes shape in a narrative text, part of the pleasure of reading *On Chesil Beach* is the excruciating awareness of the inexorable difference the novel establishes between the two protagonists' masculine and feminine subject positions, inexorable because of the moment they occupy in history. The novel achieves that awareness by giving equal time to Florence's and Edward's perspectives until the ending, where the swerve to Edward's point of view only underlines the irony of his present belief that he understands the past. I think that Herman's approach overlooks this irony and, in so doing, misses a crucial part of the novel's point.

I am conscious as I write this that the cognitive approach would advise more caution than I am exercising in assigning agency to the actions performed by a text such as *On Chesil Beach*. In the previous paragraphs I have ascribed actions and reasons to the narrator, the novelist, the text, and something I call "the novel," which I suppose is my working attempt at a substitute for the controversial term "implied author." I am intrigued by how intensely Herman is invested in getting rid of the implied author, and I am fascinated by his characterization of the communication model of narrative transmission as positively dangerous. He says, "There is a danger associated with reader constructs and frameworks based on them. . . . The danger is that of losing sight of the heuristic status of these models and hypostatizing the entities they encompass—of forgetting that reader constructs are ways of describing phases or aspects of the inferential activities that support worldmaking, not preconditions for understanding stories" (p. 152). I find this puzzling. What harm or injury is risked by thinking of reader constructs as preconditions for understanding stories? Again I am moved to ask, "What is at stake?" The problem Herman wishes to solve by banishing the implied author is clear: he is committed to assigning narrative actions, and therefore also the reasons that motivate them, to the author, thus obviating the need for the implied author. Carefully he counters the anti-intentionalist arguments of Wimsatt, Beardsley, and Booth, and logically he arrives at the conclusion that he can appropriately impute the reasons for telling to the author, by which I think he means the flesh-and-blood person, McEwan himself. He also rejects the extradiegetic narrator as the potential agent of narrative choices or actions, reasoning that a "non-personified, uncharacterized" narrator removes the need to "draw inferences concerning the teller's (in contradistinction to the author's) reasons for narrating events" (p. 48). I am persuaded by his refutation of arguments posed against intentionality within the Anglo-American critical tradition of the 1950s and 60s. But I want to know how the cognitive narrative theorist answers the poststructuralist characterization of "the author" as a product of discourse. After Bakhtin, Foucault, and Barthes, the idea of the author-as-person pales in the light shed by an awareness of any given text's place in the larger discursive system. And after Lacan, the author as unified subject with discernible reasons for actions becomes a chimerical figure, just another product of discourse. For this reason, the implied author (or what I pusillanimously call "the novel") is, I believe, a more appropriate object of analysis, because it is a discursive structure, not a person. I certainly appreciate Herman's faith in empiricism, for instance, his contention that the literary critic can look to "textual structures" to find "warrant for inferences" about the beliefs and attitudes that motivate particular narrative choices. In analyzing the moves of the implied author, that is exactly what I want to do. And yet I can't put aside my poststructuralist, feminist theoretical conviction that the object of Herman's analyses, the author, the person, McEwan himself, is an irreducible Other. So is my friend David Herman: No matter how adept I might become at Theory of Mind, I am not capable of deducing from his actions or utterances what his real intentions are in every case— can he be certain about mine? Or about Ian MacEwan's, either? Thanks to the workings of the unconscious, the sway of ideology, and the discursive constructedness of all subjective experience and of representation itself, not even I can know precisely why I make the choices I do, in storytelling or in any other activity.

The implication that the critic *can* know the Other is what puts the cognitive narrative approach in starkest contrast to the feminist approach. To be sure, the CAPA model is congruent with feminist narrative theory in its emphasis on the Context of narrative acts. Attempting to pin down the Actions performed by narrating, however, or to know with certainty the Person performing those actions, or especially to Ascribe intentions to the performer of narrative acts, reflects an assumption of critical authority that I would have to call immodest at best, oppressive at worst. The cognitive narrative theorist—however logical, empirical, and indeed brilliant he may be in drawing inferences—cannot know the reasons governing the actions of someone who occupies a completely different subject position from his own. In the belief that he can, I see a genuine danger: the danger of arrogating to himself the authority to account for the subjectivity of others, that is, of practicing a politics that is never made explicit in the approach itself. The universalism of the cognitive approach overlooks the differences born of identity positions. As long as persons occupying various identity positions continue to be in differential relations of power with one another, it is too early in the history of cultural theory to put those differences aside.

What I like best about Herman's approach, however, is his way of thinking about characters. In contrast with what I see as his personalization of the author, he depersonalizes characters in a way that holds them up for rigorous analysis as textual constructions.[10] Characters, for Herman, are collections of traits intersecting with plot. Building here on Seymour Chatman's conception, Herman is beautifully demonstrating how not to confuse the significance of fictitious persons with that of real ones. Commenting on the way Florence and Edward draw on emotionologies "to make sense of their own and others' conduct," Herman very usefully says that "the novel uses fictional individuals to explore, reflexively, the scope and nature of models of what a person is" (p. 131). I could not agree more. I would only add that gender and sexuality (not to mention race, class, nationality, etc.) are central enough to contemporary culture's assumptions about "what a person is" that our critical models ought to take them into account as primary categories of analysis. Not to do so is to serve the interests of dominant culture and its pernicious insistence that because identity differences *should* not matter, they *don't* matter. Unfortunately, they still do—part of the point of learning "what a person is" through studying texts is to bring that awareness to our interventions in the deployment of power in the extradiegetic world.

A FEMINIST NARRATIVE THEORIST RESPONDS TO BRIAN RICHARDSON'S ANTIMIMETIC NARRATIVE APPROACH

Contemporary narrative theorists of all stripes owe a big debt to Brian Richardson's immersion in postmodernist fiction. His approach—which he and others have called "unnatural" narratology to underline the way it builds upon and responds to the linguistically based "natural narratology" so influentially proposed by Monika Fludernik—takes seriously the need for bringing classical narratological insights together with the history of the material world. The formal features of texts that interest Richardson are always linked to the historical times and geographical spaces in which the texts are written and read. In this respect, his work parallels that of the contextually situated narrative theorists who focus in our analyses on gender, race, sexuality, or postcolonialism. What is "unnatural" about Richardson's work is not actually his narratology but rather the antimimetic texts he likes to write about. His analyses point to the many departures from the realist tradition that take place in contemporary novels, while the analyses also expand the narrative-theoretical lexicon to give names to these new developments in fiction. It is difficult to imagine reading a book like *Midnight's Children* without applying the insights Richardson has brought to novels of this kind, and it is impossible to achieve a thorough structural or stylistic analysis of Rushdie's works that would not use what Richardson has added to narrative theory. Richardson has taught us how to read what he calls in his contribution to this volume the "playful and outrageous kinds of texts" of literary postmodernity (p. 25).

I admire the breadth of a perspective on literature that allows Richardson to make declarations like his claim that the biggest difference between fiction and reality is death. Whereas in fiction "characters can plead with their authors to spare their lives, temporality can be run backwards so the dead come back to life, or a figure can die several times . . . and miraculously appear alive again in the next chapter," Richardson observes that in life "there is only one death, and it is irreversible" (p. 23). I also admire the ethical commitment that inspires Richardson's statement of the difference between "altering the historical record in a work of fiction and falsifying historical facts in nonfictional discourse." The former, according to Richardson, "is a serious kind of play, the latter a sordid lie" (p. 23). Part of what makes this tendency toward aphorism in Richardson's prose so striking is its adherence to a set of binary categories: fiction versus life, deathlessness versus mortality, playing versus lying, seriousness versus contemptibleness, fictional works versus nonfictional discourse. That he is comfortable navigating such territory suggests that Richardson is no poststructuralist, committed though he is to comprehending the products of postmodernism. I know from my own structuralist-influenced work on narrative that this binary habit of thought comes in handy when you are working on taxonomies of narrative structure, and Richardson has used it to advantage. However, in addition to raising specific questions about identity positioning, the responsibility of the feminist critic is to question binarisms whenever they crop up, and so, before discussing the role of gender in the structure of Rushdie's novel, I will engage Richardson's excellent discussion on one point of distinction where I think he draws the lines too brightly.

That distinction is the starting point for Richardson's argument: the difference between mimetic and antimimetic narrative texts. Everything that he has to say about antimimetic narrative gestures rings true to me, and every example he musters to illustrate his taxonomies of postmodernist narrative is persuasive. (His section on Story, Time, and Progression is typical of the comprehensiveness of his corpus, containing impressive and useful catalogues of recent novels from all over the world which play with variations on narrative conventions.) I question, though, the lines he is drawing between narrative in the realist tradition and narrative that departs from the conventions of realism. For Richardson, realism is mimetic and postmodernism is antimimetic. In a general way this is certainly true, but some of the examples Richardson mentions inspire me to question the firmness of the distinction. For instance, Richardson claims *Tristram Shandy* as a forebear of antimimetic fiction because of its many transgressions of narrative level and temporality, including those that link it directly to *Midnight's Children,* such as the narrator's complaints about the difficulty of getting to the scene of his own birth before he meets his death. Such ruptures of the narrative fabric are metalepses, and Richardson rightly points out that they violate the realist contract, the traditional readerly expectation that the novel will not betray any awareness of the fictitiousness of its storyworld. As Richardson puts it, "Mimetic narratives typically try to conceal their constructedness and appear to resemble nonfictional narratives, while postmodern narratives flaunt their artificiality and break the ontological boundaries that mimetic works so carefully preserve" (p. 20).

Well, yes and no. I have always thought of Tristram's antics as a kind of hyper-verisimilitude, a constant reminder that the way time progresses in fiction, for instance, is purely conventional and that paying attention to the time that it would actually take to put the words on the page is a way to remember what is *really* real, that is, that someone has written the text. Robbe Grillet, Richardson's other canonical example of an antimimetic novelist, claims he "do[es] not transcribe" but "constructs," but I have often wondered how Robbe Grillet differs in that practice from a canonical realist like Henry James. Robbe Grillet's novels can be read as exercises in focalization through a non-normative consciousness, constructing a world as it might look if you were viewing it from the subject position of someone with an extreme cognitive or emotional disability. How different is that, really, from constructing the world that "Maisie knew"? It is a difference in degree of disability (a non-normative person's as opposed to an ordinary child's), but not necessarily in kind of narrative construction.

Richardson mentions James's annoyance at those moments in Trollope's fictions where the narrator draws attention to his authorial power over the fates of the characters, thus committing a "serious crime," as James has it, against the mimetic effect. But if Trollope is not an example of the typical practices of the realist tradition, then who is? Charlotte Brontë, maybe, but then we would have to overlook the antimimetic effect of Lucy Snowe's explicit refusal to bring *Villette* to narrative closure, not to mention those many metaleptic passages of *Jane Eyre* directly addressed to her Reader; or maybe George Eliot, but then we must ignore the profound effect of the seventeenth chapter of *Adam Bede,* "in which the story pauses" while the narrator discusses the parallels between her novelistic project and the paintings of the Dutch Masters; or maybe Dickens, but then what about the unsettling effect of the constant switching between first- and third-person narrators and past- and present-tense narration in *Bleak House*?; or maybe Thackeray, but then there are those pesky references to his characters as puppets in *Vanity Fair.* In other words, realist novels have been indulging in antimimetic practices for as long as realist novels have been written. Sometimes they do it just for play, but sometimes they do it for a more serious purpose ironically modeled on *Tristram Shandy*'s hyper-verisimilitude. For realist novelists such as Harriet Beecher Stowe or Elizabeth Gaskell who earnestly wish to change the world, the metaleptic effect can bring the implied reader back to an awareness of the "really real," the extradiegetic world where the novelist writes and where actions like those being represented in the fiction cry out for real-world action. To be sure, Richardson is fully aware of the potentially subversive politics of Rushdie's antimimetic narration. As a feminist critic interested in the history of fiction's interaction with the material world, I see these antimimetic gestures more as a continuity from realist to postmodernist narrative than as a break between them. Without question, Rushdie presents an extreme example of antimimetic practice, though, just as Richardson argues.

Turning to gender, I find I am much more tuned in to the figure of Padma than Richardson appears to be. For him, Padma is simply the woman to whom the narrator "reads his written texts aloud" and notes her comments (p. 157). Richardson does not discuss her technical function as narratee. A lower-caste woman who does the cooking and housework while Saleem writes, who shares his bed despite his claim of impotence, and who frequently comments on both the style and the substance of Saleem's story, "our Padma" is a continuous presence in the narrative discourse. The frequent epithet of "our" is a gesture of condescension or patronage, typically used in casual British English to refer to a young brother or sister, or to a servant of the house. If Padma is not literally a servant, her illiteracy and her household tasks mark her as Saleem's social inferior, and yet her emphatic criticisms often shape or even distort the way he tells the story, especially the pacing. Like a narratee in an extradiegetically narrated realist novel, Padma is sometimes referred to in the third person but more often in second-person direct address, a practice that heightens the antimimeticism of the text. (Where is Padma supposed to be when Saleem is commenting on her in the third person, if she is present when he speaks directly to her?) Saleem's reports of Padma's nodding, fidgeting, and expostulating while he reads are constant reminders that his selection of details at least partly reflects what this inferior figure already knows and what she desires to know, as well as his own desires variously to gratify or to thwart her. The narratee is thus a gendered and classed filter standing between Saleem and the implied reader, and the actual reader's interpretation and evaluation of the story will vary according to his or her potential to share the attitudes associated with the social and cultural positions Padma occupies. Her announcement at the novel's end that she and Saleem will marry is a parody of the realist convention that requires marriage for the protagonist to achieve comic closure, but in its extreme irony it also serves as the only kind of closure an antimimetic text like *Midnight's Children* could provide.

That Rushdie would choose such a woman to be Saleem's narratee is interesting; that he would name her "Padma" is fascinating to the consumer of twenty-first-century popular culture, although it is admittedly a detail utterly irrelevant to narratology per se. Thinking about how gender affects the reception as well as the production of texts, feminist criticism often takes into account as many intertexts as possible, even when to do so is to commit an anachronism. Nearly a quarter of a century after writing *Midnight's Children*, Salman Rushdie married Padma Lakshmi, a model and cookbook author who rose to B-list celebrity status in the late 2000s as host of the reality television competition series, *Top Chef.* They divorced just three years later, but for now their names are still closely linked in Google searches and in the popular memory—and hence in the minds of readers of *Midnight's Children* who are tuned in to this intertext. This Padma presents a strong contrast to "our Padma": gorgeous, tall, classy, and accomplished, she self-presents as a hyper-sexy woman of steel, like a character in an action movie being played by Angelina Jolie. Her out-of-wedlock pregnancy in the 2009–10 season only intensified her image as a postfeminist icon, the woman who can have and do it all, all by herself. One of the things that makes Lakshmi interesting to a feminist theorist is her famous scar, a pronounced seven-inch vertical gash along the front of her upper arm, the result of a car accident in her teens. The other is her history of being the first Indian fashion model to have an international career. In 2001 she told *Vogue* magazine that at first her scar was a serious impediment to getting jobs, but a life-transforming photo shoot with Helmut Newton (and a newly developed cultural taste for bodies marred by tattoos and piercings) turned it into a trademark. Now she favors dresses and tops that bare her shoulders and arms, and she poses—as she often did as a couple with Rushdie—with her scarred arm turned to the camera. On *Top Chef* she comes across as a super-feminine dominatrix, always polite but subordinate to no one (not even to Tom Colicchio, her aggressively authoritative co-host), but ironically the thing she does best is the same thing that "our Padma" does: cooking. Like Saleem's Padma, Padma Lakshmi has a body marked by race, sexuality, sex, and gender, and furthermore, this Padma is marked by the angry-looking flaw in the beautiful skin of her upper arm. But Lakshmi's glamour and personal power are not compromised by her scar, nor can they be by her race and gender. Seeing her pictured with Rushdie, I get the sense that in the end she must have left him in the dust; "our Padma" completes her story with a marriage, but this Padma's story continues, as her degree of personal celebrity continually rises postdivorce. Lakshmi hovers in the back of my mind as I read Rushdie's novel, and the contrast she presents to Saleem's Padma places the latter at an even greater disadvantage with respect to the role she plays in the narrative transaction. Rushdie could not possibly have anticipated this development while writing *Midnight's Children* (if he could have, perhaps he would not have Saleem hammer so insistently on the derivation of the name "Padma," which he paraphrases as "dung lotus"), but the connection nevertheless signifies for the feminist reader. I would predict that my friend Brian Richardson, as a feminist reader himself, would find this connection intriguing. His antimimetic approach would not be likely, though, to discover it or to bring it to bear on his reading of Rushdie's text.

NOTES

1. Ruth Page does this with reference to linguistics, building on the work of Debra Tannen and others.

2. See Lanser ("Toward a Feminist Narratology") and Warhol (*Gendered Interventions*). Alison Case followed the example of *Gendered Interventions* to look at gender-crossing among narrators of Victorian novels. Women scholars doing gender-blind work in narrative theory in the 1980s included Cohn, Banfield, and Lanser herself in her first book (*Fictions of Authority*). Diengott declared that feminism and narratology were antithetical methodologies that could not (and should not) be synthesized.

3. The women whose contributions to narrative theory made it onto that syllabus in the spring of 2010 are (in alphabetical order): Kathryn Abrams, Paula Gunn Allen, Rita Charon, Hillary Chute, Amy Coplan,, Mieke Bal, Hélène Cixous, Dorrit Cohn, Melba Cuddy-Keane, Ellen Dissanayake, Monika Fludernik, Susan Stanford Friedman, Carolyn Grose, Emma Kafalenos, Suzanne Keen, Susan Sniader Lanser, Laura Mulvey, Beth Newman, Martha Nussbaum, Ruth Page, Judith Roof, Marie-Laure Ryan, Dan Shen, Ellen Spolsky, Michelle Scalise Sugiyama, Katharine Young, Lisa Zunshine, and myself. This leaves out important past and present work by Nancy Armstrong, Alison Booth, Hilary Dannenberg, Helen Davis, Rachel Blau duPlessis, Amy Elias, Judith Fetterley, Susan Fraiman, Joanne Frye, Catherine Gallagher, Jane Gallop, Laura Green, Diane Price Herndl, Marianne Hirsch, Molly Hite, Margaret Homans, Barbara Johnson, Irene Kacandes, Elizabeth Langland, Deidre Lynch, Kathy Mezei, Sharon Marcus, Helena Michie, Nancy Miller, Mary Anne O'Farrell, Ellen Peel, Sally Robinson, Valerie Rohy, Hilary Schor, Naomi Schor, Eve Sedgwick, Linda Shires, Amy Shuman, Sidonie Smith, Hortense Spillers, Rebecca Stern, Susan Suleiman, Julia Watson, Susan Winnett, Kay Young, and many others whose research continues to develop the project of gender- and sexuality-inflected narrative theory.

4. See Alpert. The projected date is based on the rate of increase of female full professors between 1975 and 1988. I wish I could find statistics indicating that the rate has sped up since then, but anecdotal evidence suggests that it has not.

5. See Woolf, *A Room of One's Own* (73).

6. For examples of admirable rhetorical treatments of novels foregrounding race, gender, and sexuality, see Rabinowitz ("'Betraying the Sender'") and the section on Sandra Cisneros's "Barbie-Q" in the introductory chapter to Phelan's *Living to Tell about It,* especially pages 6–12.

7. Rather than using "we" to refer to readers as cognitive narrative theorists have often done, Herman in his most recent work has more scrupulously referred in the third person to "interpreters."

8. Keen ("A Theory of Narrative Empathy," 2006), who sees "narrative empathy as rhetorical," distinguishes among strategic uses of it that are "bounded" (addressed to an in-group), "ambassadorial" (addressed to an audience of "chosen others with the aim of cultivating their empathy for the in-group"), and "broadcast" (calling on every reader to empathize, by stressing universality in "our common vulnerabilities and hopes") (223). In their identification of moments of empathy in Twain's text, Phelan and Rabinowitz are concentrating on "broadcast" strategies but are not taking into account the possibility of "empathic inaccuracy" that attention to the other two categories would allow.

9. In addition to Rabinowitz's *Before Reading* and his essay "Betraying the Sender," Brian Richardson's "Singular Text, Multiple Implied Readers" serves as a model for acknowledging the multiplicity of reading positions implicit in narrative texts.

10. Alan Palmer, who refers to "the effect of characters' mental functioning" as something created by text (325), summarizes the cognitive approach to literary character in a manner different from, but compatible with, Herman's formulation: "A character's name is a space or a vacuum into which readers feel compelled to pour meaning: characteristics, dispositions, states of mind, causations" (329) This resistance to treating characters as people is congruent with poststructuralist feminist narrative methods.

RESPONSE
by David Herman

> So when an institution . . . is the bearer of a tradition of practice or practices, its common life will be partly, but in a centrally important way, constituted by a continuous argument as to what [that institution] is and ought to be. . . . Traditions, when vital, embody continuities of conflict.
> —Alasdair MacIntyre, *After Virtue* 222

Let me begin by expressing my gratitude to all of my co-authors, from whom I have learned so much—not only through their insightful, field-extending contributions to this volume but also through the example they have set, and continue to set, as pioneers and innovators in the domain of narrative studies. Robyn Warhol's emphasis on keeping issues of gender (and other "politically significant and historically grounded differences" [p. 11]) front and center in narrative research, Brian Richardson's ongoing efforts to come to terms with the amazing formal and imaginative possibilities of experimental literary fictions, and Jim Phelan and Peter Rabinowitz's productive insistence on viewing narrative as a communicative or rhetorical transaction rather than an object or artifact—all of this work is foundational for contemporary scholarship on stories and storytelling. It is thus a privilege to be able to participate in a dialogue with this accomplished group of scholars, who have worked tirelessly to promote research and teaching in the field and to help make it an increasingly active (and exciting!) area of inquiry.

Indeed, taking my cue from the quotation by MacIntyre that I have used as an epigraph for this response, I view it as a sign of the vitality of narrative theory that we have now reached a stage where open, vigorous debate about the methods and aims of scholarship on stories has become not only possible but necessary—that is, a basic or constitutive part of research activity in the field. From this perspective, the contrasts among the approaches assembled in the present volume suggest that the domain of narrative inquiry is entering an optimal stage of disciplinary development. If incipient areas of study are too inchoate to be bearers "of a tradition of practice or practices," a larger tradition that at once informs and is informed by current research; and if moribund disciplines are those in which current practices are only the echo of past achievements, with prior research dictating what sorts of questions can be asked and how they can be answered; by contrast, disciplines that are coming into their own are marked by productive "continuities of conflict" in which practitioners are more or less visibly engaged, even when framing statements about particular, localized research questions. Accordingly, in writing the present response, I have set myself the goal of highlighting not the commonalities but the differences among my own and my co-authors' perspectives.[1] Without substantial areas of agreement among practitioners, of course, there would be no coherent, identifiable field of study, and the organization of our volume around a shared list of topics confirms that problems of narration, character, the reader, and so on, constitute central concerns for scholars of story. But as the contrasts among our contributions also suggest, narrative theory has now evolved into a bona fide scholarly tradition—one that not only accommodates but also thrives on different assessments of what should count as best practices within the tradition and how those practices ought to be developed going forward.

In the remainder of my response, in dialogue with my co-authors' contributions, I set out three basic assumptions undergirding the approach to the mind–narrative nexus that I have sketched in the previous chapters. I frame each of these three assumptions by contrasting them with what I see as key assumptions subtending my co-authors' accounts—respectively, Warhol's assumption that an approach that foregrounds issues of narrative and mind is unable to address matters of culture and context; Richardson's assumption that a sharp line separates "mimetic" and "antimimetic" narratives, and that different frameworks for inquiry are required for the narratives falling on either side of this putative divide; and Phelan and Rabinowitz's assumption that the narrative communication diagram is the best way to characterize narrative as a transaction or exchange between authors and readers.[2] In explaining why I disagree with each of these assumptions, I also seek to clarify the different premises that underlie my own approach. Because of space limitations I will not be able to engage in detail with my co-authors' readings of their focal narratives; rather, I will target what I take to be founding assumptions on which their interpretations rest. By contrasting these assumptions with the ones informing my own focus on issues of worldmaking, and thus working toward a vantage point from which the grammar of narrative inquiry can be surveyed anew (in the Wittgensteinian sense), I continue to develop the analogy between metanarratology and metaphilosophy that I described in the introduction to this book.

PARADIGMS IN DISPUTE
CONTRASTING ASSUMPTIONS FOR NARRATIVE THEORY

> *Assumption 1:* An approach that foregrounds issues of narrative and mind is not tantamount to an internalist focus on representational processes or contents in the human brain, and it need not exclude considerations of cultural difference, material embodiment, emotional engagement, or any other aspect of the larger social and physical contexts in which people produce and interpret stories. Instead, according to the research in which I seek to ground my approach, the mind is by definition embodied and emerges from the interplay between intelligent agents and the sociocultural as well as material environments those agents seek to negotiate. In short, minds are always embedded in broader contexts for action and interaction.

In her contribution to our introductory chapter, Robyn Warhol writes that "[o]f the contemporary approaches current in narrative theory, cognitive narratology of the kind that David Herman practices is the least closely linked to feminist narrative theory, because the study of processes in the human brain necessarily privileges similarities among people over differences. . . . feminist narrative theorists are not yet willing to make the jump from the culturally constructed to the universal, which seems to resonate with . . . essentialism" (p. 11). But an approach to narrative and mind need not—and, arguably, must not—focus solely on processes internal to the brain. I say "must not" because important strands of work in the philosophy of mind, robotics, psychology, and other fields underscore that the mind, though inextricably linked with brain physiology, is not reducible to it. This work stems from early research by Vygotsky and Gibson and is now being elaborated in different ways by theorists developing ecological, externalist, and enactive approaches to cognition (A. Clark; Noë, *Action* and *Out of our Heads*). Despite important contrasts among their methods and emphases, these approaches converge on a picture of the mind as fundamentally decentralized and distributed, cutting across brain, body, and world. Such research provides warrant for the claim that although human beings share basic sensorimotor capacities because of which their social and material environments present a comparable range of affordances, or opportunities for action, there will be variation in how any one person or group exploits those affordances in a given case—for reasons that narrative theory itself can help bring to light.

From a post-Cartesian perspective of the sort just described, there is no contradiction between assuming the existence of shared capacities for negotiating experience, on the one hand, and assuming that those capacities will manifest themselves differently in different cultural contexts and physical environments, on the other hand. Humans do have species-distinctive mental capacities and dispositions. That said, however, their opportunities for action—the worldly affordances that help constitute their perceptual and conceptual horizon (Gibson; Noë, *Action*)—will be inflected by gender-based preconceptions and stereotypes, among other normative frameworks specifying what it is possible or appropriate to do in what range of contexts (see chapter 7). Further, in ways that are relevant for feminist narratologists concerned with the material bodies of story producers and story interpreters, the research in which I ground my approach suggests how mind-constituting affordances are rooted in nature as well as in culture. Just as different animals experience the world differently, because of differences of organismic structure, among human beings differences of sex and age, as well as the different modes of embodiment that have been socially constructed as forms of (dis)ability, impinge on the structure and quality of experience—and also on the particular strategies individuals, communities, and cultures use when it comes to engaging with their larger environments.

Indeed, in my contributions to this volume, I have opted not to use terms such as "cognitive approaches to narrative" and "cognitive narratology," precisely because I wished to avoid any conflation of the term "cognitive" with what some scholars of mind have characterized as "cognitivism," or the view that the mind can be reduced to disembodied mental representations that are disattached from particular environments for acting and interacting. As Varela, Thompson, and Rosch put it in their influential critique, "cognitivism consists in the hypothesis that cognition . . . is the manipulation of symbols after the fashion of digital computers. . . . the mind is thought to operate by manipulating symbols that represent features of the world or represent the world as being a certain way" (8). Proposing an alternative approach, Varela, Thompson, and Rosch use the terms "enactive" (and "enactivism") to suggest that "cognition is not the representation of a pregiven world by a pregiven mind but is rather the enactment of a world and a mind on the basis of a history of the variety of actions that a being in the world performs" (9). Likewise, a focus on the way the mind works with and through stories need not entail a cognitivist separation between mental representations and the social and material environments that help shape—indeed, partly constitute—the mind.

My approach thus stresses the need to study not detached, disembodied representational contents but rather minds-in-context; the key issue is how worlds are made and remade thanks to the way a culture's or subculture's storytelling practices are geared on to humans' always-situated mental capacities and dispositions. In other words, I assume that methods of narrative worldmaking are always anchored in specific communicative contexts and are used (like other tools, whether physical, cultural, or psychological) to come to terms with specific social as well as material contingencies. In chapter 2, I argue that acts of narration can be parsed as such because of how they are embedded in larger contexts for (inter)action, which enable storytellers' acts to be glossed in terms of reasons for acting. In chapters 3 and 4, I ground processes of narrative worldmaking in modes of temporal and spatial embodiment, and chapter 5's focus on emotion discourse, along with its exploration of the interplay between what I call "model persons" and "models of persons," is meant to highlight the advantages of an approach to the mind–narrative nexus that remains situated at the level of *persons* and *person–environment interactions*.[3] Chapter 5, like my approach as a whole, thus disputes reductionist programs for research alluded to by Warhol in the remark I quoted above—programs based on the assumption that the concept of person, and person-level phenomena, must yield to some other, more fundamental level of explanation, such as neuronal activity in the brain, information-processing mechanisms, or other causal factors operating at a subpersonal level. I hold, instead, that it is at the personal rather than subpersonal level that narrative scholars are optimally positioned to contribute to—and not just borrow from—frameworks for understanding the mind. Finally, my contributions to chapters 6 and 7 engage directly with the issues of culture and context that surface in the study of narrative worldmaking as a collaborative, norm-governed practice. Any approach to narrative inquiry that takes seriously post-Cartesian accounts of the mind as embodied, situated, and extended must also come to terms with how storytelling practices at once shape and are shaped by culturally embedded norms, including norms associated with master narratives bearing on gender.

> *Assumption 2:* Disputing the existence of any sharp divide or dichotomy between "mimetic" and "antimimetic" narratives, I assume that the approach outlined in my contributions is extensible to narratives of all sorts. In other words, the approach is not limited to or affiliated with any

particular narrative genre or subgenre, whether it be the realist novel or experimental fiction. My focus is on basic mental dispositions and abilities bound up with—both supporting and supported by—storytelling practices of all sorts.

I admire not only Brian Richardson's illuminating analyses of *Midnight's Children* but also his wide-ranging discussion of many other innovative fictional texts. At the same time, I disagree with what I take to be one of the central assumptions of Richardson's approach: namely, that the study of what Richardson terms antimimetic narratives requires a different analytic framework than the study of what he calls mimetic narratives. More than this, I remain uncertain about what exactly constitutes an antimimetic narrative, because I feel that Richardson's account simultaneously hyperextends the text-type category of "narrative" and downplays the complexity of mimesis itself. Further, I believe that Richardson conflates several non-equivalent rubrics or categories, including "natural," "ordinary," "conventional," "representational," "mimetic," and "realistic," in a way that obscures the scope of his argument. By contrast, an approach that focuses on the mind-narrative nexus by exploring how storyworlds are made and remade can capture differences among narrative genres and subgenres but without assuming a dichotomous opposition between kinds of stories. Such an approach can also avoid becoming entangled in the network of binary distinctions (e.g., natural/unnatural, conventional/nonconventional, representational/nonrepresentational) introduced in Richardson's account—distinctions that do not bear closer scrutiny individually and that also fail to hang together coherently as a group.

In the first place, some of the techniques used in the texts that Richardson discusses strike me as being not antimimetic but rather antinarrative—that is, purposely designed to thwart the worldmaking process.[4] This difference is a crucial one because it entails different assumptions about the nature of narrative and about the best way to study it. For example, the passages from Beckett's *Worstward Ho* and from Borges' "The Aleph" that Richardson quotes in chapter 4 (p. 105) seem to me designed not just to inhibit but to derail attempts to build a storyworld, which, however, the passages also paradoxically invite. By blocking efforts to configure into a world the WHEN, WHAT, and WHERE dimensions of the spatiotemporal domains that they evoke, these texts reflexively explore the (fuzzy) border between two different text-types: namely, "narrative" and "list" (or "description") (see Herman, *Basic Elements* 75–105). The border in question is that between texts providing prompts for co-constructing a storyworld and texts engaging in a non- or antinarrative listing of locales that do not add up to a world. But the magical realist features of the Rushdie passage that Richardson cites immediately after the Borges text (pp. 105–6), are of a different sort. Rather than undermining attempts to connect objects, places, and time-frames into a storyworld, these features invite readers to recenter themselves in a fictional world that is governed by different physical laws (and that therefore accommodates different possibilities) than the world of everyday experience.

To extrapolate: my approach assumes that narratives can more or less reflexively call attention to the methods of worldmaking on which they themselves rely, breaking frame to comment on the world-building procedures that they activate. But I also assume that a text drops out of the domain of narrative if, during the process of interpretation, certain key questions lose their point—questions about the manner in which the WHEN, WHAT, WHERE, WHO, HOW, and WHY dimensions can be configured into a storyworld. Hence, unlike Richardson's, my approach assumes that a continuum or scale connects narratives that he instead arranges dichotomously, into discrete categories. The increments of the scale at issue correspond to different degrees of reflexivity about the world-building procedures that a given text cues readers to set into play. Narratives that are relatively more reflexive about procedures of world construction, like Rushdie's or (parts of) McEwan's, can be distinguished both from narratives that, like Twain's and Austen's, are relatively less reflexive about world-creation and also from texts that, like Beckett's and Borges', bracket the actual building of a world in order to foreground the complexity or impossibility of the construction process itself.[5] Thus, whereas Richardson opposes mimetic and antimimetic narratives, my approach assumes that a continuum spans texts that engage in more or less reflexive modes of narration, and that past a critical threshold for narrativity this continuum then shades off into non- or antinarrative texts.

My second objection to Richardson's approach is that in setting up an opposition between mimetic and antimimetic narratives, he also downplays the complexity of mimesis itself.[6] I understand what is traditionally called a mimetic representation to be one that is based on or mediated by a *model* of the world of everyday experience. Or rather, mimetic representations rely on a constellation of models, some of them deriving from narratives and other texts. Since it is impossible to gain wholly direct, unmediated access to the world of experience without deploying models deriving from other texts and from prior encounters with the world, no narrative could even in principle "reproduce a pre-existing reality"—to cite the phrase that, as Richardson notes in chapter 1 (p. 22), Robbe-Grillet used to repudiate prior novelistic practices. Indeed, since what has gone by the name of mimesis can be reconceived as a particular strategy for deploying world-models, a strategy that differs in degree but not in kind from the more reflexive use of world-models in the experimental texts on which Richardson focuses, in my own approach I choose not to use the term *mimesis* or its cognates or antonyms—for example, in my account of the interplay between model persons and models of persons in chapter 5. Nor do I appeal to the mimetic-synthetic-thematic triad. Used by Richardson in his own treatment of character in chapter 5 (pp. 132–35, 37) and by Phelan and Rabinowitz in a more general way throughout their contributions, this triad in my view problematically draws sharp lines between domains that are overlapping and interlinked.[7]

I turn finally to a third, related objection to Richardson's approach—namely, the way it relies on a network of binary distinctions that are fraught when taken individually and that furthermore are not brought into a coherent relationship with one another over the course of Richardson's account. I have already voiced my concerns about an approach premised on a dichotomized or binarized distinction between what Richardson calls mimetic and antimimetic narratives, and I have similar concerns about other binary pairs that Richardson affiliates with the mimetic/antimimetic dichotomy, including the natural/unnatural, realist/antirealist, and conventional/anticonventional distinctions. For example, as it is used in Richardson's account, the natural/unnatural binary effectively empties out the complexity and diversity of stories told in contexts of face-to-face interaction. By equating everyday storytelling with conventional narration,[8] in the narrow sense of telling stories with predictable plotlines, clichéd endings, and so forth, Richardson voids face-to-face storytelling of the rich, multidimensional structure so brilliantly analyzed by Elinor Ochs and Lisa Capps, among others. More generally, I dispute the implied equivalence between the left- and right-hand terms across this series of binary distinctions. Thus, everyday storytelling, besides being the site of remarkable artfulness and verbal creativity, regularly involves tales about supernatural events and other physical impossibilities; so there is no more warrant for equating such narration with the mimetic (as Richardson uses that term) than there is for equating it with the conventional.

These conceptual difficulties can be avoided if instead of positing a sharp division between kinds of narrative in the way that Richardson does, one situates storytelling practices on a continuum and works to identify principles for worldmaking that are instantiated differently by the narrative practices located at different places along that continuum. And as I see it, identifying the principles in question requires an exploration of the nexus of narrative and mind.

> *Assumption 3:* The narrative communication diagram, despite its wide-spread use in the field, is not the only (and I would argue not the optimal) way to explore how narrative worlds are made, why, and with what consequences and effects. It is thus time to take a critical look at this heuristic model by exploring its genealogy and in particular the way it has been shaped, from the start, by anti-intentionalist arguments. The alternative heuristic framework that I propose, the CAPA model, can do everything the narrative communication diagram can do but with greater parsimony—and in a way that avoids questionable presuppositions and entailments associated with the standard diagram.

I agree with Jim Phelan and Peter Rabinowitz's assumption that narrative can be productively studied as a form of purposeful communicative action, that is, as a transaction or exchange between authors and readers. As my contributions to Part One suggest, though, I have concerns about the history, current use, and larger implications of the narrative communication diagram on which Phelan and Rabinowitz rely to characterize narrative in these terms. As I have argued in this volume, a focus on the mind-narrative nexus entails exploring not only how narrative worlds are made but also what motivates, and results from, their making. But this same focus on narrative and mind calls into question previous heuristic constructs, including the communication diagram, that have been used to study narrative worldmaking under its profile as an exchange, transaction, or (as it might also be put) collaborative practice. In critiquing Phelan and Rabinowitz's use of the diagram, I will concentrate on how they deploy the constructs of the implied author and the implied reader, keeping in mind that Phelan and Rabinowitz subdivide the second of these constructs into what they call the authorial audience and the narrative audience.

As discussed in chapter 2, Booth's idea of the implied author emerged as a response to the anti-intentionalist position that Wimsatt and Beardsley had staked out in "The Intentional Fallacy." I suggest, by contrast, that such anti-intentionalist claims should instead be attacked at their root. The claims can be countered by showing how they are at odds with relevant research in fields including philosophy of mind, comparative ethology, and the study of language acquisition, among others; this research indicates that ascribing *reasons for acting,* which take the shape of clusters of propositional and motivational attitudes such as belief and intention, is a core feature of human *reasoning about actions,* including communicative actions such as storytelling. In turn, by refusing to concede that reading for authorial intentions counts as an instance of the genetic fallacy, one no longer needs to appeal to the implied author as a narratological workaround—as a way of not committing the intentional fallacy while still accommodating humans' proclivity to interpret texts as resulting from communicative actions that, like all other actions, are inferred to have been performed for particular reasons.

Along these lines, I am not persuaded by Phelan and Rabinowitz's justifications, in their section "Authors" in chapter 2 (pp. 29–33), for using the idea of the implied author. In the previous paragraph as well as in chapter 2, I have proposed alternative ways of addressing the issues that Phelan and Rabinowitz mention in their second, third, and fourth justifications, which concern authorial intentions and the identity relations between story creators and the stories they create. Likewise, in response to Phelan and Rabinowitz's first justification, which is actually a version of their third, one can acknowledge that narration involves self-presentation without interposing the implied author, as a kind of intermediary agent, between the producer of the story and the story he or she produces. Positing such an agent amounts to reifying what I would instead characterize as an attitudinal stance that an interpreter defeasibly Ascribes to one or more storytelling Persons—on the basis of narrational Actions performed in particular Contexts of telling.

As my use of capitalization here suggests, in disputing Phelan and Rabinowitz's account, I am drawing on the CAPA (Context, Action, Person, Ascription) model that I mentioned in chapter 2. In proposing this model as an alternative to the narrative communication diagram, my working assumption is that all social intercourse—and *ipso facto* all communicative interaction—can be analyzed in the terms the model affords. Further, I suggest that CAPA avoids problems to which both anti-intentionalist accounts and Phelan and Rabinowitz's approach are subject. The advantages of CAPA include the following:

(a) It assumes that ascriptions of communicative intentions to story creators, far from being extraneous to the process of narrative interpretation, are rooted in the fundamentals of becoming a person who is capable of recognizing others as such. Here I allude to ideas discussed in chapter 5—more specifically, the work by P. F. Strawson and others suggesting that insofar as I treat observed behavior as the conduct of a person (or as the result of such conduct), I will make sense of what's going on in terms of the mental as well as material predicates that I ascribe to the person engaged in that conduct.

(b) It accounts for the phenomena also targeted by the narrative communication diagram but does so with a reduced roster of explanatory

entities, and in particular without relying on the ideas of the implied
author or the implied reader.

(c) It offers a more unified picture of processes of narrative interpretation
and everyday reasoning practices, as well as a single framework for
studying the action of producing a narrative world, on the one hand,
and the nonverbal as well as verbal actions of characters *within* narrative worlds, on the other hand.

(d) It keeps constantly in view how inferences concerning story creators'
intentions—inferences about the reasons underlying local textual
choices as well as more global representational purposes—arise from
defeasible, context-bound, ascriptional practices. By contrast, models positing an implied author and an implied reader deflect attention
away from how these and related constructs, rather than functioning
as external, quasi-autonomous constraints on what kinds of inferences
can be drawn from what sorts of textual cues and patterns, themselves
emerge from processes of narrative interpretation.

To continue highlighting differences between my own CAPA-informed
approach and Phelan and Rabinowitz's approach, I will hone in on issues
connected with items (b) and (d) in the preceding list. My overall claim is
that the approach to narrative worldmaking that I have outlined in previous
chapters, and that seeks to bridge narrative scholarship and research on the
mind, in part via the CAPA model, allows for the study of narrative as a transactional process (or practice) but in a way that avoids problems associated
with the narrative communication diagram.

(b) Reducing the roster of explanatory entities

At the end of the section titled "Authors" in their contribution to chapter 2,
Phelan and Rabinowitz write: "we recognize that in many critical contexts
there is no significant payoff to identifying the authorial agency [responsible
for how a text is constructed] by the term 'implied author' . . . rather than
simply 'author' . . ." (p. 33). Yet many of the claims that Phelan and Rabinowitz go on to make hinge on the idea of the implied author, which functions
as an enabling condition for their model. For example, in chapter 2 Phelan
and Rabinowitz follow Booth in defining unreliable narration by appealing
to the concept of the implied author (pp. 33–37), and the same goes for their
account of the relation between textual and readerly dynamics in chapter 3,
where they speak of "discourse-level dynamics arising from the interrelations

of implied author, narrator, and audience" (p. 58). Since engaging with narratives of all sorts entails assessing degrees of reliability and having responses that are cued by textual designs, Phelan and Rabinowitz's hedge concerning the implied author as optional, or dependent on critical payoff, seems to be at odds with their modus operandi.

Nonetheless, the hedging statement does raise questions about the nature and degree of the critical payoff that might be expected, in general, from the heuristic apparatus in which the concept of the implied author is embedded. Compared with CAPA, the narrative communication diagram proliferates explanatory entities and levels, which are made necessary by an initial postulation of the implied author as a sort of cardinal hypothesis. But is this apparatus—the full range of heuristic constructs included on the production and reception sides of the communication diagram—really needed to model how story interpreters use textual cues to co-construct narrative worlds?

Consider the incident discussed in Phelan and Rabinowitz's contribution to chapter 6, in which Huck recounts how the widow Douglas "grumbles" (= prays) over her food (p. 142). In my view, the analyst need not appeal to an implied author or an authorial (or narrative) audience to account for the nature and communicative functions of the disparity between Huck's and Twain's takes on this episode. In interpreting this incident, I ascribe to Twain the aim of evoking a storyworld that features a narrator-protagonist whose construal of events diverges from the construal that I provisionally assume the author—and not some implied author—intends readers to develop. These divergent construals, as Phelan and Rabinowitz note, themselves serve broader communicative goals; but again, I can generate inferences about those goals without appealing to a shadow agent hovering between author and narrator. Nor do I need to multiply types of readers or audiences to account for the divergent methods of event-construal that give this incident its structure and effects in the larger context of Twain's novel. As I suggested in chapter 6, the implied reader is a name for the profile that an interpreter infers the reader targeted by an author to possess. Thus, in describing the authorial audience in chapter 1 as "the hypothetical group for whom the author writes . . . [and who] ground his or her rhetorical choices" (p. 6), Phelan and Rabinowitz do point to a key aspect of discourse understanding in general and narrative understanding in particular (see also endnote 7 in my contribution to chapter 2). But the question is how best to characterize this recursive ascription of intentions, whereby I impute to an author the intention of having me use textual cues as the basis for ascribing to him or her reasons for narrating events in a particular way. To explain this ascriptional process, Phelan and Rabinowitz, in their contribution to chapter 6, rely on the multi-tiered model associated with the narrative communication diagram, in which a narrator is an imitation of an author and communicates with a different audience (the narrative audience) than the audience whom the author targets (the authorial audience) (p. 140). Arguably, though, assuming that narratives like Twain's involve a nested structure of communicative goals does not require assigning a distinct reading position—or audience type—to each level of this structure.

Just as I don't need to posit distinct explanatory mechanisms to account for how the subgoal of chopping onions relates to the higher-order goal of making spaghetti sauce, appealing to two distinct audience types is not required to account for (the communicative effects of) the praying episode in Twain's novel. Instead, I ascribe to Twain the aim of triggering, through the design of this episode, ascriptions to him of an intention to evoke part of a world whose nature can sometimes—and to a greater or lesser extent—be brought into sharper focus via the narrating Huck's intermittent inability to grasp fully what's going on around him. From this perspective, a characterized narrator's own acts of telling require for their uptake not readers occupying audience positions located at two different levels in conceptual space, but rather interpreters working at a single level to situate Huck's goals within Twain's larger worldmaking project. Or to put the same point another way: a multi-tiered communicative design does not entail, in turn, a multiplication and stratification of audience positions; it entails only narrative designs, inferences about nested communicative goals, and a process of textual navigation in which interpreters, by way of the recursive ascriptions of intention just described, tentatively map the designs onto the inferred goals (and vice versa).

(d) The rhetoric of rhetorical theory, the idea of audience, and the problem of "speaking for"

More than this, however, I disagree with Phelan and Rabinowitz's suggestion that interpreters of texts like Twain's must obligatorily take up the (multileveled) reading positions described in their approach, if they are to "understand what it *feels like* to read *Huckleberry Finn*"—to use a phrase from their discussion of the praying incident in chapter 6 (p. 142). In my view, in its rhetoric if not its stated assertions, Phelan and Rabinowitz's approach backgrounds the defeasibility of the inferences on which their approach is premised—specifically, inferences about what sorts of readers are being targeted

by story creators like Twain. Through the repeated use of nominalized constructions (such as *Twain and his audience* or even *the authorial audience*),
the idea of audience becomes detached from an interpreter's assumptions
about whom an author may have been targeting and takes on the role of an
autonomous, quasi-external criterion for successful reading. Equally telling,
and related to the way Phelan and Rabinowitz frame their statements about
audiences, is the repetition of statements featuring inclusive uses of the first-
person plural pronouns "we" and "our." In statements of this sort, because of
how they contribute to a downplaying of the defeasibility or context-bound-
edness of inferences concerning the profile of readers targeted by an author,
Phelan and Rabinowitz effectively conflate their own reading experiences
with the nature of the reading experience as such.

These two problems, whereby inferences about reader profiles are reified or hypostatized and then used as a basis for making broad claims about
reader response, surface together in a statement that appears in Phelan and
Rabinowitz's contribution to chapter 7: "the narratorial dynamics of the Evasion weaken our engagement with the narrative audience as our puzzlement
about Twain's shift in tactics . . . greatly interferes with our concerns about
the world of the novel and with our satisfaction in the ethical dimension of
the implied author–narrator–audience relationships" (p. 162). In this statement, inferences about what sorts of story-recipients Huck may be targeting—that is, ascriptions of particular communicative intentions or goals to
Twain via Huck's own acts of telling—are reified in the form of *the narrative
audience,* the nominalized label for which masks how this construct emerges
from particular acts of ascription, performed by specific interpreters. At the
same time, Phelan and Rabinowitz's repetition of the first-person plural pronoun "our" elides the difference between the sort of reader whom they infer
Twain to be targeting and other possible profiles that might be assigned to
that target reader. The upshot (for me at least) is the sense that a wider range
of possible responses to the text is being truncated or reduced in the service
of a particular interpretation that, again, masks its own particularity via rhetorical strategies.[9] Through the reiteration of first-person plural pronouns,
other readers, who may be inclined to ascribe other sorts of intentions to
Twain, are being spoken for. I have a similar reaction to Phelan and Rabinowitz's claim that when Huck tears up the letter to Miss Watson "we feel our
strongest sympathy for and our greatest ethical approval of his actions" (p.
36), as well as their claim that the ending of the novel causes an "experiential
disappointment" (p. 161). In the first claim, exactly whose evaluative standards license the assertion about degrees of sympathy and approval? And in
the second claim, precisely whose experience is at issue?

I CONCLUDE with a remark about Phelan and Rabinowitz's comments, in chapter 1, concerning a posteriori versus a priori approaches to narrative study. If, as Phelan and Rabinowitz assert, an a posteriori approach to narrative study seeks "to understand and assess the variety of things narratives have done and the variety of ways they have done it" (p. 5), then it seems to me that their own approach has no special advantage in this respect when compared with any number of other approaches, including mind-oriented, transmedial, diachronic, and other perspectives. Indeed, I dispute the suggestion that rhetorical theorists can avoid preselecting particular issues and concerns when it comes to the study of narrative. Phelan and Rabinowitz's definition of narrative (p. 3), for instance, foregrounds (by specifying in more detail) the communicative or transactional aspects of narrative over its semantic or world-creating properties—properties that Phelan and Rabinowitz refer to in comparatively gross, summative terms ("something happened to someone or something"). More generally, any approach prioritizes certain kinds of questions about stories and storytelling—and certain ways of addressing those questions. Hence to foster best practices in the field, narrative theorists should spotlight the analytic priorities associated with various approaches, reflexively examining the presuppositions and entailments carried by different ways of framing questions about the phenomena under study. My hope is that the present response, along with my other contributions to the volume, can help lay groundwork for this metanarratological enterprise. My aim throughout has been to outline, within the broader context of contemporary scholarship on narrative, an approach that enables theorists to formulate what I see as especially productive questions about stories. These questions emerge when analysts bring together traditions of narrative scholarship and research on the mind to explore what stories are, how they work, and what they can be used to do.

NOTES

1. The situation is slightly more complicated when it comes to my rebuttal, in the next section, of Warhol's characterization of cognitive narratology. I dispute Warhol's characterization, but I do so in order to emphasize how my own approach explores, by drawing on alternative traditions of research, issues that also concern feminist narratologists.

2. I should clarify that these assumptions are not necessarily held exclusively by the co-authors with whom I initially associate them. For example, all of my co-authors, not just Phelan and Rabinowitz, rely on the narrative communication diagram (in various ways) in their contributions.

3. Along these lines, Warhol's claim in chapter 5 that characters are merely "functions of discourse" (p. 121), having "no psychology, no interiority or subjectivity" (p. 119), removes any basis for exploring what I see as a key question for narrative theory: namely, how culturally situated practices of engaging with the minds of persons both shape and are shaped by readers' engagements with fictional minds.

4. Writing in 2005, Richardson himself used the term "anti-narrative" to designate "narratives that ignore or defy the conventions of natural narratives" (24).

5. For reasons broached in this paragraph as well as my next one, I question the analogy that Richardson proposes toward the end of his contribution to chapter 1, in which he compares "[a] theory of narrative that excludes antimimetic works" with "a theory of art that treated all art as representational and could not discuss abstract art" (p. 25). As I see it, narrative is by definition a kind or mode of representational practice: if a text does not represent situations and events in some world or another (however different that world may be from the world of everyday experience), then it is not a narrative. Rushdie's novel, for example, is surely representational in this basic sense.

6. Contrast Ricoeur's multidimensional account of mimesis, which distinguishes among three distinct levels or modes of mimetic representation: prefiguration, configuration, and refiguration. See also Fludernik, *Narratology* (16–18).

7. As I have already suggested, mimesis necessarily involves world-models recruited from textual, cultural, and other sources, such that what my co-authors term "mimetic" components of stories overlap with what they call "synthetic" components, or features pointing to a narrative's status as a constructed artifact. On another front, Doležel ("Thematic") and Prince (*Narrative as Theme* 1–13) provide insights into how reading for themes requires parsing a text in terms of models or frames that are inferred to organize its construction—models allowing thematic meanings to be mapped onto particular units or classes of units. From this perspective, to explore what a text thematizes is to interpret it via a model for meaning generation that readers ascribe to story creators; and in turn that model both informs and is informed by the construction of the storyworld with which the narrative's themes are more or less densely interwoven. Here the overlap between the "thematic" and "synthetic" components is apparent.

8. See, for example, the section "Endings" in Richardson's contribution to chapter 3 (pp. 80–81).

9. Phelan and Rabinowitz's discussion of "the fuzziness of the authorial audience" in chapter 6 (pp. 141–42) did not allay my concerns in this connection, because they locate the fuzziness not in their inferences concerning what sorts of readers Twain

may have targeted but in the way Twain himself targeted them. Hence in Phelan and Rabinowitz's account Twain's target audience comes across as knowably fuzzy rather than, as it is in CAPA, fuzzily knowable.

RESPONSE
by Brian Richardson

GENERAL

It is a pleasure to read the extremely impressive, perspicuous, and valuable work of the other authors of this book. It is also, however, necessary to draw attention to the general mimetic orientation that runs throughout this volume. From my perspective, each author skews his or her theory of narrative in a different manner and to a different degree. Phelan and Rabinowitz, understandably enough, view their definition as a "default" position, to which other variants or permutations might be added. They often leave a generous place in their theoretical framework for the synthetic component of narrative, though the vast majority of their work revolves around mimetic and thematic concerns. I feel that their concept of the synthetic elements, especially the more extreme and unnatural ones, should be developed much further. Some chapters, such as the otherwise excellent discussion "Time, Plot, Progression," seem to contain rather less space for the more unusual practices of postmodern and antimimetic fiction.

They claim to provide a model that can capture "most of those works that are widely considered to be narratives in our culture" (p. 4). The key terms here are "most" and "our culture." What is the residue left out of "most"? As I indicate throughout this book, I feel there is an entire literature from Aristophanes to postmodernism that does not fit within such parameters; "most" is simply not enough for a comprehensive narrative theory. As to "our culture," which of our cultures do they refer to? Most postmodernists would say that ours is a postmodern culture that is creatively represented by postmodern practices, ones that prominently defy more mimetic or realistic narrative practices. Phelan and Rabinowitz, such an argument would run, provide a model better suited to later nineteenth-century literary practices than our distinctive twenty-first century works.

Phelan and Rabinowitz are rhetorically effective in presenting themselves as normative, opposing their position to that of Warhol and me, who are averred to limit our focus to feminist or antimimetic texts. Instead, I believe that Warhol and I are adding two essential perspectives that need to be present if narrative studies are not to be hopelessly one-sided and incomplete: that is, either woefully andocentric or indefensibly mimetic. My own goal is not to provide some alternative, minority, or postmodern poetics, but rather to show what a complete, comprehensive narrative theory might look like. It would include the mimetic texts, models, and analyses that other theorists provide, in this book as well as in most other guides, overviews, and handbooks of narrative theory, *and* it would also include and theorize the neglected antimimetic works that have been around almost as long as mimesis itself. This is why in many of my chapters I sketch or point to the standard or common positions that are useful and valid but need to be complemented by the antimimetic perspective if we are to have a thorough narrative theory.

I believe it is just as inaccurate to assume that all narrative is mimetic as it is to claim that all narrative is antimimetic. In 1925 Boris Tomashevsky stated that there are two types of literary styles: one of them, common in the nineteenth century, conceals its literary devices and makes them seem imperceptible and natural. The other, unrealistic style "does not bother about concealing the devices and . . . frequently tries to make them obvious, as when a writer interrupts a speech he is reporting to say he did not hear how it ended, only to go on and report what he has no realistic way of knowing" (94). This other side of the history of literature is repeatedly neglected or forgotten.

Robyn Warhol provides an exemplary, indeed paradigmatic, feminist account of narrative theory in this volume. She works with a primarily mimetic text and also points out its more self-reflexive and nonillusionistic moments, most notably when discussing the sly, self-referential discourse on endings at the end of *Persuasion*. One can easily imagine her taking an entirely antimimetic feminist work such as Monique Wittig's *Les Guérillères* and performing the same careful, cunning, theoretical exploration of that text. But in this case, there is no pressing need to do so, since other feminist scholars and theorists have already provided such analyses (on Wittig, see Lanser, *Fictions*, 267–79). Finally, the very politics that Warhol expresses may well incline her toward a more realist text that is arguably more accessible to a larger audience and its lessons more readily transferable than an analysis of a feminist avant-garde work might be.

The narratological system presented by David Herman is extremely impressive, beautifully molding experimental cognitive research, analytical philosophy, and postclassical narrative theory into a powerful and compelling synthesis. It is the most resolutely mimetic of the accounts in this volume. But it is also, perhaps necessarily, a very general poetics; by focusing on the features shared by or readily extended from nonfiction to fiction, Herman runs the risk of appearing to yield to overgeneralization, reductionism, and even missing altogether that which many of us value most in narrative fiction. Herman often seems to be looking at a distant planet through a powerful telescope, one that is unable to discern the unusual, dark topographies invisible from earth. As useful as Herman's macrocosmic study may be, it is not always clear how it might be extended to cover more unusual narratives. I do hasten to add that he has written brilliant, theoretically informed studies of experimental texts such as Patrick Modiano's *La Place de L'Étoile* and the "Sirens" episode in *Ulysses;* it is simply not always apparent to me how other radical experiments could be placed effectively within his theoretical framework. Rather than trying to force antimimetic practices into a mimetic theory they were designed to subvert, we need instead to produce a more dialectical theory that can encompass both traditions.

I find that the positions set forth by Phelan and Rabinowitz and, especially, Herman do not provide much help for dealing with many of the most distinctive and innovative aspects of a work like *Midnight's Children*. The issue is even more pronounced if the subject of analysis were a more radically antimimetic text like Beckett's *Molloy,* a text that does not embody but challenges or rejects the largely mimetic framework set forth by these theorists. Is there a story here, in any accepted sense of the term? Is there only one story? Who or what is (or are) the narrator(s)? What kinds of unnatural figures are the characters? What space do they inhabit? Who is the narratee or the implied audience of such strange texts? A primarily mimetic approach will not get us very far; it might postulate that the work is like a madman's delusion, or a dubious fantasy, or an imaged scene in hell, or an allegory of collapse, or some bizarre parody, or an exemplification of alienation in capitalist society, or whatever. But such approaches are entirely inadequate; more importantly, they trivialize Beckett's astounding creative achievements. The omission of Beckett's examples from most of the current discussions of narrative theory is a very serious one: Beckett is one of the most important and influential figures in both Anglophone and Francophone literature; from the late 1960s to the early 1980s he was widely regarded as the greatest living author writing in English, and he was awarded the Nobel Prize in Literature. What must one make of a narrative theory that has little or nothing to say about such an eminent, important, and influential author?

My own, very different approach will no doubt be judged by some to be idiosyncratic; I would respond that both this objection and my position are, in one form or another, reinscribed in some of the very texts I analyze. Rushdie's wayward narrator, Saleem Sinai, is frustrated by his literal-minded and convention-bound narratee, Padma, who insists on a more traditional style of narration and is impatient with postmodern divagations, or what she terms "all this writing-shiting" (20). This opposition echoes similar ones in numerous experimental works by authors from Laurence Sterne to Vladimir Nabokov and Italo Calvino, each of whom has included naïve, uncompre-hending narratees within their works as negative models whose interpre-tive practices are to be avoided by more astute readers. Ian McEwan, as we will shortly see, has even invented a naïvely mimetic character who cannot understand the work of the author who created him.

My position may be accused of being secondary or derivative, a kind of epiphenomenon of the more basic or foundational mimetic model of nar-rative. To this, I respond that while an antimimetic narrative practice does presuppose the conventions of mimesis, it does not follow that it is somehow subordinate or less substantial. Irony presupposes literal meaning, writing can be invented only after spoken languages exist, non-Euclidian geometry covers a different terrain than does its prior, Euclidian counterpart, and an Einsteinian universe can be conceived only after one has a thorough knowl-edge of the Newtonian physics it supersedes. In each case, the earlier term is a precondition for the emergence of the later one; in none of the cases is the temporally prior one superior to the subsequent knowledge that is built on its foundations.

CHARACTER

My own response to the other theorists in this volume might best be clarified by looking at the concept of character, the point at which our respective theo-retical formulations seem to be the most divergent. Phelan and Rabinowitz offer a rich model that includes mimetic, synthetic, and thematic compo-nents. As I have argued above, I believe that the mimetic component is far more fragile than they indicate. More importantly, the synthetic component is much more complex, multiform, and dynamic than they suggest; indeed, we need to devote more attention to unnatural figures such as characters that merge with other characters, ones that are too fragmented or contradictory to constitute a single individual, those who know themselves to be fictional creations, or impossible ones who can die more than once. I also assert that an additional category, the intertextual, is necessary to do full justice to the distinctive nature and origins of literary characters. It is inadequate to affirm that Saleem is primarily a mimetic, thematic, or synthetic construct, though one can, admittedly, get a lot of mileage out of the latter two categories. Saleem is perhaps above all a reincarnation of Tristram Shandy. Saleem writes, "Our names contain our fates; living as we do in a place where names have not acquired the meaninglessness of the West, and are still more than mere sounds, we are also victims of our titles" (348–49). Here, he is alluding to Sterne—in fact almost literally taking a page from Walter Shandy's *Tristrapaedia* on the power that names have over the destinies of the characters who bear them—even as he playfully suggests he is identifying a distinctively non-Western nomenclature. Again, we need the intertextual background to fully comprehend Saleem's name and fate, as well as an antimimetic approach to appreciate how naming can become destiny in ludic, fictional texts.

Warhol rightly insists on the fictionality of fictional characters and on the significance of their ideological underpinnings. The other authors in this volume insist on the mimetic component, and to be sure it seems to me that part of the purpose of realistic fiction is to provide verisimilar characters. If they were not realistic, it would make no sense to ask of them, as one might ask of real people, how did things actually go after that concluding happy marriage had become a memory? Authors can and do write sequels that chart the fates of such characters; often it is the mimetic component that provides a crucial motivation for such continuations. On the other hand, it is important to insist on the inevitable entanglement of the intensely ideological with the ostensibly mimetic: throughout history, especially the history of literary portraits of women, authors have deliberately or unwittingly propagated sexist stereotypes in the name of realism.

I would also add that that even those accounts that stress the fictionality of characters, such as structuralist character theory, often have an unacknowledged mimetic bias. When describing a character as a cluster of predicates, structuralists rarely consider the possibility of insufficient or inherently contradictory predicates (though Roland Barthes, in a footnote, does praise Philippe Sollers for writing a novel, *Drame,* which "gets rid of the person" [105]). Though antipsychological and opposed to the concept of an essential self, structuralists typically provide an actantial model that imagines figures (e.g., the "hero") repeatedly making choices between logically incompatible options, rather like humans do. The possibility of crossing these forking paths in a way that defies logic is usually not imagined by the theorists, though a range of authors from Borges to Robbe-Grillet, Robert Coover, Harold Pinter, and Caryl Churchill have embodied just such internally contradictory narrative possibilities. As Luc Herman and Bart Ver-vaeck have pointed out: "In postmodern novels characters lose many of their human traits: they blend into one another, they say they are the invention of the narrator or the text, they disappear as suddenly as they appear. Structur-alism hardly knows what to do with such non-anthropomorphic characters, which proves the extent of its remaining anthropomorphism" (70).

At his most general, Herman hedges his bets, defining characters as human or "more or less prototypical members of the category of 'persons'" (p. 125). One may partially assent to such a claim, hoping that it will be suf-ficiently qualified and emended as the argument proceeds. But as Herman's section continues, its object becomes narrower: fictional individuals "can be inferred to possess more or less extensive constellations of personal traits" (p. 127). Again, there is some wiggle room here, though we see a dominant mimetic paradigm firmly in place. At this point I want to protest that some characters may not possess many human traits at all, that they may possess them in the wrong ways, that they may defy such a mimetic recuperation, and that it is insufficient to subsume these fascinating possibilities as mere variants of the "more or less prototypical" person—some are not less proto-typical but instead antithetical. What is prototypical about a character who knows himself to be a fictional character, or one who, like Saleem, feels the unnatural consequences of becoming invisible ("present but insubstantial; actual, but without being or weight. . . . I discovered, in the basket, how ghosts see the world" [438])? It appears that Herman, like Richard Gerrig and Ralf Schneider, two theorists he cites favorably, seems to be ignoring all non- or antimimetic aspects of literary characterization. At its worst, such a monocular approach will ignore or negate the impressive conceptual work on nonmimetic aspects of characters done by earlier theorists such as Joel Weinsheimer, Thomas Docherty, and Aleid Fokkema; further, it threatens to return us to the kind of naive or vulgar mimeticism that prevailed at the beginning of the twentieth century and that drove scholars like A. C. Bradley to ask seriously where Hamlet was when he learned of his father's death and how many children Lady Macbeth had. Literary theory does not need to go back to this narrowly confined space.

In short, a comprehensive theory of character needs several different components. Any single approach, whether mimetic, synthetic, or ideologi-cal, is a necessarily impoverished one; much more work still needs to be done to retain and extend the analysis of antimimetic figures.

SPECIFIC POINTS

In the first portion of this book I often used the positions of Phelan and Rabinowitz to frame my own discussions; there is consequently little need to rearticulate specific differences that have already been noted and argued. Nevertheless, a few points may be mentioned here. I am surprised that, after their fine discussion of the narrator, they don't go on to mention nonhuman or posthuman narrators, as well as the fact that a narrative does not need to have a single, overarching anthropomorphic narrator figure: postmodernism shows us the possibility of what I have called the "death of the narrator" (*Unnatural* 1–3, 134–40). Similarly, Phelan's excellent and important identification of six varieties of unreliable narration are all based on a mimetic paradigm; these would be nicely complemented by the addition of a few of the outrageous, distinctively postmodern types of unreliability, as I have suggested elsewhere (*Unnatural* 103–5).

In the same vein, their notion of the synthetic is markedly realistic in their discussion of space, setting, and perspective. They write that a plot may demand a certain kind of location and thus the meeting of the wolf and the girl in a rewriting of "Little Red Riding Hood" could not take place in a prison cell; furthermore, that the plot of *Huck Finn* depends on the Mississippi providing the protagonists with a means of transportation. But these statements are true only of *realistic* narratives; in a postmodern rewriting of "Red Riding Hood," such as Angela Carter's "The Company of Wolves" (in which the young woman, ignoring her dead grandmother, winds up making love to the wolf man), any setting, internal or external, is possible. Likewise, a river is necessary and its corresponding constraints apply only in a mimetic text that adheres to the canons of verisimilitude; Marco Polo didn't need a river (or any other particular means of transportation) to get around the imaginary China of Calvino's *Invisible Cities*.

I suspect that many of these absences stem from the insistently mimetic nature of their definition of narrative: "somebody telling somebody else, on some occasion, and for some purposes, that something happened to someone or something" (p. 3). I would offer instead the more flexible formulation: "Narrative is the representation of a causally related series of events." And I would immediately go on to point out how some texts, like Beckett's "Ping," seem designed to challenge even this definition.

I also wish to note that Phelan and Rabinowitz's formulation of narrative audiences in this volume is especially effective and supple. The one area I would want to extend is in fact one that Rabinowitz addressed in 1994: the possibilities of multivalent or multiple authorial audiences. I would like to stress that the implied reader of the antimimetic text has a double consciousness; she notes the mimetic convention that is being abrogated as well as the playful antimimetic effect that is produced. Postmodern texts such as *Molloy* or *Gravity's Rainbow* presuppose other narrative models, for example, the modernist paradigm, that the novels then go on to transgress or transcend. *Lolita* presupposes knowledge both of the modernist paradigm and of the conventions of the detective novel. Modernist novels such as *The Waves* or *The Sound and the Fury* often play on and frustrate the expectations based on the conventions of the realist novel, and gay or minority texts are often addressed to both a more general and a more specific authorial audience. In works written to elude censors, two audiences are addressed: one that is intended to miss and another that is intended to find the text's hidden, subversive meaning. For many works, it is often enough to identify the authorial audience and follow how it is constructed and engaged; with more complex texts, one would do well to seek to identify the multiple possible audiences, poetics, and paradigms being addressed, invoked, or eluded.

ROBYN WARHOL provides an excellent overview and compelling analysis of feminist narrative theory. I find her discussions of authors, plots, endings, space, and the susceptible reader to be especially important. One point where we do differ is on the possible gendering of concepts like the implied reader (p. 144). The implied reader is indeed a virtual being, as Warhol notes, but that does not mean it can't be gendered. Most entities in and behind a fictional narrative are in some important sense virtual: not only implied readers but implied authors, narrators, even characters; I don't see why one should not recognize gendered identities. And many of these entities are distinctly gendered, as Patrocinio Schweickart has argued (38–44); the stories of Hemingway are clearly directed to a decidedly male authorial audience. Many other virtual entities are likewise gendered, such as gods, unicorns, faeries, GPS voice systems, and so on.

Like many other feminists, Warhol has an ambivalent response to the question of aesthetic value. On the one hand, she states that the feminist narrative theorist cannot separate narrative values from aesthetic values, and the conjunction of these terms implies a third term: political values, implying that these are all intertwined. The same affirmation appears in the final statement of her final section. On the other hand, she makes and documents many aesthetic judgments at the level of style. Jane Austen regularly made similar judgments; for her there was no shadow of a doubt concerning the reality and significance of aesthetic value.

Warhol states that "if the reason there were so few 'great' women writers was that not enough women had written texts that match the aesthetic standards of their male contemporaries and critics, then, according to feminism, there was something wrong with a set of standards that could so effectively exclude the creative efforts of half of humanity" (p. 165). This is no doubt largely true. It may also be that Warhol is too generous here: I strongly suspect that a corollary problem was that the same standard was often prejudicially applied: when women writers did satisfy established aesthetic criteria, their work was dismissed by male critics because of their authors' gender. This is no doubt why many women writers of the nineteenth century used male pseudonyms (George Sand, Currer Bell, George Eliot) in order to gain a less biased reading. In my judgment, the brilliant work of Edith Wharton, one of the greatest American authors, is insufficiently acknowledged; I have no doubt that her gender has played a major part in this undervaluation. This situation is at least equally true of women authors who extend or transgress modernist paradigms, such as Elizabeth Jane Howard, Eva Figes, Anna Kavan, Angela Carter, Monique Wittig, and many others. In these cases, the problem is not the aesthetic standard but the biased way in which it is applied. Ultimately, I believe that an aesthetic argument, more so than a political, historical, or even a narratological justification, is the best way to ensure that great, neglected women authors of earlier periods continue to be read in the twenty-first century.

AMONG THE MANY impressive points made by David Herman in his sections, one of the most helpful is his bold attempt to bring a robust concept of intentionality back into literary discourse. Elsewhere, however, his approach, stressing the most general features of most narratives, has the curious consequence of seeming not to need many of the distinctions that narrative theorists have developed over the past fifty years. He wants to dispense with the implied author and is dubious about the implied reader; he can do without a focalizer; he is even wary about the concept of the narrator. He even seems at points to minimize the fiction/nonfiction difference, a distinction I have argued is crucial. His comments on the narrator are revealing: for his approach, which acknowledges the need to ascribe intentions to narrating agents, the category of "narrator" will be "more or less salient depending on the profile of a given narrational act" (p. 46). One might easily suggest that this is largely true of most other concepts as well: all the elements of narrative theory that Herman is prepared to do without are not as important for the theory and analysis of conversational narratives or most eighteenth-century fiction.

However, the numerous wayward, devious, and duplicitous narrators of modernism richly reward the concepts of both the narrator and unreliability; indeed, it is very hard to teach the work of Joyce, Faulkner, or Nabokov without these conceptual tools. The same is true of the concept of the implied reader or authorial audience. Herman suggests that "expressions like *the implied reader* can have the effect of occluding the way they, too, designate interpretations that stem from inferences made by actual readers" (p. 152). This simply does not strike me as a serious problem. The concept of the implied reader may not always be absolutely necessary for understanding every audience response; though still helpful, it is probably not essential for a general understanding of the reception of the fables of Aesop or *Pilgrim's Progress*. Once again, for modernist works where the authorial audience (or implied reader) differs radically from the narrative audience (or narratee), it can be extremely useful if not, in fact, indispensible. It is perhaps even more essential in cases where more than one authorial audience is being addressed, as in children's stories that have one meaning for the child and a very different one for an adult.

Likewise, the notion of the implied author is particularly helpful when dealing with a single work by multiple authors. To take Herman's own example, the multiple creators of the film *The Cement Garden* succeeded in producing "the effect of a single act of narration" (p. 50); the same is true of Conrad and Ford's collaboration on Part 2, Chapter 5 of *Nostromo*. Why not simply call this a single implied author, since this is the effect the different individuals involved were trying to produce? Other works notoriously fail to achieve such a fusion of sensibilities: it is evident which part of *Pericles* was written by Shakespeare and which by the anonymous journeyman playwright; similarly, most readers can readily tell that chapters of *The Whole Family* read as if they were written by different authors. In these cases, we clearly have multiple actual authors who fail to achieve the effect of a single act of narration. I see no problem in saying that in these works we can infer the presence of two or more implied authors.

Another classic example is the case where an author fabricates an implied author who is very different from the actual writer. Generations of readers were shocked when it was discovered that the historical Thomas Mann had powerful homoerotic desires, and thus was quite unlike the implicitly heterosexual implied author he had constructed in all his published works (see

Tobin). This kind of opposition is so powerful that it has itself been the subject of fictions, such as Henry James's "The Private Life" and Borges' "Borges and I." Postmodern writers presuppose the notion whenever they attempt to transgress it. Some actual writers will be unable to maintain their former "implied authorial self" and, as in the case of the final works of Hemingway, merely produce an unintended parody of what Wayne Booth calls their "career implied author." Can one articulate these various relations without the concept of the implied author? Certainly. But I find that the concept gives us a very useful tool for assembling and discussing this entire range of possibilities. The danger of hypostatizing this figure is outweighed by its utility. This leads to the larger methodological question of when to retain, add, or discard narratological categories. My answer (and the practice of most narrative theorists) is simple: we keep or develop the concepts that have a demonstrated utility. The concept of the implied author is very useful for me to explain these and other textual features and relations (see my "Implied"). In a case like this one, it's best to keep Occam's razor in your pocket.

MISSING THEORY

If my account of the mimetic bias of narrative theory is correct, it should be no surprise that all the other theorists in this volume (and most other volumes) use realistic texts for their central examples, that their conceptions of narrative are largely mimetic and that their range of reference is, with very few exceptions, exclusively mimetic. This is of course entirely understandable; a particular theoretical approach naturally gravitates toward certain texts or classes of texts, just as starting from a particular narrative usually leads in the direction of some theories rather than others. For this reason, we might usefully speculate on what the other accounts leave out of their theories and analyses, and then ask what specifically an antimimetic approach would add to the discussion of the creative authors analyzed by the other theorists in this volume.

An antimimetic analysis of *Huckleberry Finn* would begin with the book's first sentences: "You don't know about me without you have read a book by the name of *The Adventures of Tom Sawyer,* but that ain't no matter. That book was made by Mr. Mark Twain, and he told the truth, mainly. There were things he stretched, but mainly he told the truth" (3). Here we have a fictional character commenting on the work of the author who created him, and testifying (with a few qualifications) to its basic veracity before going on to relate the continuation of the story himself. This is an antimimetic violation of mimetic conventions—a character cannot know the fictional work within which he or she is a fictional character—as well as a familiar type of metalepsis, or violation of the ontological boundaries between a real author and a fictional being. This practice also has a rich genealogy, going back at least as far as Don Quixote and Sancho Panza's incredulous reading of the inaccurate continuation of their story (published by a real author) at the beginning of the second volume of *Don Quixote.* Twain's opening goes on to set up an intertextual drama that is intermittently returned to in the novel, most obviously in Tom Sawyer's determination to free Jim by reproducing scenarios he has read in books, especially romantic or chivalrous ones, as Tom becomes a contemporary Quixote. The novel's rhetorical situation here is not merely doubled, as Phelan and Rabinowitz point out at the beginning of their section of this book, but arguably tripled by this additional level of metafictional intertextuality.

This thread would seem to be a useful one to use to explore other intertextual allusions and parodies in a novel so critical of book learning and the uses to which it is put. In a deliberate but revealing exaggeration, Twain once blamed the Civil War on Walter Scott's novels, which were extremely popular in the antebellum South, because of their "romantic sense of the chivalry of combat" and their insistence on the "nobility of serving sentimental causes that were probably doomed to fail" (Beaty 449). Twain's remarks are part of a continuing dialogue on the use and abuse of reading that was a regular subject of metacritique in novels that documented the unfortunate fates of insufficiently critical readers, including Flaubert's *Madame Bovary* (a modern rewriting of *Quixote*), Hardy's *Jude the Obscure,* Conrad's *Lord Jim,* and extending forward to Faulkner's "Old Man," whose protagonist decides to commit a robbery after reading a number of popular crime stories. (He is immediately apprehended, to the surprise of no one but himself.)

If one were to do an antimimetic analysis of one of Jane Austen's works, one would select *Northanger Abbey,* her other posthumously published novel. This work engages in an exploration and critique of contemporary fiction, and it interrogates and lays bare a number of the basic elements and techniques of the novel. It opens by describing the characters of the Morland family and simultaneously critiquing expected patterns of plot development and character construction. Thus, Austen writes of Mrs Morland: "She had three sons before Catherine was born; and, instead of dying in bringing the latter into the world, as anybody might expect, she still lived on" (367). Anyone, that is, whose readerly expectations were too conventional. When Austen presents Catherine reading a novel about another character, the self-reflexive practice is self-consciously noted and defended: "If the heroine of one novel be not patronized by the heroine of another, from whom can she expect protection and regard?" (385), the narrator muses. The plot centers on reading and representation, specifically on the protagonist's overly enthusiastic response to her reading Ann Radcliff's *The Mysteries of Udolpho* and the mistaken judgments this causes when she applies its scenarios to her own situation. The antimimetic tone is most clearly sounded in the narrator's wry reflections on ending in Chapter 29, and her metafictional observation that readers "will see in the tell-tale compression of pages before them, that we are hastening together to perfect felicity" (540).

David Herman has selected Ian McEwan's *On Chesil Beach* to work with. It is certainly an excellent choice for his theoretical framework. Readers of contemporary literature, however, might point out that this novel is one of his least experimental and therefore least typical novels. This text, although almost entirely realistic, does, however, have passages that stray from the narrow mimetic path, as when the narrator notes: "while one had heard of wealthier people going in for psychoanalysis, it was not yet customary to regard oneself in everyday terms as an enigma, as an exercise in narrative history, or as a problem waiting to be solved" (26). This comment is particularly revealing since McEwan's characters sometimes *are* exercises in narrative history; this is particularly true of the extrapolated, fictionalized later lives of characters presented as real by the duplicitous narrator of his earlier novel, *Atonement* (2001).

Among McEwan's more adventurous and innovative fictions are his novel *The Company of Strangers* (1981), whose labyrinthine geography mirrors its snake-like plot, and *The Child in Time* (1987), a masterful work that creates an impossible temporality that cannot be included within Herman's framework. Still more important is *Atonement* (2001). In this work one finds, yet again, a novel whose theme is the incommensurability of fact and fiction, a novel that provides an intertextual commentary on modern British fiction. McEwan has stated that its "every sentence contains a ghostly commentary on its own process" (59). It also includes a fictional letter from an actual novelist (Elizabeth Bowen) to the fictional narrator that discusses the aesthetics of fictional representation. The work also includes a playful, powerful drama about the nature of its narrator, one which traditional, mimetic readers often find annoying or perfidious, but which can be thoroughly enjoyed by readers with a more expansive, postmimetic sensibility (see Phelan, *Experiencing* 109–32). Most telling of all is a brief passage in *Saturday* (205) in which the protagonist, an excellent brain surgeon, is befuddled by modern literature; his literalist imagination just can't make sense of nonrealist fiction. Dismissing some of the books his literary daughter has given him to read, he recalls incomprehensible heroes who "were granted a magical sense of smell, or tumbled unharmed out of high-flying aircraft. One visionary saw through a pub window his parents as they had been some weeks after his conception, discussing the possibility of aborting him" (66). These figures are, respectively, the protagonists of Rushdie's *Midnight's Children* and *The Satanic Verses* and McEwan's own *The Child in Time*. The implied reader will get the intertextual joke, and the comprehensive narrative theorist will want to be sure to move beyond the merely mimetic sensibility that McEwan here mocks.

One cannot fault Warhol for failing to select an admittedly unusual (if highly revealing) text by Austen, especially since she discloses key antimimetic passages in *Persuasion*. Nor should one chide Herman for passing on the most complex, innovative, and acclaimed work of McEwan: his goal is not to explicate the work of McEwan, but to illustrate his own theory. But these choices do suggest how the theoretical parameters we select go on to influence the narratives we gravitate toward and decide to foreground. They also reveal how much one's theoretical perspective leaves out, whether in the analysis of a text or in our understanding of an author's corpus. A mimetic approach naturally leads to mimetic examples, and naturally neglects unnatural narratives.

The other theorists have (most understandably, in the case of Warhol) left alone their chosen authors' most complex and self-conscious interactions with the nature of literary narrative, engagement with novelistic tradition, and perceived limitations or failures of mimesis. Nevertheless, like Salman Rushdie, each of these novelists has written a book that alludes to and critiques contemporary practices of representation. These self-consciously fictional works dramatically point out the radical difference of fiction, that is, the distance between fictional narrators and human storytellers, the ways that characters are not like people, and the artificiality of conventional methods of emplotment and resolution. They are all part of a larger and continuous dialogue on the nature and goals of narrative representation that extends back to Aristophanes' metadramas *The Frogs* and *The Thesmophoriazusae*. Twain, Austen, and McEwan are all, in varying degrees in different works, profoundly antimimetic authors. Many basic elements of narrative theory that we have been examining in this volume—the nature and purpose of plot, character, perspective, and mimesis itself—are debated within their works of fiction, but there is very little mention of these metacritical acts by the other theorists. Neither is it entirely clear how such an analysis could be included in Herman's paradigm or, to a lesser extent, that of Phelan and Rabinowitz, without a major revision of those models.

There is no getting around the incontrovertible fact that many compelling narratives in the history of literature are substantially antimimetic or contain significant antimimetic scenes and reflections. And a primarily mimetic theory cannot, in principle, do justice to antimimetic practices; it can tell only half the story. What is necessary for narrative theory is a reorientation of the model of narrative away from a predominantly mimetic conception toward a more flexible and comprehensive one that can encompass mimetic and antimimetic forms alike. To this end, postmodern, unnatural, and antimimetic theorists will continue to conceptualize and foreground the fascinating, unusual, extreme, and impossible worlds of narrative fiction.

WORKS CITED

Abbott, H. Porter. *The Cambridge Introduction to Narrative*. 2nd edition. Cambridge: Cambridge University Press, 2008.

———. "Story, Plot, and Narration." In *The Cambridge Companion to Narrative*, edited by David Herman, 39–51. Cambridge: Cambridge University Press, 2007.

Alber, Jan. "Impossible *Storyworlds*—and What to Do with Them." *Storyworlds: A Journal of Narrative Studies* 1 (2009): 79–96.

Alber, Jan and Rüdiger Heinze, eds. *Unnatural Narratives – Unnatural Narratology*. Berlin: de Gruyter, 2011.

Alber, Jan, Stefan Iversen, Henrik Skov Nielsen, and Brian Richardson. "Unnatural Narratives, Unnatural Narratology: Beyond Mimetic Models." *Narrative* 18 (2010): 113–36.

———. "Introduction." *A Poetics of Unnatural Narrative* (forthcoming).

Albright, Evelyn May. *The Short-Story, Its Principles and Structure*. New York: Macmillan, 1907.

Aldama, Frederick Luis. *Your Brain on Latino Comics*. Austin: University of Texas Press, 2009.

Alpert, Dona. "Gender Inequity in Academia: An Empirical Analysis." *Initiatives* 53 (1990): 10–12.

Austen, Jane. *The Complete Novels of Jane Austen*. Volume 2. New York: Random, 1950.

———. *Northanger Abbey*. 1818. Peterborough, ON: Broadview Press, 2002.

———. *Persuasion*. 1818. Harmondsworth: Penguin, 1989.

Austen-Leigh, James Edward. *A Memoir of Jane Austen*. 1869. New York: Oxford University Press, 2002.

Austin, Michael. *Useful Fictions: Evolution, Anxiety, and the Origins of Literature*. Lincoln: University of Nebraska Press, 2010.

Baker, Lynne Rudder. *The Metaphysics of Everyday Life*. Cambridge: Cambridge University Press, 2007.

———. *Persons and Bodies*. Cambridge: Cambridge University Press, 2000.

Bakhtin, Mikhail M. *The Dialogic Imagination: Four Essays*. Edited by Michael Holquist. Translated by Caryl Emerson and Holquist. Austin: University of Texas Press, 1982.

Bamberg, Michael and Molly Andrews, eds. *Considering Counter-Narratives: Narrating, Resisting, Making Sense.* Amsterdam: John Benjamins, 2004.

Banfield, Ann. *Unspeakable Sentences: Narration and Representation in the Language of Fiction.* Boston: Routledge and Kegan Paul, 1982.

Barthes, Roland. *Image-Music-Text.* Translated by Stephen Heath. New York: Farrar, Straus and Giroux, 1977.

Beaty, Jerome, ed. *The Norton Introduction to the Short Novel.* 3rd Edition. New York: W. W. Norton, 1982.

Bechdel, Alison. *Fun Home: A Family Tragicomic.* New York: Houghton Mifflin Harcourt, 2006.

Beckett, Samuel. "Cascando." In *Collected Shorter Plays,* 135–44. New York: Grove, 1984.

———. "Ping." In *The Complete Short Prose, 1929–1989,* edited by S. E. Gontarski, 193–96. New York: Grove, 1995.

———. *Worstward Ho.* New York: Grove, 1983.

Birkin, Andrew. *The Cement Garden.* Laurentic Films, 1993.

Bland, D. S. "Endangering the Reader's Neck: Background Description in the Novel." In *The Theory of the Novel,* edited by Philip Stevick, 313–31. New York: The Free Press, 1967.

Booth, Wayne C. *The Rhetoric of Fiction.* 2nd edition. Chicago: University of Chicago Press, 1983.

Bordwell, David. *Narration in the Fiction Film.* Madison: University of Wisconsin Press, 1985.

Borges, Jorge Luis. *Collected Fictions.* Translated by Andrew Hurley. New York: Penguin, 1998.

Boyd, Brian. *On the Origin of Stories: Evolution, Cognition, and Fiction.* Cambridge, MA: Harvard University Press, 2009.

Brenner, William H. *Wittgenstein's Philosophical Investigations.* Albany: State University of New York Press, 1999.

Bridgeman, Teresa. "Time and Space." In *The Cambridge Companion to Narrative,* edited by David Herman, 52–65. Cambridge: Cambridge University Press, 2007.

Brockmeier, Jens. "Explaining the Interpretive Mind." *Human Development* 39 (1996): 287–95.

Brontë, Charlotte. *Jane Eyre.* 1847. New York: Penguin, 2006.

Brooks, Cleanth and Robert Penn Warren. *Understanding Fiction.* 3rd edition. Englewood Cliffs, NJ: Prentice Hall, 1979.

Brooks, Peter. *Reading for the Plot: Design and Intention in Narrative.* Cambridge, MA: Harvard University Press, 1984.

Bruner, Jerome. *Acts of Meaning.* Cambridge, MA: Harvard University Press, 1990.

———. "The Narrative Construction of Reality." *Critical Inquiry* 18 (1991): 1–21.

Bulson, Eric. *Novels, Maps, Modernity: The Spatial Imagination, 1850–2000.* New York: Routledge, 2006.

Butler, Judith. *Gender Trouble: Feminism and the Subversion of Identity.* New York: Routledge, 1990.

Calvino. Italo. *If on a winter's night a traveler.* Translated by William Weaver. New York: Harcourt Brace Jovanovich, 1981.

Case, Alison. *Plotting Women: Gender and Narration in the Eighteenth- and Nineteenth-century British Novel.* Charlottesville: University of Virginia Press, 1999.

Chatman, Seymour. "Backwards." *Narrative* 17.1 (2009): 31–55.

———. *Story and Discourse: Narrative Structure in Fiction and Film.* Ithaca: Cornell University Press, 1978.

Cherny, Lynn and Elizabeth Reba Weise, eds. *Wired Women: Gender and New Realities in Cyberspace.* Seattle: Seal Press, 1996.

Cixous, Hélène. "The Character of 'Character.'" *New Literary History* 5 (1974): 383–402.

Clark, Andy. *Supersizing the Mind: Embodiment, Action, and Cognitive Extension.* Oxford: Oxford University Press, 2008.

Clark, Herbert. *Using Language.* Cambridge: Cambridge University Press, 1996.

Cohen, Keith. "Unweaving Puig's *Spider Woman*: Ekphrasis and Narration." *Narrative* 2.1 (1994): 17–28.

Cohn, Dorrit. *The Distinction of Fiction.* Baltimore: Johns Hopkins University Press, 1999.

———. *Transparent Minds: Narrative Modes for Presenting Consciousness in Fiction.* Princeton: Princeton University Press, 1978.

Cole, Barbara Tiller. *White Lies and Other Half-Truths.* Amazon.com: Createspace, 2008.

Collins, Patricia Hill. *Black Feminist Thought: Knowledge, Consciousness, and the Politics of Empowerment.* New York: Routledge, 1991.

Crane, R. S. "The Concept of Plot and the Plot of *Tom Jones*." In *Critics and Criticism*, edited by Crane, 616–47. Chicago: University of Chicago Press, 1952.

Crenshaw, Kimberlé W. "Mapping the Margins: Intersectionality, Identity Politics, and Violence against Women of Color." *Stanford Law Review* 43.6 (1991): 1241–99.

Cuddy-Keane, Melba. "Virginia Woolf and Beginning's Ragged Edge." In *Narrative Beginnings: Theories and Practices,* edited by Brian Richardson, 96–112. Lincoln: University of Nebraska Press, 2009.

Culler, Jonathan. *Structuralist Poetics: Structuralism, Linguistics, and the Study of Literature.* Ithaca: Cornell University Press, 1975.

Dannenberg, Hilary P. *Coincidence and Counterfactuality: Plotting Time and Space in Narrative Fiction.* Lincoln: University of Nebraska Press, 2008.

———. "Plot." In *Routledge Encyclopedia of Narrative Theory,* edited by David Herman, Manfred Jahn, and Marie-Laure Ryan, 435–39. London: Routledge, 2005.

Davidson, Donald. *Essays on Actions and Events.* Oxford: Oxford University Press, 1980.

Denby, David. *Great Books.* New York: Simon and Schuster, 1996.

Dewey, John. *Art as Experience.* New York: Capricorn Books, 1934.

Diengott, Nilli. "Narratology and Feminism." *Style* 22.1 (1988): 42–51.

Docherty, Thomas. *Reading (Absent) Character: Towards a Theory of Characterization in Fiction.* Oxford: Oxford University Press, 1985.

Doležel, Lubomír. "A Thematics for Motivation and Action." In *Thematics: New Approaches,* edited by Claude Bremond, Joshua Landy, and Thomas Pavel, 57–66. Albany: State University of New York Press, 1995.

———. *Heterocosmica: Fiction and Possible Worlds.* Baltimore: Johns Hopkins University Press, 1998.

Donald, Merlin. *Origins of the Modern Mind: Three Stages in the Evolution of Culture and Cognition.* Cambridge, MA: Harvard University Press, 1991.

Duchan, Judith F., Gail A. Bruder, and Lynne E. Hewitt, eds. *Deixis in Narrative: A Cognitive Science Perspective.* Hillsdale, NJ: Lawrence Erlbaum, 1995.

DuPlessis, Rachel Blau. *Writing beyond the Ending: Narrative Strategies of Twentieth-Century Women Writers.* Bloomington: Indiana University Press, 1985.

Easterlin, Nancy. *A Biocultural Approach to Literary Theory and Interpretation.* Baltimore: Johns Hopkins University Press, 2012.

Eco, Umberto. *The Role of the Reader: Explorations in the Semiotics of Texts.* Bloomington: Indiana University Press, 1979.

Emmott, Catherine. *Narrative Comprehension: A Discourse Perspective.* Oxford: Oxford University Press, 1997.

Eliot, George. "Silly Novels by Lady Novelists." *The Westminster Review* 66 (1856): 442–61. Reprinted in *The Essays of George Eliot.* Edited by Thomas Pinney. New York: Columbia University Press, 1963.

Even-Zohar, Itamar. "Constraints of Realeme Insertability in Narrative." *Poetics Today* 1.3 (1980): 65–74.

Finch, Casey. "The Tittle-Tattle of Highbury: Gossip and the Free Indirect Style in *Emma*." *Representations* 31 (1990): 1–18.

Fludernik, Monika. *Towards a "Natural" Narratology.* London: Routledge, 1996.

Fludernik, Monika, ed. "Second-Person Narrative." *Style* 28.3 (1994).

Fokkema, Aleid. *Postmodern Characters: A Study of Characterization in British and American Postmodern Fiction.* Amsterdam: Rodopi, 1991.

Fowler, Henry W. *A Dictionary of Modern Usage.* 1926. Edited by David Crystal. Oxford and New York: Oxford University Press, 2009.

Fraiman, Susan. "Jane Austen and Edward Said: Gender, Culture, and Imperialism." *Critical Inquiry* 21 (1995): 805–21.

Garofalo, Daniela. *Manly Leaders in Nineteenth-Century British Literature.* Albany: State University of New York Press, 2008.

Genette, Gérard. *Narrative Discourse: An Essay in Method.* Translated by Jane E. Lewin. Ithaca: Cornell University Press, 1980.

———. *Narrative Discourse Revisited.* Translated by Jane E. Lewin. Ithaca: Cornell University Press, 1988.

Gerrig, Richard J. *Experiencing Narrative Worlds: On the Psychological Activities of Reading.* New Haven: Yale University Press, 1993.

Gibson, J. J. *An Ecological Approach to Visual Perception.* Boston: Houghton-Mifflin, 1979.

Gilbert, Sandra and Susan Gubar. *The Norton Anthology of Literature by Women.* 1986. New York: W. W. Norton, 2007.

Goldie, Peter. *On Personality.* London: Routledge, 2004.

Goodman, Nelson. *Ways of Worldmaking.* Indianapolis: Hackett, 1978.

Graff, Gerald and James Phelan, eds. *The Adventures of Huckleberry Finn: A Case Study in Critical Controversy.* 2nd edition. Boston: St. Martin's Press, 2004.

Green, Georgia M. *Pragmatics and Natural Language Understanding.* Hillsdale, NJ: Lawrence Erlbaum, 1989.

Greimas, A. J. *Structural Semantics: An Attempt at a Method.* Translated by Daniele McDowell, Ronald Schleifer, and Alan Velie. Lincoln: University of Nebraska Press, 1984.

Greimas, Algirdas J. and Joseph Courtès. *Semiotics and Language: An Analytical Dictionary.* Translated by Larry Crist et al. Bloomington: Indiana University Press, 1983.

Greimas, A. J. and Jacques Fontanille. *The Semiotics of Passions.* Translated by Paul Perron and Frank Collins. Minneapolis: University of Minnesota Press, 1993.

Grice, Paul. *Studies in the Way of Words.* Cambridge, MA: Harvard University Press, 1989.

Grishakova, Marina. *The Models of Space, Time and Vision in V. Nabokov's Fiction: Narrative Strategies and Cultural Frames.* Tartu: Tartu University Press, 2006.

Hansen, Per Krogh, Stefan Iversen, Henrik Skov Nielsen, and Rolf Reitan, eds. *Strange Voices in Narrative Fiction.* Berlin: de Gruyter, 2011.

Harding, D. W. "Regulated Hatred: An Aspect of the Work of Jane Austen." 1940. In *Regulated Hatred and Other Essays on Jane Austen,* edited by Monica Lawlor, 5–26. London: Athlone, 1998.

Harding, Sandra. *Whose Science? Whose Knowledge? Thinking from Women's Lives.* Ithaca: Cornell University Press, 1991.

Harré, Rom and Grant Gillett. *The Discursive Mind.* London: Sage, 1994.

Hartsock, Nancy. *The Feminist Standpoint Revisited and Other Essays.* Boulder: Westview Press, 1998.

——. *Money, Sex, and Power: Toward a Feminist Historical Materialism.* New York: Longman, 1983.

Head, Dominic. *Ian McEwan.* Manchester: Manchester University Press, 2007.

——. "*On Chesil Beach:* Another 'Overrated' Novella?" In *Ian McEwan,* edited by Sebastian Groes, 115–22. London: Continuum, 2009.

Heinze, Rüdiger. "Violations of Mimetic Epistemology in First-Person Narrative Fiction." *Narrative* 16.3 (2008): 279–97.

Heise, Ursula. *Chronoschisms: Time, Narrative, and Postmodernism.* Cambridge: Cambridge University Press, 1997.

Herman, David. *Basic Elements of Narrative.* Oxford: Wiley-Blackwell, 2009.

——. "Beyond Voice and Vision: Cognitive Grammar and Focalization Theory." In *Point of View, Perspective, Focalization: Modeling Mediacy,* edited by Peter Hühn, Wolf Schmid, and Jörg Schönert, 119–42. Berlin: de Gruyter, 2009.

——. "Directions in Cognitive Narratology: Triangulating Stories, Media, and the Mind." *Postclassical Narratology: Approaches and Analyses,* edited by Jan Alber and Monika Fludernik, 137–62. Columbus: The Ohio State University Press, 2010.

——. "Formal Models in Narrative Analysis." *Circles Disturbed: The Interplay of Mathematics and Narrative,* edited by Apostolos Doxiadis and Barry Mazur, 447–80. Princeton: Princeton University Press, 2012.

——. "Introduction." In *The Emergence of Mind: Representations of Consciousness in Narrative Discourse in English,* edited by David Herman, 1–40. Lincoln: University of Nebraska Press, 2011.

——. "Introduction." In *Narratologies: New Perspectives on Narrative Analysis,* edited by David Herman, 1–30. Columbus: The Ohio State University Press, 1999.

——. "Narrative Theory and the Intentional Stance." *Partial Answers* 6.2 (2008): 233–60.

——. "Post-Cartesian Approaches to Narrative and Mind." *Style* 45.2 (2011): 265–71.

——. "Storied Minds: Narrative Scaffolding for Folk Psychology." *Journal of Consciousness Studies* 16.6–8 (2009): 40–68.

——. *Story Logic: Problems and Possibilities of Narrative.* Lincoln: University of Nebraska Press, 2002.

Herman, Luc and Bart Vervaeck. *Handbook of Narrative Analysis.* Lincoln: University of Nebraska Press, 2005.

Hobson, Peter. *The Cradle of Thought.* London: Macmillan, 2002.

Hogan, Patrick Colm. "The Brain in Love: A Case Study in Cognitive Neuroscience and Literary Theory." *Journal of Literary Theory* 1.2 (2007): 339–55.

hooks, bell. *Feminist Theory: From Margin to Center.* Cambridge, MA: South End Press, 1984.

Horwich, Paul. "Wittgenstein's Meta-philosophical Development." In *From a Deflationary Point of View,* 159–73. Oxford: Oxford University Press, 2005.

Hutto, Daniel D. *Folk Psychological Narratives: The Sociocultural Basis of Understanding Reasons.* Cambridge, MA: MIT Press, 2008.

Iser, Wolfgang. *The Implied Reader: Patterns of Communication in Prose Fiction from Bunyan to Beckett.* Baltimore: The Johns Hopkins University Press, 1972.

Jahn, Manfred. "More Aspects of Focalization: Refinements and Applications." *GRAAT* 21 (1999): 85–110.

James, Henry. Quoted in B. C. Southam, ed. *Jane Austen: The Critical Heritage: Volume 2, 1870–1940.* New York: Taylor and Francis, 1996.

James, Henry. *Theory of Fiction: Henry James.* Edited by James E. Miller, Jr. Lincoln: University of Nebraska Press, 1972.

Jannidis, Fotis. "Character." *The Living Handbook of Narratology,* edited by Peter Hühn, John Pier, Wolf Schmid, and Jörg Schönert, 14–29. Berlin: de Gruyter, 2009.

———. *Figur und Person: Beitrag zu einer historischen Narratologie.* Berlin: de Gruyter, 2004.

Jehlen, Myra. "Reading Gender in *Adventures of Huckleberry Finn.*" In Graff and Phelan, 496–509.

Joyce, James. *Ulysses: The Corrected Text.* Edited by Hans Walter Gabler. New York: Random House, 1986.

Kafalenos, Emma, "Toward a Typology of Indeterminacy in Postmodern Narrative." *Comparative Literature* 44 (1992): 380–408.

Keen, Suzanne. "A Theory of Narrative Empathy." *Narrative* 14.3 (2006): 207–36.

Kirkham, Margaret. "The Austen Portraits and the Received Biography." *Women and Literature* 3 (1983): 29–38.

Kramp, Michael. *Disciplining Love: Austen and the Modern Man.* Columbus: The Ohio State University Press, 2007.

Langacker, Ronald W. *Foundations of Cognitive Grammar,* vol. 1. Stanford: Stanford University Press, 1987.

Lanser, Susan Sniader. *Fictions of Authority.* Ithaca: Cornell University Press, 1992.

———. *The Narrative Act: Point of View in Prose Fiction.* Princeton: Princeton University Press, 1982.

———. "Toward a Feminist Narratology." *Style* 20.3 (1986): 341–63.

Lathan, Sharon. *Mr. and Mrs. Fitzwilliam Darcy: Two Shall Become One.* Naperville, IL: Sourcebooks Landmark, 2009.

Lejeune, Philippe. *On Autobiography.* Translated by Katherine Leary. Minneapolis: University of Minnesota Press, 1989.

Levinson, Stephen C. "Activity Types in Language." In *Talk at Work,* edited by Paul Drew and John Heritage, 66–100. Cambridge: Cambridge University Press, 1992.

Lynch, Deidre, ed. *Janeites: Austen's Disciples and Devotees.* Princeton: Princeton University Press, 2000.

MacIntyre, Alasdair. *After Virtue: A Study in Moral Theory.* 3rd edition. Notre Dame: University of Notre Dame Press, 2007.

Mäkelä, Maria. "Possible Minds: Constructing—and Reading—Another Consciousness as Fiction." *FREE Language INDIRECT Translation DISCOURSE Narratology: Linguistic, Translatological and Literary-Theoretical Encounters.* Edited by Pekka Tammi and Hannu Tommola, 231–60. Tampere: Tampere University Press, 2006.

Malle, Bertram F. "Folk Explanations of Intentional Action." In *Intentions and Intentionality: Foundations of Social Cognition,* edited by Bertram F. Malle, Louis J. Moses, and Dare A. Baldwin, 265–86. Cambridge, MA: MIT Press, 2001.

Margolin, Uri. "Character." In *The Cambridge Companion to Narrative,* edited by David Herman, 66–79. Cambridge: Cambridge University Press, 2007.

———. "Of What Is Past, Is Passing, or to Come: Temporality, Aspectuality, Modality, and the Nature of Literary Narrative." In *Narratologies: New Perspectives on Narrative Analysis,* edited by David Herman, 142–66. Columbus: The Ohio State University Press, 1999.

Margolis, Stacy. "*Huckleberry Finn*; Or, Consequences." In Graff and Phelan, 310–22.

McCarthy, Mary. *The Company She Keeps*. New York: Harcourt, Brace, 1942.

McDowell, Linda. *Gender, Identity, and Place: Understanding Feminist Geographies*. Minneapolis: University of Minnesota Press, 1999.

———. *Towards an Understanding of the Gender Division of Urban Space*. Malden, MA: Blackwell, 2002.

McEwan, Ian. *The Cement Garden*. New York: Simon and Schuster, 1978.

———. Interview by Adam Begley. *Paris Review* 162 (2002): 30–60.

———. *On Chesil Beach*. New York: Anchor Books, 2007.

———. *Saturday*. New York: Doubleday, 2005.

McHale, Brian. *Postmodernist Fiction*. New York: Methuen, 1987.

Michie, Helena. *Sororophobia: Differences among Women in Literature and Culture*. Oxford: Oxford University Press, 1992.

Miller, D. A. *Narrative and Its Discontents: Problems of Closure in the Traditional Novel*. Princeton: Princeton University Press, 1981.

———. *The Novel and the Police*. Berkeley: University of California Press, 1988.

Miller, J. Hillis. *Reading Narrative*. Norman: University of Oklahoma Press, 1998.

Mink, Louis. "Narrative Form as Cognitive Instrument." In *The Writing of History: Literary Form and Historical Understanding*, edited by Robert H. Canary and Hentry Kozicki, 129–49. Madison: University of Wisconsin Press, 1978.

Morrison, Toni. "Jim's Africanist Presence in *Huckleberry Finn*." In Graff and Phelan, 305–310.

Nabokov, Vladimir. *The Annotated Lolita*. Edited by Alfred Appel, Jr. New York: McGraw Hill, 1970.

———. *Pale Fire*. New York: Putnam, 1962.

Nelles, William. "Historical and Implied Authors and Readers." *Comparative Literature* 45 (1993): 22–46.

Nelson, Roy Jay. *Causality and Narrative in French Fiction from Zola to Robbe-Grillet*. Columbus: The Ohio State University Press, 1990.

Nielsen, Henrik Skov. "The Impersonal Voice in First-Person Narrative Fiction." *Narrative* 12 (2004): 133–50.

Noë, Alva. *Action in Perception*. Cambridge, MA: MIT Press, 2004.

———. *Out of Our Heads: Why You Are Not Your Brain, and Other Lessons from the Biology of Consciousness*. New York: Hill and Wang, 2009.

Ochs, Elinor and Lisa Capps. *Living Narrative*. Cambridge, MA: Harvard University Press, 2001.

O'Farrell, Mary Ann and Lynne Vallone, eds. *Virtual Gender: Fantasies of Subjectivity and Embodiment*. Ann Arbor: University of Michigan Press, 2002.

Page, Ruth. *Literary and Linguistic Approaches to Feminist Narratology*. New York: Palgrave. 2006.

Palmer, Alan. *Fictional Minds*. Lincoln: University of Nebraska Press, 2004.

———. *Social Minds in the Novel*. Columbus: The Ohio State University Press, 2010.

Pavel, Thomas G. *Fictional Worlds*. Cambridge, MA: Harvard University Press, 1986.

Peel, Ellen. "Subject, Object, and the Alternation of First- and Third-Person Narration in Novels by Alther, Atwood, and Drabble: Toward a Theory of Feminist Aesthetics." *Critique* 30 (1989): 107–22.

Perry, Menakhem. "Literary Dynamics: How the Order of a Text Creates Its Meanings." *Poetics Today* 1.1/2 (1979): 35–64, 311–61.

Phelan, James. "Dual Focalization, Retrospective Fictional Autobiography, and the Ethics of *Lolita*." In *Narrative and Consciousness: Literature, Psychology and the Brain*, edited by Gary D. Fireman, Ted E. McVey, and Owen J. Flanagan, 129–48. New York: Oxford University Press, 2003.

———. "Estranging Unreliability, Bonding Unreliability, and the Ethics of *Lolita*." *Narrative* 15.2 (2007): 222–38.

———. *Experiencing Fiction: Judgments, Progressions, and the Rhetorical Theory of Narrative*. Columbus: The Ohio State University Press, 2007.

———. "The Implied Author, Deficient Narration, and Nonfiction Narrative: Or, What's Off-Kilter in *The Year of Magical Thinking* and *The Diving Bell and the Butterfly*?" *Style* 45.1 (2011): 127–45.

———. *Living to Tell about It: A Rhetoric and Ethics of Character Narration*. Ithaca: Cornell University Press, 2005.

———. "Rhetoric, Ethics, and Narrative Communication: Or, from Story and Discourse to Authors, Resources, and Audiences." *Soundings* 94.1–2 (2011): 55–74.

———. *Worlds from Words: A Theory of Language in Fiction*. Chicago: University of Chicago Press, 1981.

Phelan, James and Peter J. Rabinowitz. "'A True Book, with Some Stretchers'—and Some Humbug: Twain, Huck and the Reader's Experience of *Huckleberry Finn*." *Foreign Literature Studies (Wuhan, China)* 4 (2010): 13-23.

Phelan, James and David H. Richter, eds. *Fact, Fiction, and Form: Selected Essays of Ralph W. Rader*. Columbus: The Ohio State University Press, 2011.

Prince, Gerald. *Narrative as Theme*. Lincoln: University of Nebraska Press, 1992.

———. "On a Postcolonial Narratology." In *A Companion to Narrative Theory*, edited by James Phelan and Peter Rabinowitz, 372–81. Malden, MA: Blackwell, 2005.

———. "Reader." In *Handbook of Narratology*, edited by Peter Hühn, John Pier, Wolf Schmid, and Jörg Schönert, 398–410. Berlin: de Gruyter, 2009.

Propp, Vladimir. *Morphology of the Folktale*. 1928. Translated by Laurence Scott. Austin: University of Texas Press, 1968.

Rabinowitz, Peter J. "'The Absence of Her Voice from that Concord': The Value of the Implied Author." *Style* 45.1 (2011): 99–108.

———. *Before Reading: Narrative Conventions and the Politics of Interpretation*. 1987. Rpt. Columbus: The Ohio State University Press, 1998.

———. "Shakespeare's Dolphin, Dumbo's Feather, and Other Red Herrings: Some Thoughts on Intention and Meaning." *Style* 44 (2010): 342–64.

Radway, Janice. *Reading the Romance: Women, Patriarchy, and Popular Literature*. 2nd edition. Chapel Hill: University of North Carolina Press, 1991.

Reddy, Michael J. "The Conduit Metaphor: A Case of Frame Conflict in Our Language about Language." In *Metaphor and Thought*, edited by Andrew Ortony, 284–324. Cambridge: Cambridge University Press, 1979.

Reichenbach, Hans. *Elements of Symbolic Logic*. New York: Macmillan, 1947.

Richardson, Brian. "Anti-Narrative." In *Routledge Encyclopedia of Narrative Theory*, edited by David Herman, Manfred Jahn, and Marie-Laure Ryan, 24–25. London: Routledge, 2005.

———. "Beyond the Poetics of Plot: Alternative Forms of Narrative Progression and the Multiple Trajectories of *Ulysses*." *A Companion to Narrative Theory*, edited by James Phelan and Peter Rabinowitz, 167–80. Malden MA: Blackwell, 2005.

———. "Beyond Poststructuralism: Theory of Character, the Personae of Modern Drama, and the Antinomies of Critical Theory." *Modern Drama* 40 (1997): 86–99.

———. "Beyond Story and Discourse: Narrative Time in Postmodern and Non-Mimetic Fiction." *Narrative Dynamics*, edited by Brian Richardson, 47–63. Columbus: The Ohio State University Press, 2002.

———. "Denarration in Fiction: Erasing the Story in Beckett and Others." *Narrative* 9 (2001): 168–75.

———. "Endings in Drama and Performance: A Theoretical Model." *Current Trends in Narratology*, edited by Greta Olsen, 181–99. Berlin: de Gruyter, 2011.

———. "The Implied Author: Back from the Grave or Simply Dead Again?" *Style* 45.1 (2011): 1–10.

———. "Nabokov's Experiments and the Nature of Fictionality." *Storyworlds: A Journal of Narrative Studies* 3 (2011): 73–92.

———. "A Poetics of Probability: Systems of Causation within Fictional Worlds." Chapter Two, *Unlikely Stories: Causality and the Nature of Modern Narrative*, 61–88. Newark DE: University of Delaware Press, 1997.

———. "Singular Text, Multiple Implied Readers." *Style* 41.3 (2007): 259–74.

———. "A Theory of Narrative Beginnings and the Beginnings of 'The Dead' and *Molloy*." *Narrative Beginnings: Theories and Practices*, edited by Brian Richardson, 113–26. Lincoln: University of Nebraska Press, 2008.

———. *Unnatural Voices: Extreme Narration in Modern and Contemporary Fiction*. Columbus: The Ohio State University Press, 2006.

Ricoeur, Paul. *Time and Narrative*. 3 vols. 1983, 1984, 1985. Translated by Kathleen McLaughlin and David Pellauer. Chicago: University of Chicago Press, 1984, 1985, 1988.

Ritivoi, Andreea Deciu. "Explaining People: Narrative and the Study of Identity." *Storyworlds* 1 (2009): 25–41.

Robbe-Grillet, Alain. *For a New Novel: Essays on Fiction*. Translated by Richard Howard. New York: Grove, 1965.

———. "Order and Disorder in Film and Fiction." Translated by Bruce Morrissette. *Critical Inquiry* 4 (1977): 1–20.

Rorty, Amélie Oksenberg, ed. *The Identities of Persons*. Berkeley: University of California Press, 1976.

Rouse, Joseph. "Social Practices and Normativity." *Philosophy of the Social Sciences* 37.1 (2007): 46–56.

Rushdie, Salman. *Midnight's Children*. 1980. New York: Random, 2006.

———. *The Satanic Verses*. 1988. New York: Picador, 1997.

Ryan, Marie-Laure. *Possible Worlds, Artificial Intelligence and Narrative Theory*. Bloomington: Indiana University Press, 1991.

———. "Toward a Definition of Narrative." In *The Cambridge Companion to Narrative*, edited by David Herman, 22–35. Cambridge: Cambridge University Press, 2007.

Said, Edward. *Culture and Imperialism*. New York: Vintage, 1994.

Schiffrin, Deborah. *In Other Words: Variation and Reference in Narrative*. Cambridge: Cambridge University Press, 2006.

Schneider, Ralf. "Toward a Cognitive Theory of Literary Character: The Dynamics of Mental Model Construction." *Style* 35.4 (2001): 607–40.

———. "Reader Constructs." In *Routledge Encyclopedia of Narrative Theory*, edited by David Herman, Manfred Jahn, and Marie-Laure Ryan, 482–83. London: Routledge, 2005.

Schweickart, Patrocinio P. "Reading Ourselves: Toward a Feminist Theory of Reading." In *Gender and Reading: Essays on Readers, Texts, and Contexts*, edited by Elizabeth Flynn and Patrocinio P. Schweickart, 31–62. Baltimore: Johns Hopkins University Press, 1986.

Seager, Joni and Lise Nelson, eds. *Companion to Feminist Geography*. Malden, MA: Blackwell, 2005.

Sedgwick, Eve Kosofsky. *Between Men: English Literature and Male Homosocial Desire*. New York: Columbia University Press, 1985.

Seemann, Axel. "Person Perception." *Philosophical Explorations* 11.3 (2008): 245–62.

Shaw, Harry E. "Why Won't Our Terms Stay Put? The Narrative Communication Diagram Scrutinized and Historicized." In *A Companion to Narrative Theory*, edited by James Phelan and Peter J. Rabinowitz, 299–311. Oxford: Blackwell, 2005.

Shen, Dan. "Breaking Conventional Barriers: Transgressions of Modes of Focalization." *New Perspectives on Narrative Perspective*, edited by Willie van Peer and Seymour Chatman, 159–72. Albany: State University of New York Press, 2001.

Shklovskii, Viktor. *Theory of Prose*. Translated by Benjamin Sher. Elmwood Park, IL: The Dalkey Archive, 1990.

Shusterman, Richard. *Pragmatist Aesthetics: Living Beauty, Rethinking Art*. Oxford: Blackwell, 1992.

Slors, Marc, and Cynthia Macdonald. "Rethinking Folk-Psychology: Alternatives to Theories of Mind." *Philosophical Explorations* 11.3 (2008): 153–61.

Stanzel, F. K. *A Theory of Narrative*. Translated by Charlotte Goedsche. Cambridge: Cambridge University Press, 1984.

Stearns, Peter and Carol Stearns. "Emotionology: Clarifying the History of Emotions and Emotional Standards." *American Historical Review* 90 (1985): 13–36.

Sternberg, Meir. *Expositional Modes and Temporal Ordering in Fiction*. Baltimore: Johns Hopkins University Press, 1978.

———. "Proteus in Quotation-Land: Mimesis and the Forms of Reported Discourse." *Poetics Today* 3.2 (1982): 107–56.

Strawson, Galen. "Against Narrativity." *Ratio* 17 (2004): 428–52.

Strawson, P. F. *Individuals*. London: Methuen, 1959.

Talmy, Leonard. *Toward a Cognitive Semantics*, vol. 1. Cambridge, MA: MIT Press, 2000.

Taylor, Charles. *Sources of the Self: The Making of Modern Identity*. Cambridge, MA: Harvard University Press, 1989.

Tobin, Robert Deam. "Why Is Tadzio a Boy? Perspectives on Homoeroticism in *Death in Venice*." In Thomas Mann, *Death in Venice: A New Translation, Background and Contexts, Criticism*, edited by Clayton Koelb, 207–32. New York: W. W. Norton, 1994.

Tomasello, Michael. *The Cultural Origins of Human Cognition*. Cambridge, MA: Harvard University Press, 1999.

Tomashevsky, Boris. "Thematics." *Russian Formalist Criticism: Four Essays*. Translated and edited by Lee T. Lemon and Marion J. Reis, 61–98. Lincoln: University of Nebraska Press, 1965.

Tooby, John and Leda Cosmides. "Does Beauty Build Adapted Minds? Toward an Evolutionary Theory of Aesthetics, Fiction and the Arts." *SubStance* 94/95 (2001): 6–27.

Turner, Mark. *The Literary Mind*. Oxford: Oxford University Press, 1996.

Twain, Mark. *Adventures of Huckleberry Finn. A Case Study in Critical Controversy*, edited by Gerald Graff and James Phelan. Boston: Bedford-St. Martin's, 2004.

Tyrkkö, Jukka. "'Kaleidoscope Narratives and the Act of Reading." In *Theorizing Narrativity*, edited by John Pier and José Ángel García Landa, 277–306. Berlin: de Gruyter, 2008.

Varela, Francisco J., Evan Thompson, and Eleanor Rosch. *The Embodied Mind: Cognitive Science and Human Experience*. Cambridge, MA: MIT Press, 1991.

Vonnegut, Kurt. *Slaughterhouse-Five*. 1969. New York: Random, 1991.

Vygotsky, Lev S. *Mind in Society: The Development of Higher Psychological Processes,* edited by Michael Cole, Vera John-Steiner, Sylvia Scribner, and Ellen Souberman. Cambridge, MA: Harvard University Press, 1978.

Walsh, Richard. *The Rhetoric of Fictionality: Narrative Theory and the Idea of Fiction.* Columbus: The Ohio State University Press, 2007.

Warhol, Robyn R. *Gendered Interventions: Narrative Discourse in the Victorian Novel.* New Brunswick: Rutgers University Press, 1989.

———. *Having a Good Cry: Effeminate Feelings and Popular Forms.* Columbus: The Ohio State University Press, 2003.

———. "The Look, the Body, and the Heroine: A Feminist-Narratological Reading of *Persuasion.*" *Novel* 26.1 (1992): 5–19.

Warhol-Down, Robyn. "Teaching Gender and Narrative." *Teaching Narrative Theory,* edited by David Herman, Brian McHale, and James Phelan, 237–51. New York: Modern Language Association, 2010.

Werth, Paul. *Text Worlds: Representing Conceptual Space in Discourse.* Edited by Michael Short. London: Longman, 1999.

Wilde, Oscar. *The Importance of Being Earnest.* 1895. New York: W. W. Norton, 2006.

Whitehead, Alfred North. *Science and the Modern World.* 1927. New York: Macmillan, 1956.

Williams, Jeffrey J. *Theory and the Novel: Narrative and Reflexivity in the British Tradition.* Cambridge: Cambridge University Press, 1998.

Wilt, Judith. "Jane Austen's Men: Inside/Outside 'The Mystery.'" *Men by Women,* edited by Janet Todd, 59–76. New York: Holmes and Meier, 1981.

Wimsatt, William K. and Monroe C. Beardsley. "The Intentional Fallacy." 1946. In *The Norton Anthology of Theory and Criticism,* edited by Vincent B. Leitch et al., 1374–87. New York: W. W. Norton, 2001.

Winterson, Jeanette. *Written on the Body.* New York: Vintage, 1994.

Wittgenstein, Ludwig. *Philosophical Investigations.* 1953. Translated by G. E. M. Anscombe, P. M. S. Hacker, and Joachim Schulte. Revised 4th edition by P. M. S. Hacker and Joachim Schulte. Oxford: Wiley-Blackwell, 2009.

Woloch, Alex. *The One and the Many: Minor Characters and the Space of the Novel.* Princeton: Princeton University Press, 2003.

Woolf, Virginia. *A Room of One's Own.* 1929. Boston: Harvest Books, 1989.

———. *The Waves.* 1931. New York: Harcourt, 1950.

Wollstonecraft, Mary. *A Vindication of the Rights of Women.* 1792. New York: W. W. Norton, 2009.

Zalewski, Daniel. "The Background Hum: Ian McEwan's Art of Unease." *The New Yorker* 85.2 (2009): 46–61.

Zoran, Gabriel. "Towards a Theory of Space in Narrative." *Poetics Today* 5 (1984): 309–35.

Zunshine, Lisa. *Why We Read Fiction: Theory of Mind and the Novel.* Columbus: The Ohio State University Press, 2006.

INDEX

THEORY AND INTERPRETATION OF NARRATIVE

James Phelan, Peter J. Rabinowitz, and Robyn Warhol, Series Editors

Because the series editors believe that the most significant work in narrative studies today contributes both to our knowledge of specific narratives and to our understanding of narrative in general, studies in the series typically offer interpretations of individual narratives and address significant theoretical issues underlying those interpretations. The series does not privilege one critical perspective but is open to work from any strong theoretical position.